Cinematic Worldbuilding

Everybody has a story in them. Some people lack the language and the tools to tell that story effectively. As an avid tabletop role-playing game player, I'm amazed at people's ability to tell stories on the spot. Both the players and the game masters are creating worlds in their minds and playing out the events, using improv, in real-time. Being an author and screenwriter, I know how difficult it is to create consistent and well-constructed characters, themes, and conflicts. I believe that storytellers looking to level up in the classroom, their hobby, or career could learn a lot from games like Dungeons & Dragons, Pathfinder, and others. This book seeks to give people the tools and language to create and master their worlds and characters, using TTRPG mechanics and rulesets as foundational elements. This book will contain insights and interviews from some of today's most respected game masters, players, actual play actors, and we'll also hear from some of the people behind the scenes responsible for creating these games, and how they view worldbuilding and storytelling for their audiences.

Nicholas LaRue is an author, screenwriter, and film critic. His first book, *Behind the Scenes of Indie Film Marketing,* debuted at #2 in Film & Television on Amazon. Nic's website, FilmSnobbery.com (est. 2008), is dedicated to being a voice for the indie film community. His work frequently brings him all over the country, speaking at conferences and film festivals. He is an avid TTRPG player who has a passion for dynamic storytelling and compelling characters. Nic is also the author of *Behind the Scenes of Indie Film Marketing: A FilmSnobbery Field Guide* (Routledge/Focal Press, June 2024).

Cinematic Worldbuilding
A TTRPG Approach to Storytelling

Nicholas LaRue

CRC Press
Taylor & Francis Group
Boca Raton London New York

CRC Press is an imprint of the
Taylor & Francis Group, an **informa** business

Designed cover image: Canva

First edition published 2026
by CRC Press
2385 NW Executive Center Drive, Suite 320, Boca Raton FL 33431

and by CRC Press
4 Park Square, Milton Park, Abingdon, Oxon, OX14 4RN

CRC Press is an imprint of Taylor & Francis Group, LLC

ISBN: 978-1-032-88516-2 (hbk)
ISBN: 978-1-032-88515-5 (pbk)
ISBN: 978-1-003-53820-2 (ebk)

DOI: 10.1201/9781003538202

Typeset in Minion
by Deanta Global Publishing Services, Chennai, India

Dedicated To

My wife, Angelique

Author, Screenwriter, Friend

Devin Watson

Contents

Preface

ABOUT THE AUTHOR

Nicholas LaRue is an author, screenwriter, film critic, and founder of FilmSnobbery.com, a website dedicated to being a voice for the indie film community. Nic has worked in the Hollywood studio system as the Head of Post-Production for Raleigh Studios, served as the Director of Marketing for Miglionico Design, and is currently the CEO of LaRue Entertainment Group, LLC, which serves as the holding company and entertainment industry consulting arm of FilmSnobbery.

INTRODUCTION

Storytelling is the thing humans do best. Everyone has a story in them. Some of them are epic space operas, and others are about the interesting person you met when you were out for a walk last week. Some stories turn into books, others into movies. We have hundreds of channels and more than a handful of streaming services dedicated to showing the stories that rooms full of dedicated and talented professionals concoct every year from your favorite studios.

Do you have a story you want to tell but are having trouble keeping it from going off the rails? Are you someone who has read "Save the Cat" and Syd Field's books on screenwriting but can't seem to get past the first act of your tale? Maybe it's time to try something different. Something...radical.

This book is going to teach you to play by a fresh set of rules that traditional screenwriting instructors offer. We're going to play by TTRPG standards. "What the heck is a TTRPG" you ask? TTRPG stands for tabletop role-playing game. You might recognize the brand names associated with it more than the acronym. Ever hear of Dungeons & Dragons (also referred to as D&D)? How about Pathfinder, the TTRPG created by the good folks at Paizo? Maybe you're more familiar with the World of Darkness rulebooks for Werewolf: The Apocalypse or Vampire: The Masquerade?

There are TTRPGs for most of today's most famous properties, including Dune, the Marvel Universe, Doctor Who, and more. Some of the more creative fans of TTRPGs have even taken to creating their own universes and rulebooks like DeAngelo Murillo, who wrote the rulebook for his Emerald Templars system and is currently working on his next game, Celestial Masquerade. Tabletop role-playing games are having a big moment right now. Online actual play shows like Critical Role and Dimension 20 have entered the mainstream conversation, taking Dungeons & Dragons out of basements and libraries to theaters and stadiums.

Learning anything new can be overwhelming, which is why we are including advice and information from leading TTRPG players, game masters, creators, and other folks who make their living by creating fantastical worlds and adventures for their players to live and play in. We are also going to feature words of wisdom from working screenwriters whose work you can currently see on television, at your local movie theater, or on your favorite streaming platform. We also hope you'll take advantage of the resources we've added at the end of this book, like map grids and character sheets, and use them when you're fleshing out your own worlds and characters.

We're going to take the narrative and game mechanic principles of TTRPGs and apply them to screenwriting. In this book, we are going to look at worldbuilding, character creation, conflict, story structure, and everything else that goes into creating a screenplay, and we're going to add a TTRPG twist to it. This will allow you to create more consistent worlds and more fully alive and nuanced characters that actors will love to inhabit. Using the methods throughout this book, you'll hopefully be able to look at the way you tell your stories differently, defeat writer's block, and finish your screenplay.

Software like Final Draft or Fade In can fill in the gaps when it comes time to put fingers to keys and worry about formatting. Having your story laid out, your characters feeling like they're in the room with you, and a confident purpose born out of efficient preparedness will have you racing through pages and eager to let your imagination off the leash.

As we make our way through this book, we'll default to referring to the Dungeons & Dragons 5th Edition rule sets while referencing other rule sets from other game systems in specific cases. Those will be called out separately to help avoid confusion.

Let's get started.

HOW TO USE THIS BOOK

The intention of this book is to provide a fun and informative examination of the screenwriting process by using TTRPG theory, methods, and mechanics to create better and more immersive stories. Also, there are interviews spread throughout this book from a variety of points of view from people of different backgrounds, ethnicities, player/Game Master experience levels, and societal points of view. I hope their contributions to this book will give you a better understanding of the concepts that are being presented from a less academic perspective. Their passion for their craft and the care they take as both performers and storytellers are the main reasons they were selected to be in this book. We couldn't include large quotes from everyone we interviewed but want to include as many voices as possible. As you read this book, you'll see a small quote labeled as a **"Point of Inspiration."** These quotes stood out as particularly poignant moments in my conversations with a contributor, and I felt that while they might not fit within the larger conversation, they should still be included somewhere within the text.

While I wrote the content of this book, the academic nature of it means I can't offer my direct opinions or share personal stories related to the content I'm presenting....Or can I? In the spirit of this book, which is about breaking the rules and finding the fun within the work, of which I hope you're passionate about, I have injected a few **"From the Author"** asides and digressions that I hope you'll find interesting.

There is a list of contributors in the back of this book that has their headshot and brief biography giving their expertise in their chosen fields. There are some people who were interviewed for this book who prefer to use pseudonyms and/or online handles to identify themselves. Being sensitive to their privacy and safety concerns is of the utmost importance, with great care given to respect their wishes.

Periodically, you will see bold sections labeled **"Exercise,"** followed by instructions to perform a task or assignment. You are certainly not obligated (unless this text is being used in a classroom setting, in which case, follow your instructor's directions) to complete any of these, but you may find some value in trying them.

There are many terms used in both the screenwriting and TTRPG worlds. The end of this book contains a glossary of terms that covers both separately so you can look up anything you are unfamiliar with. If you're still struggling, there are many online resources available to you with just a few key terms input into your favorite search engine.

What this book is:

- This book is designed for beginner screenwriters to take inspiration from, for TTRPG enthusiasts to crib tips and tricks from experts in the field, and for writers who feel stuck in their attempts to finish their work and are looking for a new approach to writing. It is to be used as a reference when you need it. It was designed to complement a classroom text, not replace it.

- This book is meant to be an informal chat between peers about the nature and pitfalls of screenwriting, and as such, you may not agree with what the author or the contributors' points of view are.

- This book is designed to:

  - Inspire—Learn the secrets your favorite game masters used to create worlds beyond number. Your story might be the next critical success!

  - Engage—Storytelling is hard, but it can also be fun using the tools found within this book.

  - Educate—If you missed that creative writing or screenwriting class, no problem, this book will give you the foundation you need to start your worldbuilding journey.

- This book caters mainly to screenwriters but is also intended to be picked up and read by anyone looking to use TTRPGs as a creative element in building their stories.

What this book isn't:

- This book is NOT designed to replace formal creative writing or screenwriting education.

- This book is NOT a replacement for any TTRPG rulebooks or supplemental texts. Any advice from GMs/DMs in this book is not meant to override the advice from the GM/DM you are currently playing with at your table.

This book does not specifically endorse any one game platform, player, or Game Master, but attempts to present a broad spectrum of options to potential players and writers who might intend to use the methods and/or advice given.

CHAPTER 1

What Is a TTRPG?

IT'S NOT ALL DUNGEONS AND/OR DRAGONS

POINT OF INSPIRATION

"There's a golden rule at my table. No one person's fun should be more important than another person's at the table. The only wrong way to play any game is to be an asshole."—Justin Miller (Noir)

If you are new to tabletop role-playing games, you might immediately gravitate toward the most popular of them, *Dungeons & Dragons*. The idea of being a headstrong paladin or a wise wizard appeals to many people looking to escape the real world for a few hours a week. Slaying evil sorcerers and saving villages with your friends is fun. But did you know that D&D is just the tip of the iceberg when it comes to the variety that TTRPGs come in?

TTRPGs are more than a group of five or six people sitting around a table telling a fantasy story of swords and sorcery. Sometimes you play TTRPGs with only two people. Sometimes they can even be solo adventures that you undertake by yourself. Writer and producer Tatiana Gefter, who created the Soul Operator audio drama, has this to say about playing solo TTRPGs and how they relate back to storytelling:

DOI: 10.1201/9781003538202-1

One of the explicit instructions is that there is no wrong way to play. The prompt system with Welcome to the Habitrail is broad enough that you can do almost anything and be able to justify it to the prompt that you received. A lot of them are reactionary, so you pull a couple of tarot cards, choose the one that you know best fits, and then whatever happens is typically something that your character is reacting to. In a scripting sense, that works really well, because I can have whatever it is, happen at any point of the episode, and have the characters react to it however they would, and it's totally fine, completely correct.

There is no wrong way to play any solo TTRPG, because it is so deeply personal. Many of them are explicitly introspective experiences. You can play as a character, or you can play as yourself. It kind of depends on how deep into your own psyche you want to get. There's a game called Anamnesis created by Samantha Leigh, who has made several solo games, and it's literally about rediscovering who you are. A game like that is beautiful and an incredible gameplay experience for yourself, but it's not necessarily one that I would use for the show, because I look for games that either have an established world or some through-line that can be worked into a script and a plot that would be reasonably easy for an audience to follow. The benefit is that people don't have to have played the game to get it, but people who have played the game get this Easter egg experience with Welcome to the Habitrail specifically, because all the episode titles are tarot cards in the game that correspond with the prompt that inspired the episode. So, if you've played the game, or you have it, you can kind of get an idea of what might happen in that episode. Which I also thought was a really cool thing to tie into this bridging of mediums.

People arrive at TTRPGs in many ways. Some get into it by finding books left behind by older siblings or parents. Some discover these games by finding the players or creators on social media. Others stumble upon a game in progress at their local game or comic book store. Jes Wade, a huge organizer of charity games in the TTRPG space and a pillar of the gaming community, shares their experience in discovering D&D:

I got into TTRPGs back in 2019. My partner and I used to loiter around Target, and we always had to go to the game section, and I would see the D&D starter set, and I was like, wouldn't it be fun if we gave it a try? I pestered a bunch of people until finally someone on my rugby team asked, "what if we played on the rugby camping trip?" So, we all made characters at the tent, basically, and then sat around the campfire for the entire weekend playing and had an amazing time. It was perfect. I tore my ACL right afterwards, and I couldn't do anything. I really threw myself into playing D&D because that's all I could do from my couch. It was right before the pandemic happened, and shortly after, I was introduced to the D&D Twitter community. There are people just like me that want to play D&D all the time!

Shortly after, I learned that D&D is not the only tabletop role-playing game that you can play, and my eyes were blown open, which was a really cool experience. In my day job and throughout my professional career, I have always worked for nonprofits. I started working for the Boys and Girls Club in college, and I was there for five years. Worked for the American Cancer Society, March of Dimes. Fundraising is what I do now, day and night, because I am also a charity TTRPG content creator, and so the way I view TTRPGs is, it's not only a great way to immerse yourself in stories, it's not only a great way to find lifelong friends, but it's also an amazing vessel to raise funds for very worthy causes.

"I've been very blessed and thankful to have a great community that not only wants to support me but also the causes that I want to support."

Katie Downey, who goes by GoblinKatie online, shares how she got into TTRPGs:

I started playing back in high school. My first game was Dungeons and Dragons, Second Edition, and I played that for a while, and then I got into LARPing (Live Action Role Playing). I love LARPing. So many of my weekends were eaten up with LARPing. I kind of fell out of tabletop (gaming), and in 2019, my buddy Dustin got a hold of me and asked if I would do a D&D stream. I heard D&D, and was like, Yes! What's a stream?

That was the introduction, and the next day, my buddy Adam contacted me about doing a D&D podcast. I got thrown into the deep end, and I hadn't played D&D since the second edition, so I apparently skipped a lot of the interesting editions.

Not limited to the fantasy genre alone, TTRPGs come in all flavors. Want to take on the personas of your heroes and heroines? Licensed properties from your favorite movies and television shows allow you to play as your favorite characters, or people who live in the same story world as the characters you love, giving you the freedom to expand those worlds with your gameplay.

If you're a person into fantasy games, Dungeons & Dragons and Pathfinder are good places to start. Maybe flying through space is more your style and you prefer a science fiction setting? Star Trek Adventures and the Doctor Who TTRPG have you covered. The creators behind D&D and Pathfinder even have their own flavors of space adventures with Spelljammer and StarFinder. Do you like your gameplay to be a little darker or more horror-oriented? The World of Darkness system of games is perfect for that and completely adaptable to be played together. You can howl at the moon in Werewolf: The Apocalypse or slake your thirst for blood with Vampire: The Masquerade.

Perhaps none of the mainstream options fulfill that creative storytelling itch that you're looking to scratch. There are hundreds, if not thousands, of independently produced and designed games for almost any style of play and genre. Like movies and television, there's something for everyone, and in fact, there are many similarities between how we develop and tell stories in movies and television and how game developers, game masters, and players tell stories and create characters when they're immersed in their fictional worlds.

Some of these gamers and creators have taken their hobbies one step further and shared their gameplay with audiences online via streaming services like Twitch or Discord. This is called actual play and has become a popular way for hobbyists to turn their passion for storytelling into a sustainable, professional job. Much like independent filmmakers, many are creating without the help of large studios, complete with sets, casting, and marketing to their audiences. Most importantly, they're telling the stories that are special to them and the communities they're a part of.

As you move through your own creative journey, find other creators that resonate with you and the type of stories you want to tell. Study their work, take the methods, and adapt them to your own storytelling style. Reach out to collaborate with people you respect to create something bigger than you could make by yourself. Don't be afraid to be audacious and share your work with audiences. Be bold. Find the audiences that appreciate the work you do and get them to advocate for you.

Being a creative is not just something you do; it's something you are.

THE GAME MASTER

As a screenwriter, you are the person behind the keyboard creating the world, the characters that live in it, and you control all their actions. You tell them what to say, and you decide who lives and who dies. Being a GM, also called a Game Master (or DM, which stands for Dungeon Master if we're talking in strictly D&D terms), is similar. You create the world where players' characters live in and all the people that those characters interact with. The only thing that the Game Master doesn't control is the players themselves or their actions. Instead, the success of their endeavors is left up to a roll of the dice.

GMs/DMs come in all shapes and sizes and come into gaming in many ways. Actor, DM, and one-third of the acclaimed legacy internet program Totally Rad Show cast, Jeff Cannata shares what brought him into the DM scene.

> I got a BFA in theater at UC Santa Barbara, and moved to Los Angeles right after college and started working, doing a lot of plays, television, soap operas, commercials, you name it. I was a working actor in Los Angeles, generating my own work, writing, and doing improv. I did a lot of comedy improv. I had a sketch group, and sort of dates me, but it was early days of the internet, pre-YouTube.
>
> We were making shorts for Atom Films, when that was a thing, and creating content. Then I started doing a show called the Totally Rad Show, and that was one of the first internet video shows on a channel called Revision3, which existed because YouTube did not, and how it happened was that I had a friend of a friend who knew Alex Albrecht, who was one guy I started the show with, and Alex and a buddy of his had gone down, I think it was to Comic Con

or some convention, and had played Dungeons and Dragons for the first time as adults. They came back from that and said, "we want to do this more. Let's generate a group to play D&D", and they reached out to people they knew would be interested as well. I was on that list as a friend of a friend, and I also had very much wanted to play Dungeons and Dragons my whole life, but I genuinely didn't have enough friends when I was a kid. I didn't have other humans to play tabletop games with, so I would read the rules and just pine away, wanting to play games like Ultima and Wizards of Might and Magic and Pools of Radiance, and all the games on that were aping the thing on a computer.

Anyway, so I'm a full adult now going, oh yeah, I would love to do this. So we started playing Dungeons and Dragons with a buddy of theirs that had been DMing quite a long time, and brought us together, and that's where I met Alex Albrecht and Dan Trachtenberg, and we became friends right away, and started hanging out together, talking about movies and video games and all the stuff that we were into, and decided, hey, we can make this show called the Totally Rad Show. Let's do it. So, we made that show, which ran for seven years. We played a lot of D&D during that time, and at a certain point, I don't even remember how it happened exactly, but maybe the guy that was DMing couldn't do it, I don't even remember the particulars of it, but at some point somebody said, Well, we need another DM to do this, and everybody kind of looked at me, and I went, Yeah, I'll give it a shot. Foolish me was like, hey, I'll do all the work. I fell in love with it. I automatically just knew this was what I liked. The creator, the facilitator. I call it Dungeon Master—The Facilitator of Fun. Some people think of it as an antagonist. I don't. I think of it as a facilitator of fun. You're there to ensure everybody has a great time. I really enjoyed that role. I enjoyed coming up with fun surprises. Another way I described DMing is like throwing 1000 surprise parties, and it's always fun when you thrill your players, and you get into a groove and they surprise you, and you surprise them, and everybody's having a great time.

That's how it started. We had a group that we played frequently (not as frequently as any of us would have liked, which is a common refrain for people who play tabletop games), but we played often enough that we had fun. People were digging what I was doing, and Alex was in that group, and Dan was in that group, and other of my buddies were in that group. Fast forward to well after the Totally Rad Show wrapped up, Alex was hired by this company called Caffeine, that was starting up its own streaming technology, its own streaming service, and they were looking for content to create, and he said, I've always wanted to make my dream version of a Dungeons and Dragons show that has a big budget, and we can do sets and big models and his vision was always to do it with actors. Obviously, Critical Role had been doing it with voice actors. But he wanted to cast the show, not just have it be a bunch of already established friendships, but literally cast the show, and that's what he did.

He called me up and he said, Hey, Jeff, would you like to DM the show that I'm doing (The Dungeon Run)? And I was like, oh, man, I don't know, it seems like a lot of work. And he's like, no, no, no. Just use the module that you've already done. Do what you've done with our group. It's only going to be 10 episodes. You could do it. And I was like, okay, I could do 10 episodes. I can do an arc in 10 episodes. We did 150 of them. I would never have said yes if he had said 150 right at the beginning.

The GM isn't God in the game, as they might be mistaken to be. There are rules for the game for fairness and balance toward the players, which they're constrained by, and to add structure to, what is essentially an open-world sandbox endeavor. GMs are, of course, fully capable and often encouraged to "homebrew," or introduce their own rules and mechanics to their games at their discretion, but the penalty is knowing that it won't make the game more interesting or fun for their players. The same goes for screenwriting. While you sit in front of a blank page with endless possibilities, there are still expectations that follow certain rules, some arbitrary, others industry-imposed, to create and format your work into a specific shape, size, and conformity to standards.

Sometimes things don't always go smoothly, and that's why trust is a key component at any table between the DM/GM and their players. Rivals of Waterdeep player and season eleven's co-GM Brian Gray reflects on how trust is essential at the table when the GM is in a tight spot:

I think as a GM, the pressure is harder, because while the players are going through the story (and they're honestly doing a lot more to shape the story than the GM is), you're still expected to be able to, at some point, if all the people at the table look at each other and have no idea what to do. They all turn and look to you. You're expected to know what's that next story beat, and that's why I have all the notes to say, okay, well, time passes, and you do this. I have had moments where I've frozen, and thankfully, I had people who were able to get me through it. In that moment I had no idea what to do, and somebody else at the table picked up with a prompt, and they started throwing it around the room, and that gave me a chance to get back to my notes and recenter myself. I always say, trust in the people that you're playing with, or, if you don't know all the people you're playing with, trust in the person at the table that you've worked with and know that they've got your back.

This is the case in many TTRPG games. A 20-sided die decides the fate of a player's actions. It can also control whether an attempt for or against the players from the Game Master is successful or not. Want to destroy the monster plaguing the nearby town? Roll to see if you hit. If you miss, the monster might slay you instead. Roll high enough, and you might just hit the monster hard enough to vanquish it and bring peace back to the local peasants.

The dice are powerful, but they aren't creative. They determine outcomes but don't set the scenarios. That job is for the GM and the players. Depending on who your GM is, the system being played, and the makeup of the table or game session, the experience can be vastly different. There is definitely a difference between a newer GM and a veteran who has been playing for many years with a variety of players. A newer GM who is playing with seasoned gamers can get away with running an adventure on rails if they understand how to communicate effectively with their players and nimbly swivel or dodge with their choices to keep the game fun and fast-paced. Conversely, a GM who has only played one game system for a long time but is hesitant to run scenarios outside the official adventure guides might bring a lackluster gaming experience to veteran players.

The GM sets the tone of the game. They are the keepers of all the secrets, and it is a massive undertaking to be responsible for an entire group's evening of fun for several hours at a time, sometimes over years. Many of them invest hundreds of dollars or more in gaming manuals and adventure paths to keep their players on their toes with fresh content. Along with their monetary purchases, they also spend hours reading those manuals and memorizing adventures, creature stat blocks, and deciding what voice they're going to use when playing as the cute bartender non-playable character (NPC) their players encounter at the beginning of their quest.

Professional Dungeon Master and screenwriter B. Dave Walters has a wonderful outlook on what it is to be a good DM:

> The speech I always give people what I'm talking about DM'ing at a high level, as a Dungeon Master, is this. Any TTRPG storyteller, and any storyteller by extension, has one job. Your job is to elicit an emotional response. It's the only thing you have got to do. If the people at the table are laughing, if they're crying, if they're shaking their head yes, if they're shaking their head no, if they're covering their eyes. Whatever it is, you are succeeding. Your only enemy is "meh". Your only enemy is apathy. I would say, with storytelling and screenwriting, it's the same, and it's getting harder and harder because attention spans are getting shorter and shorter.

When you are planning out the story that will eventually become your script, it's helpful to think like a Game Master. Study the manuals, watch the videos, and read scripts from movies and television shows you enjoyed or that match the genre or tone of what you're trying to write. Watch or listen to interviews with writers, filmmakers, or other people you respect and learn their processes. Just as important, listen to the people and the things happening in the surrounding environment. The random things you hear from people passing by will become the realistic hooks of dynamic dialog that will resonate with viewers or people reading your scripts.

Listening is one of the most important jobs a GM has when gaming with their players. The GM can be infinitely prepared on paper, but if they're not listening to the wants and needs of their players and their characters, they'll miss key opportunities to create memorable or emotionally poignant moments that their players will remember forever. Those same emotional beats translate to screenplays as well. Both the screenwriter and the GM have the same motivations. They both need to lead the folks on the receiving end of their stories emotionally to create an impact. They need to be aware of their players' emotional states, the flow of the session they're currently playing in, and be able to pivot if their journey takes an unexpected turn.

Being a Game Master, like many creative endeavors, takes audacity. Even in a private home game, you are still creating a world and a story thread for other people to play with, and you may feel certain feelings of inadequacy about that at first. Writers share these feelings, and the only way to overcome that anxiety, impostor syndrome, or whatever you might call it, is to actually do it.

Professional GM, terrain builder, voice actor, and cosplayer Jesse Jerdak understands this first-hand and shares his wisdom and views on what it takes to be a GM:

> I have that audacity that you were just mentioning, and so the very first thing I ever wrote is still my ongoing campaign. We've been doing it for almost five years now. We just had our 90th session in that same campaign, which is pretty cool, and I think you're absolutely right, especially for my specific skill set, what I'm known as known for in the industry, that those writing skills that help you suppress any degree of shame. You just throw your insecurities on the back burner. You commit to the bit, and I think that really helps for a DM. I can drop into a dwarf in no time, and all of a sudden, I'm five feet tall and I've got a giant red beard, and at no point am I concerned about what I'm coming off as, because I believe it, and because I believe it, my players believe it. I think it's an incredibly valuable skill set that, especially in actual play production. It would be cool to see more of that, more trained actors stepping into that role, if you're doing it specifically for entertainment purposes.

FROM THE AUTHOR

Being a first-time DM and being a first-time author or screenwriter have a lot in common in that they both require a leap of faith on your behalf. A lot of people, myself included, doubt that they can write the script or the novel, or lead a group of adventurers through a campaign to a satisfying conclusion. They'd be correct...Until they do.

Doing creative things, whether writing, filming a movie, or running a D&D campaign, all feels impossible until you go through the process. Even when you accomplish your goal, you might feel that it was a fluke the first time and that you could never do it again...Until you do it again, and again. A tip I read in a book years ago, which I can't remember the title of but is a common tip for people who want to become authors, screenwriters, or pursue other creative endeavors, is that the first step is when someone asks what you do for a living, you answer with the thing that you strive to be. If you want to be an author, call yourself an author. If you want to be a screenwriter, call yourself a screenwriter. Don't wait for permission to be called those things. Start early. You'll get there if you believe you can. Even if it takes years.

THE PLAYERS

POINT OF INSPIRATION

"Everything the players do matters and affects the world. Everything they do and don't do..."—Brogan Kelley

Playing a TTRPG differs from sitting behind your keyboard and developing your screenplay in one major way. When you are writing, it is a solitary experience, while playing a rousing session of Dungeons & Dragons is best done with a group of people. If you consider yourself the GM sitting at the head of the table, directing the story, then your main characters would be the players sitting across from you. The players serve a key role in telling the story of the adventure that the GM is presenting. While the GM sets the players on their quest, once they are let off the leash, the story can go anywhere. For a writer, that can be one of the most freeing feelings they can experience.

Every story needs characters, whether those characters are human, elf, Klingon, or a rolling garbage robot in a far-flung future. The characters we create, and the worlds we set them loose in, define our stories. Each campaign of TTRPGs like Dungeons & Dragons or Pathfinder starts with a blank character sheet for each player to create their adventurer with. Even niche games like Vampire: The Masquerade and Werewolf: The Apocalypse gives you the mandate of creating a character that is one of many varieties of vampire or werewolf. In TTRPGs, it is possible to be almost anyone or anything you can dream up. The more creative the player, the better the character they have the possibility of creating.

Writing a screenplay requires fresh and dynamic characters. Think about some of the most memorable film roles from cinema history. What makes Rocky Balboa and his story in *Rocky* so undeniable? The underdog trope is well-worn in movies and television, so why is *Rocky* considered a classic? Sylvester Stallone's performance brings Balboa to life, and Talia Shire's Adrian is a perfect complement to Rocky, fleshing out the world Rocky lives in and showing a completely different side to the character when he's not in the ring. The story, throughout the film, leads you to believe that Rocky is on track to defeat Apollo Creed during their climactic bout but dodges enveloping the trope in totality by having Rocky lose his fight but gaining respect, both from his opponent and from himself. *Rocky* isn't about physical strength but mental toughness and courage.

What would *Rocky* look like if Stallone wasn't in the title character's boots? Would the film have hit differently if an equally talented actor like Robert Redford (who actually was considered for the role) had taken the reins of the lead? Would the USS Indianapolis speech in *Jaws* have had as much impact on audiences if Robert Shaw had not deliver it? How about Waymond Wang's character, played by Ke Huy Quan, in Everything Everywhere All at Once? His character could have been played by another actor, but would another performer have made Waymond as memorable?

We're addressing two things in the above examples. The first is the person in the role, and the second is the character they're playing. TTRPG games like Dungeons & Dragons and the story that's being told at the table rely on the same. To tell the best story possible, you need the right actors in the roles of the best characters.

When the wrong mix of personalities is at the game table, it won't be long before the campaign being played or the story being told falls apart and people quit. It doesn't matter how powerful the characters they create are. If they don't play well together, they won't make it to the end of the adventure.

People who don't take care in creating their characters can suffer a similar fate. TTRPGs require a certain amount of immersion and care to be given to character creation. Folks who don't take their responsibilities as players seriously, or act with malicious nonchalance, are wasting the time of everyone else at the table and making the experience less fun and more tedious than it needs to be.

TTRPG and voice actress Kelly, who goes by the moniker TheKellHop online, talks about the kinds of characters she enjoys playing, and how playing and acting with other great people helps her rise to the top of her own ability.

> My favorite types of characters to play are characters that have sincere emotional depth. If it's for an AP, I would like to approach that depth and maybe have it changed someone who is watching or listening. When it comes to AP (Actual Play), I'll say it up and down, I very much enjoy entertaining and I very much enjoy connecting with an audience, and if I can accomplish a thought-out character arc that has meaning and value and maybe illuminates some of the simple, beautiful truths of life, I am happy.
>
> When it comes to my private games, I actually think the way I play, for actual plays, has made me a more resourceful player overall, and that has bled into my private games. When you're around people that are "at the top of their game", people who are just so talented and passionate and dedicated to telling a good story for people, it's going to rub off on you and so many of the talented people I find myself amazingly around, somehow they have rubbed off on me in such a way where I go to some of my private games and like I can bring that same passion that I feel for performing, I can bring that same passion to my private game. It's just made me a better player overall.

Going back to the concept of the "lone wolf" character, one of the more famous examples of that character who is changed by their interactions with others in their orbit would be Batman. Until the introduction of Robin, the Boy Wonder, Batman was alone in the Bat Cave, with the only interactions outside the criminal element he hunted at night being with his butler Alfred. Once Dick Grayson is introduced, it softens Batman both as a human being and also to the citizens of Gotham City. The idea that you are influenced by the people you surround yourself with is not a new one. It shows that while a "lone wolf" might be effective to a point, they will be limited in their growth potential. Kelly (TheKellHop) expands on this.

> So interestingly enough, I think that nugget of truth is found in your friends at the table. You all bring these individual concepts to the table. You know each other from day one, and those conversations about who you were, who you are, and who you're going

to be, should be continuously happening as you tell this story. As far as a conflict is concerned, a fellow PC can be like, Man, I really appreciate what you did for me back there. Or, you know, I remember when I first met you, or, you know, we've come a long way. Those nuggets of truth are just so naturally woven into an interaction that it's not something for me that's hard to keep track of. It's the art of knowing each other. I've talked about this with some friends about like, what's a piece of advice that you would give to a new player who's just starting out and, well, a big thing for me is giving. Giving fellow characters permission to change yours because if you come to that table as, "I'm a lone wolf, and I'm always going to be a lone wolf. I'm Batman, and that's what I'm here to do, and you can't change me", you're not going to tell a good story, and that's a pretty stagnant truth. But if you come to that table with a chip on your shoulder, and over time you give the other characters permission to change you, your truth is going to be so much more interesting than if you keep those walls up. One of my favorite things is seeing how my character's truth changes through interaction with the people that matter to them. The how your truth grows, how your truth shifts, and that's what helps you hold on to who you are.

The truth for me is what does this character's heart looks like, and how have I let others change it? How has that altered the story, and how does that make us better? That's where the truth of a character's personality, who they are, and who they're going to be really comes to the forefront for me.

STORYTELLING FOR ROLE-PLAYING GAMES

POINT OF INSPIRATION

"We tell these stories because we want to see ourselves in those characters, or we want to be those characters."—Joshua M. Simons

Storytelling in TTRPGs differs from movies in a few critical ways. Stories that are told in TTRPGs are first, collaborative, and second, many official adventure paths already have the story created for the Game Master and players to play with. The closest comparison would be a screenwriter coming onto a large franchise film like a Marvel movie. While they may have certain areas of the story they can make their own, many of the overarching decisions are laid out already and planned long before the decision to bring them on the project was made.

This doesn't mean the Game Master is hamstrung with keeping his adventurers on rails following the story. The wonderful thing about games like Pathfinder and Dungeons & Dragons is that anything can happen, and screenwriters should adopt that same mantra when creating their stories. Just because your outline says that a character is supposed to go to location A or interact with character B, maybe they don't. Perhaps instead of doing what is expected, try an exercise where the character or story goes in a different direction, and see what the organic outcome of that becomes.

Ashley Warren, who has worked on D&D adventure paths in the past, talks about her experience crafting those stories from an IP standpoint working with Wizards of the Coast, which publishes Dungeons & Dragons, and how that experience differs from traditional creative writing exercises:

> When I wrote some official material for Dungeons and Dragons, I appreciated the structure, because one of the core tenets that I have as a creative writing teacher is that creativity thrives with some structure. I think especially for newer writers and aspiring writers, when they're figuring out their process and those limitations are really helpful. Like working within a word count, and working within a pre-existing world or characters, because it allows you to focus on other elements and improve those other elements. I wouldn't want to only do IP work in my entire career, but I like the balance. For example, when I worked on Rime of the Frost Maiden, which is a D&D book by Wizards of the Coast, we were given something like a story Bible, which has the whole narrative plot outlined. But when you're given your actual assignments, I had a chapter that was 10,000 words, but I was only given a one-line description of what's going to happen in the chapter. So, there's still a lot of creativity there, and what you have to do when you have those kinds of projects is you have to really flex your game and narrative design muscles. You might not be coming up with the worldbuilding, but you're coming up with the actual objectives for the players, and you're coming up with those cool

moments of tension, and you are also incorporating worldbuilding. You're sacrificing creativity entirely; you just have to be stronger at the things that you're being expected to do.

I enjoy having the freedom to world build and create my own characters. I'm all about setting an atmosphere. That's what really excites me when I'm writing, and what I actually love about narrative design because you have a lot of opportunities to infuse your work with a lot of those atmospheric, immersive details, and that's really where I feel like I thrive. But it is nice to know the main objective. For instance, in a particular section, I have to come up with a really creative way to get people from point A to point B. I think that for writers of all levels, embracing the restrictions and the limitations is really important, and I think when people aspire to be professional D&D writers that's what most of that work would be. You're not necessarily going to get a job at Wizards of the Coast and be able to make whatever you want, and same with like working at like a video game company or any major company working within IP. So, you have to find your own ways to be creative within that.

I've done a lot of commissioned work, which usually means that I'm given a general directive or a plot, and then it's my job to really flesh that out. I always have a really fun time doing that. One of the first projects I did as a narrative designer was a D&D adventure, and it was like a sequel to a best-selling adventure that was on the Dungeon Masters Guild. I was given a framework for it, but I had a lot of creative control. The setting itself wasn't really sparking my passion. So, I asked myself, how do I find my own way to be really excited about this project? And I ended up changing one element entirely; a volcano, and I made the volcano have blue fire instead of orange fire or some innocuous detail like that, and then, because of that, I got to create all the lore around why there was a blue-fired volcano. Even though it was a minor detail, it really roped me into the story as the writer, and I was still working within the confines of the story, but I got to do something that I felt was really exciting. So, I would say, that's my perspective on the things that I love about stories; the elements, the characters, and what I can include within this directive. Sometimes it's nice to just jump into a project that already has those parameters set and not have to do all that yourself.

Usually, after I do a really IP heavy project, it's nice to go back to my own projects where I have full creative control, and then kind of go wild. I think I see a lot of new writers really struggle to write for IP, because they'll say they want to do XYZ outside of the scope of the project, but that's not what you're being hired to do. So, it's good practice to learn how to work within IP, because that's actually what a lot of the work that narrative designers do within that corporate space. It took me a while to figure out how I liked to work within that and within those limitations and those expectations.

EXERCISE 1.1

Write a scene for a script no longer than five pages that contain at least two characters, one location, and one premise in any genre you want. Once you've completed that scene, start over with the same characters, location, premise, and genre, but change at least one decision a character makes within that scene and compare the two. How does changing your character's decisions make the scene better or worse?

The random elements of both the dice and the players create unexpected twists and turns that don't reveal themselves until the players speak or the dice are rolled. A player, or even a Game Master, can have the character they're playing makes an inspiring speech and roll a natural one on their die, negating much of the bravado that the speech afforded them. For the purposes of comedy, this is gold, but even dramatic moments can be carried by poor dice rolls. For example, if a character is dying and can only be saved by a high dice roll, and the player fails that roll, the character perishes. The other players have now lost one of their party. They've lost someone who has adventured with them, fought with them, and developed bonds with them. It's a sad moment for the table. But that poor roll might also inspire the rest of the adventuring party to fight in that character's honor, seek revenge, or band together to form an even tighter-knit group. It might also force the players to strategize better, knowing that their current approach is costing lives.

On the other side, in a world where that player rolled well and recovered, they might also think twice about their approach lest they be felled again by their opponent. It might also become an inspiring moment for the rest of the players as they circle up the wagons to protect their recently hurt comrade until they are back up to fighting strength.

That player's presence at the table might be the difference between defeating their opponent or being stomped into the ground and left for dead. The not-knowing is one of the best parts of playing TTRPGs, and it can also be one of the most liberating parts of being a screenwriter. The Game Master facilitates the players to tell *their* story, and you are doing the same for your characters in your screenplay. A good GM isn't forcing the story down the players' throats; they are allowing the players to decide for themselves what the story is going to be.

Unless you are writing either for a large ongoing franchise series of films, or writing episodic scripts for television, there is very little chance you are responsible for creating a story every week, sometimes for an entire year or more. That sort of stamina belongs to TTRPG players and GMs. Most long-form campaigns that start at level 1 and progress to level 20 (the common level caps for games like Dungeons & Dragons and Pathfinder) can take a year to complete, assuming the players and GM are meeting weekly and the adventure progresses as expected. Sometimes it takes longer.

The short form method of TTRPG storytelling is called a one-shot. This is a self-contained adventure that players complete within one to three gaming sessions. The adventure can be something as simple as "find and defeat the BBEG (Big Bad Evil Guy) in the forest outside of the city." It might also be to defeat a few lower-level foes while trying to solve a puzzle to get out of a maze the characters are trapped in. These brief adventures are akin to short film scripts or, sometimes, even more like episodic television. Some GMs allow characters to return from previous one-shots to continue to progress mechanically in future ones, gaining experience points, loot, and other insights that may tie into something greater at a later date.

WHAT DOES THIS HAVE TO DO WITH SCREENWRITING?

POINT OF INSPIRATION

"For characters, both for writing and for acting, I now make character sheets for any character I play because it gives me a touchstone to go back to and ask, how do I feel about this? What kind of response might I have to this?"—Jennifer Kretchmer

What do rolling dice, adding stats to character sheets, and pretending to be an elf for a few hours a week have to do with writing movie scripts? Robert McKee doesn't tell me to play Dungeons & Dragons. Neither does Blake Snyder or his cat (although saving a cat would make for a fantastic one-shot adventure). If all the experts who teach at the university level aren't teaching tabletop role-playing game mechanics as a creative writing exercise, then why should we bother continuing reading this book?

All of these are great questions, easily answered.

Starting with the first question, rolling dice, writing down character stats, and becoming something other than yourself are one of the best ways to get outside of your own head and perspective and into another's. For instance, you might not be able to be a firefighter in real life, but in your role-playing adventures, you might be fighting in a tall building engulfed in an inferno. How does your character behave? How do they feel as the flames threaten that character's existence or the lives of their fellow first responders? Being able to put yourself in the shoes of your characters is critical to understanding their behavior, backstory, personality traits, and physical and emotional limitations. Being ensconced in your character enough that you care if something good or bad happens to them allows you to make better and more realistic decisions for them.

There are similarities between the TTRPG professional GM/DM and player industry and the independent film industry. 2024 Crit Award nominee for Best Indie GM, Zachary Vaudo, talks about how he sees it from his perspective:

> The funny thing to me, from my experience, it's less like the 90s indie film circuit, and it's more like the early to mid-2000s web series internet video circuit, because a lot of these productions don't have money, period. Nobody's getting paid. You don't hear about most of these folks, but the majority of games that are going on, the actual play streams that are going on, nobody is getting paid, regardless of the level at which they are producing. People are all in it for the love of the game. That could be anything from sitting in a Zoom window recording stuff, to you're all sitting in someone's living room recording to in a studio recording.
>
> My start in actual play was with ATL By Night, a Vampire the Masquerade show. The first chronicle of ATL consisted of a bunch of people that were part of the entertainment industry in

different capacities, film and stage and whatnot, and we all had an entertainer and camera mindset, and we also just enjoyed playing games. We played the game, but we were conscious of the camera, and we have this ingrained knowledge of narrative beat. Nothing was scripted out on our end. We just have this knowledge of how things go in this, but also none of us were getting paid because we were also a bunch of friends that were coming together and playing a game. The current cast of ATL comes from a variety of backgrounds, a lot of different people. Some of them have never had any camera experience before, just gamers. Some of them have had camera experience, but in different capacities. It's all different, and thus, there's a different mentality that approaches it. To jump back to the earlier point of 'for the love of the game', versus the professionals. There are professionals that are also playing it for the love of the game, outside of a professional capacity. It's just, it all comes down to your life experiences and where you came from as somebody that also likes to play games.

One of the founders of Rascal News, a new, independent, reader-supported, worker-owned online outlet for journalism about tabletop role-playing games and the people who make them, Rowan Zeoli, chimes in, understanding that indie film and the TTRPG space share a heritage of people trying to express themselves despite shortcomings in the materials or education available to them:

> Not having resources to make the technical productions or have access to the education to make the technical productions, a lot of it's happening (anyway). Even in the actual play space, that is very trans and is heavily populated with people of color, with disabled people. It is a medium of people who do not have the money to make the art match the vision they have in their head, and they're still gonna make it, anyway. I think that's really beautiful.

Film and television actor, and now professional GM Jesse Jerdak, also tags in on this and points out an aspect of being part of the wider entertainment industry that many people in the TTRPG space have yet to realize but are quickly learning:

I was getting bit parts in movies and series and stuff. I had one reoccurring role ever, and it got canceled at the pilot, so we filmed the pilot, and we didn't go past that. It broke my heart, because it was reoccurring, and you know what that means to an actor. I never quit my day job. We have a lot of people (in the TTRPG space) that are very passionate, enthusiastic, and excited in a much smaller industry trying to put corn and peas on the table and streaming to five people at a time. Don't quit your day job. It sucks, because you want to be an artist, right? You want to be pure, and you want to stay in front of people's eyeballs.

We're seeing this weird thing where people are very popular and getting a lot of exposure, and they are broke as a joke, and they are losing their houses, and they're moving back in with their parents. I saw it as an actor. People are busboys and they work at diners while they put themselves through hell to be an actor or an actress, and they go to auditions. They're still on that grind, and I don't think the performers in this industry have learned that yet, and it's tough to watch.

The broader point of Jesse's statements is that being in the entertainment industry is a lot like being an entrepreneur, and as such, you need to be responsible for treating your career like a business. Whether that career involves streaming a game to people on Twitch while running a Patreon and Etsy hustle on the side or peddling your scripts up and down the various studios and agencies in Los Angeles. Have a plan, execute your plan, and don't quit your day job.

Why do most authoritative screenwriting books not talk about role-playing and instead focus on beat sheets and note cards? The reason might be structure, and how some folks thrive when given boundaries and rules. Hollywood also likes to sell people a dream that, if you follow the rules and work hard, you might get picked from obscurity to be the next Spike Lee or Quentin Tarantino. In truth, there is no magic formula for screenwriting success. So, if you take the rules for what they are, arbitrary, then you can focus on your characters and your story instead of worrying if your slug lines are bold or not.

Writer and game designer Jonathan Wilder discusses his approach to rules in both TTRPGs and scripted storytelling. When asked about his interpretation of rules in both worlds, here was his response:

I lean towards, mostly, rules as written, but also sort of rules as intended. As someone who does design work, I find it really interesting to seek what the designers intended with certain rules, because sometimes, for whatever reason, you get a rule that just doesn't have the level of specificity needed to communicate what it's trying to, so I like to kind of have to ask, why does this rule exist? What is it trying to do?

When we talk about when you can break the rules, there's the common adage of you have to understand the rules in order to break the rules. I think that there is use to rules. You could throw out all the rules of a game, but then you're basically just playing an improv game, which has some value. I really love Fiasco, and that is a game that is pretty much just an improv game with a couple of things bolted onto it.

If the rules aren't working to an extreme extent for you, then you're probably not playing the right game. To put it in a screenwriting perspective, if the rules are holding you back so you can't tell the story that you want to tell, then maybe it's time to break through that, as long as you understand why and how you're going to accomplish that.

It's important to know the rules as they're presented to you. They might help you in places like writers' rooms, where structure is important because of the number of people involved in creating seasons of television. The story structure elements might even be helpful if your personality or learning predilection dictates needing them. Once you know the rules, then you can choose which one's help you get from a blank page to Fade Out.

A question posited to screenwriter and avid TTRPG player and Dungeon Master, Dan Hernandez (*Teenage Mutant Ninja Turtles: Mutant Mayhem*), asked if he ever used playing TTRPGs as a lubricant for ideas for screenwriting, or to get into a different headspace before or after working on a script. He replied:

I think it's very important to do that and to take those kinds of breaks, because it's nice to inhabit somebody else for a little bit. It's nice to be caught up in a story that you are dynamically creating with your friends and with other people.

Being the Dungeon Master is, I love doing it, but it's challenging, and it has its own sense of, sort of the rubric of what is a successful session is like, slightly different when you're the Dungeon Master, because it's both a compelling story and a dynamic performance, but also, are people having fun? Are people feeling excited about continuing? That can also force you to kind of think in a different mode.

One of the things that I do when I'm the Dungeon Master is I write this sort of video game-ish, what I call "cinematics" before every session. I write a piece of prose, sometimes poetry, but usually sort of prose from a privileged point of view that the character wouldn't necessarily get, whether that's like the bad guy, sort of writing in a journal, or a snippet of verse that has a clue as to what might happen in the session, things like that.

Sometimes just doing writing exercises like that can really be useful. I have found myself in writer's room situations going, oh, you know what we really need here is we need like a chase mechanic and or sometimes when you're thinking of set pieces, dynamic set pieces, a lot of times the best encounters are one's like in Call of Cthulhu. You're fighting a Shoggoth and guess what, Nyarlathotep just showed up, and now, the whole dynamic has changed.

So, what I'm really talking about is escalations, and I think by sort of seeing what works in a TTRPG encounter that started like this, and then it escalated to this. It can be directly applicable sometimes to getting in that creative head space where you go down and you say, okay, well, what are the Ninja Turtles gonna face here? The Foot soldiers. Okay, great, but it can't just be the Foot soldiers. Yeah, they're gonna take down the Foot soldiers. So, what is that escalation in, sort of in D&D encounter terms, that makes a challenge level three into a challenge level eight? That's sort of where getting out of your own head space and engaging in these other kinds of storytelling modes is really helpful sometimes, because it is directly applicable to when you're doing the technical construction of a movie or a scene or whatever. You can apply those lessons in both directions, which is pretty cool for me, because it's all I do, all the time.

This book aims to give you the tools and confidence to do something great and possibly life-changing. Pursuing a career in the arts is no easy task, but it is achievable. Grant Howitt, a founder of the TTRPG design company Rowan, Rook, and Decard, gives a comparison between the intimidating rulebooks associated with Dungeons & Dragons and his own two-page creation, Honey Heist.

> Most people's first experience of a role-playing game is Dungeons & Dragons, which is three books, really heavily produced. Everything's been copy-edited, everything's been proofread and what have you. But also, especially if you think about D&D 3.5, the rules are intensely structured. It's not balanced, but it's structured, and so it can be quite intimidating to think, well, I want to do that. I want to make something like that, because the idea is that it's got to be 900 pages long, and it's got to be perfect, and it has to detail the entire world and that sort of thing.
>
> What I find really exciting is showing people, especially kids or young designers (Honey Heist) and saying, his can be a role-playing game, and it's in black and white, and it's written by hand, and Honey Heist is more popular than most other role-playing games, and it took me about two days. You can do that. It is not hard to do this.

This book seeks to release you from the constraints of traditional screen-writing methods and get back to storytelling. Focus less on rules and structures and more on character development and worldbuilding. Also, get back to what makes writing fun and exciting.

CHAPTER 2

Story

WHAT STORY ARE YOU TRYING TO TELL?

There are many ways we tell stories. We have movies, games, books, plays, and comics. Hell, we even have mimes. Storytelling is ingrained in the fabric of our society. In a conversation with TTRPG designer and writer Christian Nommay, he spoke about a transformative trip to the Lascaux Caves in France, where he witnessed one of the earliest discoveries of human storytelling:

> The power of stories, of storytelling, is incredibly potent. There are so many things that they can do, and so many people it can heal. Whether you're telling a story around the campfire, telling stories is part of our DNA as a species. Part of my family came from Perigord noir in France. It's where you have the Lascaux Caves. It was one of the first caves that was found with prehistoric paintings, and you can visit a reconstitution, because you can't visit the original caves anymore, but they reproduced them exactly how they were found. When I visited there, I had some sort of revelation. It struck me that since we started to draw, telling stories has been a part of our lives, of what we are as a species. It's not just something to entertain us. We need this. It's something that feeds our soul.

DOI: 10.1201/9781003538202-2

As much as it's important to tell your story, you should also ask yourself, "what story are you trying to tell?" This question should be the foundation of everything you write for an audience. Very similar to how journalists write their pieces, ask yourself these questions:

1. **Who**—Who is the audience for this story?

2. **What**—What do I hope my audience gets out of this story, or what do I hope they feel about it?

3. **Where**—Where does this story take place?

4. **When**—When does this story take place?

5. **Why**—Why am I writing this story now? Why am I the best person to tell this story? (This question can be important when you are setting out to create a story that might not be your story to tell, i.e., you are a white person trying to tell a story about racial injustice or prejudice. There might be others more qualified to tell this story, or you should consult with an expert before you begin.)

6. **How**—How should this story be told? Is this a novel? A game? A comic book? A screenplay? A podcast?

EXERCISE 2.1

Think of a story you want to write and use the above "who, what, where, when, why, and how" model to answer these questions. How do you feel about your story now? Were you able to answer all the questions to your satisfaction easily?

The things you put into your stories should mean something. A hero should be more than just a noble knight in shining armor. What story are you trying to tell us by using this character? Actress and storyteller Jennifer Kretchmer explains this from her perspective.

Monsters should, in a good story, be representative of something, right? Silent Hill games are so great because those monsters represent something specific to the characters. It's always a psychological representation of the experience of the characters. It's why something like Buffy the Vampire Slayer was so great. Tying the monster (to the characters) becomes something that is very personal to the characters and to the story. You can play these TTRPG games, just picking a monster at random from whatever monster book you're working with, or finding a threat at random, and there are absolutely stories to tell where you're up against some other force. Picking at random and throwing it in for no reason can be fun, but ultimately, you're missing out on the potential of telling a story there that matters and becomes personal to the people involved.

Knowing what story you're trying to tell is the first step to outlining the tale. Even if you're a "pantser" (someone who writes organically with little planning, relying on the flow of their writing to carry them from beginning to end and not using an outline to structure their writing) rather than a "planner" (someone who outlines or otherwise meticulously writes out their story's plot points, twists, and turns, and writes with specific goals in mind to help them get to the end of their story), knowing your end goal is an important first step. Acclaimed author Ed Greenwood spoke about his approach to writing for this book and goes into some detail as to how outlining and understanding the story you are trying to tell is an essential part of the marketing and selling of your finished work. This applies, as he says, to the publishing industry, but also applies to the film industry as well, as you master creating loglines and synopses for your scripts:

I love world building, so I will do it anyway, just for me. And I'm lucky. I'm a person who can write really fast when they have to. Every single publisher has their own way of doing things, for instance, in writing groups and amongst novices who want to get published, there is a discussion of plotters versus "pantsers", and I will often be asked, well, how do you write? And I say it depends on the project. I've written 500 books, literally, and if I'm collaborating or if I'm working with a major publisher, they all have their ways of doing things, and I have to follow them, because it just doesn't work otherwise. For instance, if you are a pantser, and I have written books where I just sit down and start noodling and the player, the characters take over, and I just write what they do, you can't do that with a major New York publisher, because they want to order the cover art early. They have a catalog. In the old days, it was a glossy print catalog, perhaps the most elaborate thing they printed in a year, and it was to tell bookstores and other outlets what to order, and it had to have a summary of the story. So, I would have to outline the story before I wrote it, no matter what.

If I was a first-time author coming over the transom, selling them a book on spec, in which case they wanted a finished book, because the last thing they want is to have paid for a book, and the author can't finish a book because they've never done one before. So, they want the finished book. But then, on some occasions, and I've actually had to do this with other publishers, they will say, could you please take the finished book and write an outline no longer than this many words, because we need it for the catalog? You're going to have to outline the book, whether outlining is what you do.

Screenwriting is an art just like sculpting or painting. You are digging deep within yourself and trying to tell a story that only you can tell because it is unique to you. While there's nothing wrong with fun popcorn scripts and movies where you can turn off your brain for a couple of hours, ideally, if you're going to spend the time and money to churn out 90-plus pages of material with the expectation that someone is going to spend millions of dollars to turn that idea into a reality, you should make it mean something.

TTRPG creator, writer, and performer Connie Chang says it best when speaking about their creative process:

My general approach to any sort of art making at all is I'm making art for myself and 30 other freaks. I don't give a fuck about what anyone else thinks, so as long as the art I'm making feeds me and is so specific, unapologetic, and really takes risks. It takes a big swing, and it's gonna miss a lot of people, which I'm cool with. In fact, I think if you set out to make art that will satisfy everybody, you end up with slop. You end up with mainstream slop that doesn't say anything, because you can't say anything if you want to appeal to everything, right? I think that's a really cowardly way to make art and a way to make art that I personally really do not enjoy.

STORY STRUCTURES

As the adage says, there are many ways to skin a cat. There are many ways in which to structure and tell your story. Some of these methods date back to ancient Greece, and some were created or popularized within the last couple of decades. There is no right way, only the best and most efficient way for you to convey what you're trying to get across to your audience. You may notice that many of the methods used by playwrights, novelists, screenwriters, and others are an amalgam of each other. Every story has a beginning, a middle, and an ending, but how we arrive at each of those milestones makes the story different and adds to the ways they are consumed. Below, we cover some of the most popular story structures and give examples of the films that use them.

Story Structure Types

The Fichtean Curve

Originally conceived in 1983's The Art of Fiction by John Gardner, this sea-creature fin-shaped story structure is great for novelists and screenwriters alike and is a very simple triangle arc that starts with rising action until it reaches a tipping point climax, and then falls to the inevitable conclusion. Translated into film terms, the rising action would start at the beginning of the movie and continue until the end of the second act, where the viewer would then witness the climax and a hastened third act where everything gets wrapped up. The original *Star Wars* film, *A New Hope*, is an example of this story structure type.

The rising action is everything from Princess Leia giving the Death Star plans to R2D2 to take to Ben (Obi-Wan) Kenobi through to when Darth Vader and Kenobi face each other while the others rescue the Princess and shut down the Death Star's tractor beam holding their ship there. (This is all roughly the first hour and a half of the two-hour and one-minute-long movie, depending on which edition you're watching.)

The climax occurs when Darth Vader kills Kenobi on the Death Star while Luke, Leia, Han, and the rest escape back to the Rebel Alliance on Yavin IV.

The falling action is the defense of Yavin IV, culminating in the destruction of the Death Star by Luke Skywalker in his X-Wing (with a little help from Han in the Millennium Falcon). The film ends with an elaborate award ceremony where Princess Leia gives Luke and Han medals for their heroism.

Emphasis on the rising action in this method of story structure is great for building tension, drawing out drama, and for character development. Star Wars takes a lot of time building the universe that the characters inhabit. The climax has you wondering if the rebels can succeed when the most powerful character in the story (Kenobi) has just been defeated. By the time you arrive at the falling action phase of the movie, you know the stakes of what happens if the Rebel Alliance cannot stop the Empire, understand some of the mystical powers of the force, and have some idea of the motivations of the characters. The same relief we see on Luke's face as he watches the proton torpedoes go down the shaft to the heart of the Death Star is the same feeling the audience has. The release of all that built-up tension from the first two phases of the story structure leaves the audience with a satisfying conclusion.

The Three-Act Structure

Originating in the playwright community thanks to the ancient text Aristotle's *Poetics*, which popularized this framework back in ancient times, and then co-opted as a go-to structure for the film industry as an expedient way to tell stories by Syd Field in his book *Screenplay: The Foundations of Screenwriting*. The three-act structure has since fallen by the wayside in favor of the more modern five-act structure and Save the Cat beat sheet.

The hallmarks of the three-act structure are simple.

Act 1—Setup.

Act 2—Confrontation.

Act 3—Resolution.

Die Hard is an example of the three-act structure. Upon a non-exhaustive examination, the movie's acts would break down like this:

Act 1—The setup of the robbery by Hans Gruber and his crew, John McClane's trip to surprise his estranged wife Holly at Nakatomi Plaza during their Christmas party, and everything leading up to Hans' people taking the party guests hostage, causing John to go into hiding.

Act 2—John tries to call the cops, but his initial attempts go unheeded. He confronts his first terrorist, laying the groundwork for two of the movie's most popular catchphrases: "Now I have a machine gun. Ho. Ho. Ho" and "Yippee Kai Yay Motherfucker." Once the police and the FBI become involved, complicating his situation inside the building and escalating the cat-and-mouse game between John, Hans, and Hans' goons, the movie moves toward the final act as John systematically kills the terrorists until only a few remain.

Act 3—This act includes the final confrontation between John and Hans on the rooftop of the Nakatomi Plaza and concludes with Hans plummeting to his death, almost taking Holly with him. The post-script is the scene that follows, which shows the heroic act by Officer Al Powell, John's confidant throughout the movie, who shoots the last remaining terrorist who briefly escapes custody and attacks John and Holly.

The Hero's Journey

Popularized by Joseph Campbell in 1949, the Hero's Journey is a mono-myth and a common storytelling model that is easily accessible to novice and expert writers alike. You'll find this method used in many popular fiction and films such as Margaret Atwood's *The Handmaid's Tale, The Lord of the Rings* films directed by Peter Jackson, and *The Hunger Games* directed by Gary Ross and written by Ross, Suzanne Collins (who wrote the original book), and Billy Ray. This 12-step process is as follows, using *The Lion King* as an example:

Step One—The Call to Adventure—Simba is prodded by his uncle Scar to visit the Elephant Graveyard where he is ambushed by hyenas and is rescued by his father.

Step Two—The Refusal of the Call—Simba realizes that he is not ready to be on his own yet, much less succeed his father as the next king of the Pride Lands.

Step Three—Meeting the Mentor—There are several characters in *The Lion King* that could be characterized as the "mentor" character, as Mufasa, Timon, Pumbaa, and Rafiki all have some wisdom to share with Simba on his journey, but clearly the most important of these characters, and the most impactful on both the story and Simba, is Mufasa.

Step Four—Crossing the Threshold—Once Mufasa is killed by Scar, Simba runs away from the Pride Lands, leaving his old life behind and beginning his journey.

Step Five—Tests, Allies, and Enemies—Simba meets Timon and Pumbaa, who espouse their motto of "Hakuna Matata" and teach Simba a new and different way of living, free from guilt and responsibility.

Step Six—The Approach to the Inmost Cave—When Simba meets Nala, a lioness from his former pride, he is forced to confront elements of his past, pushing him out of the physical and emotional comfort of his new home and friends. This encounter forces Simba to start to look inside himself to see the lion he could be if he embraced his destiny.

Step Seven—The Ordeal—In *The Lion King*, this scene becomes a key moment in which Simba begins to embrace his destiny and seize the reality he fled from as a child. This scene is very emotional for both the main character and the audience.

Step Eight—The Reward—This is more subtextual in the movie than a physical reward. Simba now believes himself worthy of his father's love and position in his former pride. He resolves his personal conflicts and proceeds to the next phase.

Step Nine—The Road Back—Simba follows his path back to the Pride Lands.

Step Ten—The Resurrection—Simba confronts Scar and defeats him, taking on his father's mantle as the new king of the Pride Lands.

Step Eleven—The Return—With the defeat of Scar, Simba restores the kingdom of his father to where it once was. He is now older and wiser, he has friends, his love (Nala), and the film ends with.

Step Twelve—The Freedom to Live—This is the "happily ever after" ending of the film, where the Pride Lands are free of tyranny once more.

Game designer and creator of Pathfinder, Jason Bulmahn, has his own take on the Hero's Journey model:

> I think people like to knock the Hero's Journey because it's so tired and overused. I get that, but I also get why it's tired and overused, because it is a natural element of our storytelling. We feel it to some extent. It is the story of our own life and understanding that the way people engage with a story is important and how they interact with how the story unfolds and how it builds upon itself. There's something very human in that. That's why we play games, because it connects us to who we are. It is a way for us to tell stories that our normal lives wouldn't permit. I can't run off and go on adventures. I can't take a ring to Mount Rainier and throw it in. First of all, I can't mountain climb, and second, my knees are bad, and I don't have a Sam, but ultimately, this is a very human thing.
>
> Can you break that? Yes, you absolutely can. You can shatter that construct. You can tell stories differently. It's not about the rules. It's about understanding how to interact with standard story constructs and standard story frames that everyone's familiar with. When you step away from those, it's best to have an expertise in how people interact with that, so that when they do, they show their interactions. You know how to tell a story within them.
>
> There are a lot of different story structures. I don't think any one of them is right. I just think that all of them tell different types of stories, and you can go your own way, but I do think that means that you're kind of in uncharted waters how people will respond to it. I have broken story structure in a way that players do not find sound, that ultimately, they got pretty mad about. I told the story back when I was in college where the players were doing this big heroic thing. Halfway through it, they all get killed. I'm like, see you next week. I broke the story structure. I killed all my protagonists. I did it intentionally in an unfair fight. Why? Because the next week, they were going to wake up as undead, and I was going to have that a be a sub-story.
>
> But I have to admit, they were pretty mad at me. I learned a valuable lesson there, that I broke a covenant, and that covenant is: we are all here to tell a story together. Everybody has expectations

about what that story is going to be. Now, I think when you're doing a movie or screenplay or a show, and to be honest, an actual play drifts towards the middle between a purely free-form home game where nobody's watching. You can do whatever the hell you want. It's the story you and your buddies are telling together that week. The other end is a movie, which is filmed, edited, and prepared. This is the story you're going to see. Actual plays live in the middle, although they are kind of free form, they're still structured.

Freytag's Pyramid / 5 Act Structure

Developed by novelist Gustav Freytag in the 19th century, Freytag's Pyramid comprises five stages. This framework includes:

Exposition—This is where the story begins and gives the reader, listener, or viewer the setup for the rest of the story. It includes the settings, characters, and establishes themes that will prevail until the end of the story, unless a twist is introduced later. The inciting incident comes between the exposition and the rising action.

Rising Action—Following the introduction of the inciting incident, the rising action is where the story takes off. It establishes the conflict and stakes for the characters and the story. This can take up most of the book, film, podcast, or other media the consumer is engaging with.

Climax—This piece in the structure can be complicated, drawn out, and full of emotion, or it might be fast-paced and quick. Either way, you want to take time with this part of your story, regardless of the structure you're implementing. This is the turning point of your story, leading later to catharsis and resolution. The climax should support the themes and ideas presented in the exposition portion of your story.

Falling Action—This can be an area where secondary and tertiary conflicts are resolved and addresses changes made to the main characters because of the climax. This is a good place to expand the characters' views and show the consequences of their actions and interactions within the story world you've created.

Resolution—This is the end of the story. Tie up loose ends and leave the audience with a sense of completion or tease a continuation of the story in other sequel media.

Save the Cat Beat Sheet
Originally created by successful spec screenwriter Blake Snyder, whose credits include *Stop! Or My Mom Will Shoot*, *Blank Check* for Disney, and the TV series Kids Incorporated. He wrote the "Save the Cat" trilogy of screenwriting books that covered his vision of story structure and screenwriting methods, and he led seminars and workshops around the world for aspiring screenwriters. He was also a highly sought-after consultant for the Hollywood studio system. Blake passed away from cardiac arrest in 2009. Snyder's beat sheet method is a modified three-act structure that contains several beats within it.

Act One

Opening Image (In the first 1% of the script)—The first impression of the main character or story world before the dominant story begins.

Theme Stated (5%)—This is the story you're attempting to tell.

Set Up (1–10%)—Like most beats in the Save the Cat method, this is character-driven and shows the character's need for change, flaws, or a need for a different/better future.

Catalyst (10%)—This is the event that sets the character on their journey for the rest of the story.

Debate (10–20%)—This introduces the first of many questions that characters might have ranging from which direction to go to discussing their trepidation about the main quest/story.

Act Two

Break into Two (20%)—A challenge or event that marks the beginning of the second act.

B-Story (22%)—This could be a secondary main character's aim or a best buddy character's quest. You might also introduce a love interest or a secondary villain's objective here.

Fun and Games (20–50%)—This might be a montage, a party scene, or a series of shots where the protagonist and his friends are succeeding either in general or toward their stated story goal. This beat supports the overall premise of the story.

Midpoint (50%)—A scene of false victory or a false defeat. There might be allusions to the falsity to add tension. Either way, the characters find out that not everything is as it seems.

Bad Guys Close In (50–75%)—The characters might feel trapped, either physically or emotionally, at this point in the story. They feel surrounded, and the downward spiral for the protagonist begins.

All Is Lost (75%)—The lowest point for the main characters. This is also where the antagonist or villains are on the cusp of success, or flat-out succeed in their machinations. The stakes are at their highest at this point. This represents the death of something within the character, or the death of a friend, mentor, or close family member of the protagonist.

Dark Night (75–80%)—This is a self-reflective scene where the main character's transformation becomes defined. It might include a realization and symbolize or reflect the theme of the story.

Act Three

Break into Three (80%)—This shows the character in their final form. This begins the setup for either a tragic or happy finale.

Finale (80–99%)—If the ending of the story is happy, then the villains are defeated, and the "all is lost" part of the story is subverted. If it's a tragic ending, the character succumbs to their evil side, or the bad guys win.

Final image (99–100%)—The final image reflects the first beat in Act One. If a picture is worth a thousand words, then the final image encapsulates everything in the story that wasn't explicitly stated but is implied.

The Marvel Cinematic Universe movies, particularly the first *Iron Man* film, are a great example of the Save the Cat screenwriting method and structure.

The Snowflake Method

Created by "the Snowflake Guy" Randy Ingermanson, a theoretical physicist turned award-winning novelist who later became a writing instructor. The short version of this method begins with a central theme expressed in a single sentence or short paragraph, making up the center of the snowflake. From there, you branch out, adding character and plot details. Last, you flesh out your outline by listing every scene, drilling down further. Finally, you write your story.

The complete version of this method is ten steps, and is incredibly thorough, as one would expect something designed by a physicist to be. It encourages writers to think deeply about their story and characters before starting the writing process. According to Randy, each step builds on the previous one, and the key to success with this method is building momentum toward the completion of the story. It encourages you to write more descriptions of the settings and minor characters and to expand story threads from paragraphs to pages.

This story structure is definitely geared toward planners rather than "pantsers" and favors novelists rather than screenwriters. From a screenwriting perspective, this method would work for episodic television writers working with multiple characters and arcs throughout a season. You would start with a central theme that drives the season forward and goes from there.

Dan Harmon's Story Circle

Not exactly a narrative structure by itself, but the Dan Harmon Story Circle is a wonderful tool to test whether or not your story ideas stand up to scrutiny. This method is popular among filmmakers and writers of TV shows for the logical and consistent ways that writers can examine their stories for plot holes and other things that trip up writers.

The circle is comprised of eight parts. Four of those parts (1–3, and 8) revolve around an inner circle marked "Order," while the other four (4–7) revolve around the inner circle labeled "Chaos." Below is how these are laid out in order:

1. **YOU**—Establish the protagonist/They are in a zone of comfort.

2. **NEED**—Something isn't right/They want something.

3. **GO**—Crossing the threshold/They go somewhere to get it.

4. **SEARCH**—The road of trials / They adapt to their new surroundings and challenges.

5. **FIND**—Meeting the goddess / They get the thing.

6. **TAKE**—Paying the price.

7. **RETURN**—Bringing it home / They return to the familiar.

8. **CHANGE**—Master of both worlds / But they are now changed.

You can see that the story circle follows the Heroes Journey closely and models very well within the three-act structure. Act I is the status quo of order that the protagonist is familiar with. Act II is where chaos reigns and the protagonist's world (values, feelings, etc.) is turned upside down. Act III introduces the new order where the protagonist has overcome their fears, enemies, or other obstacles to be able to live within a new status quo.

The simple nature of the Dan Harmon Story Circle is to get you to think about your protagonist's journey from their perspective instead of focusing on the worldbuilding around the protagonist. Once you've nailed the road that your main character is leading themselves down, then you can go back and fill in the world around them with people and things that either support or get in the way of your protagonist's journey.

Seven Point Story Structure

This story structure should be somewhat familiar to TTRPG enthusiasts as it was popularized by the science fiction author Dan Wells in 2013 when he took the story structure used in the Star Trek Roleplaying Game Narrator's Guide and adapted it into a system favored by many authors since. Here is how the Seven Point Story Structure is put together:

1. Hook—The introduction to the story. From an RPG perspective, this would be what the GM uses to bring the player characters into the world the story takes place in.

2. Plot Point 1—This is where the GM would bring their players into the adventure with an inciting incident (consider in D&D when your DM asks you to roll initiative for the first time in an adventure. This is likely that time). This is also the point that brings the adventurers together as a team for the first time.

3. Pinch Point 1—The tension mounts and stakes are raised with the principal antagonist being introduced, or the key challenge presenting itself.

4. Mid-Point—A turning point. The part where the protagonist(s) go from having things happen to them to taking charge of their adventure.

5. Pinch Point 2—Things go wrong. In a traditional three-act story, this would be the "all is lost" moment that would happen at the end of Act II.

6. Plot Point 2—An unexpected discovery gives the protagonist(s) something that assists them in defeating their antagonist. You see this a lot in cartoons where, somehow, someway, a character comes along with just the right information to give the protagonist an edge against their enemy, or they finally fully realize their powers.

7. Resolution—The conflict is resolved and/or the antagonist is defeated.

This story structure puts the emphasis on plot points more than it does on characters. This can help you create the world and challenges your characters will face in advance and then place your character along the path you've already created. It favors worldbuilding over character growth, with anything significant happening to the character being saved for the Plot Point 2 part, which is just flavoring for the upcoming resolution. If you are a DM/GM and want to be a screenwriter or novelist, this might save you some time as you write, as the familiarity of it as it relates to TTRPGs will probably make you feel more comfortable. Once you master this story structure, you can branch out to more character-driven ones like the Dan Harmon Story Circle to mesh together world and character building into something that can strengthen your stories using both techniques.

Story Spine

Popularized by Pixar artist Emma Costs who sent a viral tweet about 22 tips that make you a better storyteller, with one rule in particular becominghas become a major topic of conversation among writers called The Story Spine, created by playwright Kenn Adams and detailed in his best-selling book *How to Improvise a Full-Length Play: The Art of Spontaneous Theater*. Made up of seven steps, this method of storytelling helps with the structure of any movie or narrative and has been adopted, as mentioned above, by Pixar, but also by Disney and Lucasfilm to train new writers on all their projects. These seven steps are:

1. Once Upon a Time…—Not beginning strictly with these words, but looking at it from a storytelling perspective as a worldbuilding tool to establish the setting of the story and the protagonist's life until now.

2. And Every Day…—This puts your character into their world and sets the tone for what they're doing or feeling on an average day. This may set up an emotional challenge for them to overcome later.

3. Until One Day…—Life's all roses and libraries until the aliens arrive. This is the part of the story that changes the protagonist's status quo and sets them on their journey.

4. And Because of This… (Part 1)—Think of this as an if/then statement, or a result of cause/effect. Since the character's status quo has been upset, they need to either change or find a way to return to their place of comfort.

5. And Because of This… (Part 2)—The second part of causation results from the previous part. Since the protagonist left their home due to the alien invasion, they weren't able to protect their baby sister, who is now in the clutches of the evil alien queen. So now the protagonist not only needs to find a way to get rid of the aliens, but also to save their sister.

6. Until Finally…—This is the climax of the story. The protagonist gets the information or "thing" they need to achieve their goal or defeat their enemy.

7. And Ever Since That Day…—The story resolves, and as the narrative ends for the main character, the storyteller explains the new status quo that has been achieved and how everyone has been affected by it.

This fairytale-like structure leads the protagonist from their oft humble beginnings all the way to their impending "happily ever after." It's no surprise that children's/family creators favor this method of storytelling at studios like Disney or Pixar.

This simple method is great for breaking through bouts of writer's block. If the two-part "and because of this" sections of this method look familiar, you might have seen or heard them described by South Park creators Trey Parker and Matt Stone as part of their method, which changes them slightly into "but and therefore." Cause and effect are powerful ways to lend momentum to your story in ways that feel natural to your audience, giving way to more tension and rising action leading into your climax. In addition to the "but and therefore" rule that Parker and Stone discuss, they also have the "and then" rule which states that if you can place "and then" in between your story beats, you're writing a boring story. Why is this? Because you're just leading one idea into the next without the events having any reaction to each other. No consequence to whatever happened previously. Considering Parker and Stone created not only one of the most successful cartoons on the planet as well as an award-winning Broadway hit with *The Book of Mormon*, but you might also consider looking into their method as well as The Story Spine for your next script or novel.

In Medias Res

In Latin, it means "in the middle of things," and in the context of story-telling, it means that your story begins partway through your plot to give the sense of immediate action or consequences, while the more mundane story points are filled in later either through dialog or through flashback. If you need an example of this, look no further than The Bard, William Shakespeare himself. He used this technique in some of his most famous works, such as *Hamlet*, *Macbeth*, and *The Tempest*. For Hollywood examples, you could look at the 1947 detective film *Crossfire*, or award-winning hits like *Pulp Fiction* and *Mad Max: Fury Road*.

If you are concerned about locking your audience into your film right away, then In Medias Res is probably the right story structure method for you. In television, this method is sometimes used as part of the cold open, establishing something exciting or horrifying to the plot or main characters and then leading into the opening credits, which then usually leads into a flashback or scene separate from the cold open that gives more context to the overall plot of the episode before tying in the cold open events and leading into the climax and resolution.

While not as fancy or complicated as some of the other story structures listed in this chapter, In Medias Res can have a dramatic effect on your ability to maintain a hold on your audience and get them invested in your story before having to introduce complicated concepts to them. When done correctly, the audience will stay glued to your story until the end, based on the premise that you'll fulfill the promise put forth by your opening scene(s). In Medias Res relies heavily on a social contract, and you as a storyteller need to live up to your end of the bargain to avoid turning off your audience, maybe for good.

#

Adapting and Modifying Existing Structures to Fit Your Story

TTRPG creator and storyteller Connie Chang uses their own story structure, described below along with how they explore and deliver on the themes of the AP they are trying to deliver to their audience:

> 100 times out of 100 times the hardest fucking part about running an AP is the middle. That is always the hardest part because it's the longest part, and it's the part where we have the least amount of guidance. It's the part where you're going to have to take the most risks, and it's the part where you'll fail the most, because in the beginning, anyone can nail an opening. Cold open, bam! Just think of a cool visual, bam! Get everyone in. Bam, bam, bam! You can plan that shit, and it'll look great. The opening is what will get audiences interested and their asses in seats. The middle is where you actually have to prove that your story is worth staying for. That's the hardest part. The ending…I start from the end first, and that doesn't necessarily mean I know how the story's going to end, so there's no surprise for BBEG and there's no surprise for the players. That's not what it means at all. What that means is, I know who the big bad is. I know what their plans are. I know what the world will look like if they succeed. That's the ending.
>
> For me, the big bad is the core theme of the show. So, if the big bad is, for instance, an eldritch representation of the concept of chaos itself, then chaos is probably in conflict with the other themes of fate and destiny, right? Chaos, choice, fate, predetermined destiny, all these things; really big, nebulous, intangible concepts. Then the work of the middle is to boil them down into tangible conflicts that will deepen, reinforce, reverse and/or complicate the themes that you're trying to explore over the course of your campaign.
>
> Every campaign explores different themes, right? Whether you intentionally build them out or not, start from the end there. So, what are the core themes of this campaign? Who are the core antagonists and or main big, bad bitch in charge, who's going to be the engine of the story, and be the vehicle through which I explore those themes? What kind of world am I building to hold these themes and these characters in that will allow them to explore the

story in the most enriching and thematic way possible? Then once I've got the ending kind of figured out all of those aspects, then I kind of go to the beginning. How can I foreshadow all that shit through the beginning and the middle?

You can plan that out pretty well, especially if you've got a good cast with you who's cool with talking about stuff in advance. You let them know, like, hey, we really want the opening to really kick ass. That's when we're going to get butts in seats. Let's think about this.

I guarantee you in Dimension 20 they talk about the opening. Brennan (Lee Mulligan) has a really strong idea for what the opening is going to be already. That's not completely off the cuff, right? The middle, however, and this is kind of why I think of screenwriting. There's the Act Two slump. I've got the opening. Fuck, now I actually have to deliver on the premise. Am I going to do that in a way that isn't trite, in a way that is that hasn't already been overdone, in a way that is unique and in a way that advances the themes in a spontaneous, fun, unexpected and genius way? How am I going to do that?

There' are a lot of different ways that I try to do this. One of them is specifically through the Chaos Protocol, which is our current ongoing campaign. It's planned out in advance to have eight arcs. There's going to be eight arcs, so I roughly know where each of the acts are overall, I like to work, in my head, in like a four-act structure, because I break Act Two into two acts, kind of divided by the midpoint. So, I'm able to kind of neatly group them in by arc. That really helps me out. Then within each arc, when we kind of take the timeline and zoom it in. Each arc comprises 16 streams, which we break up into 32 podcast episodes. So, every podcast episode is like half of one stream. That ends up breaking neatly into four sections as well. That was for my ADHD brain. This just helps me structure really well. So, I know the first four episodes are the beginning, the middle eight is the middle, and the last four are the end.

Connie's four-act storytelling model feels very similar to the Chinese Qǐchéngzhuǎnhé (in English translated/changed to Kishōtenketsu) structure, which is formatted as having an introduction (ki), the development (sho), the twist (ten), and conclusion (ketsu), and attributed to many Chinese and Japanese (where it is known as kishōtengō) four-line poems. An example of this would be 2016's animated feature *Your Name* directed by Makoto Shinkai.

INTEGRATING TTRPG METHODS INTO SCRIPT WRITING

Once you've figured out the story you're trying to tell, decided on the story structure you want to use, and settled on your characters, locations, themes, and other elements, then you're ready to start your script.

That's great news! Now it's time to unleash the power of your words on the blank canvas of the page. Whether you're using a notepad, a notepad app, or industry-standard software like Final Draft or FadeIn, it's time to take all the work you've done and apply it.

POINT OF INSPIRATION

The storytelling possibilities of that instant unleashing of power and something that we still haven't really codified. It's the stuff of sense of wonder, what happens when one magic collides with another in midair. All sorts of chaotic things happen....As a storyteller, I can do anything now. With that awesome power comes the awesome responsibility of trying not to write something that sucks.—Ed Greenwood, the creator of the Forgotten Realms.

You've already done a lot of the work that will drive your script forward and give you the momentum to get from Fade In to the end. All the notes and worldbuilding you've done are now useful as a reference tool whenever you feel lost, or when writer's block takes hold. You can take a moment to escape into the world you've created and look at your story with fresh eyes. Look at your character sheets, maps, and other notes you've taken as you were building the bones of your script. Take a few minutes and act out the scene yourself or with a friend, partner, or random moot on the internet.

Look at where your story starts. Get a feel for the characters that are interacting and driving your first 10–15 pages. Hear the dialog flow as you recite it back to yourself (another helpful tip is to record yourself speaking the dialog and then play it back to yourself).

EXERCISE 2.2

Write the first 10–15 pages of your script. Examine the first ten pages and eliminate all passive verbs you find. Then, get rid of any filler words in your actions to make them feel more urgent and show momentum.

Just like many TTRPGs begin with a rule book that you can refer to in times of indecision or clarification, keep your story and character notes close by to refer to as you progress through your script. If you've written stat blocks for your characters, and they've "leveled up" through the first act of your screenplay, make sure that you update your character's sheet to reflect those changes. This will be useful as your character's arc progresses through the story and will add a layer of consistency if you're ever unsure if your character's decisions are correct or are deviating from where you need them to be.

Game designer James Introcaso shares his approach to using similar methods he used when working in film and television when he is working in the medium of TTRPGs:

> When you're creating something, you're thinking about "what is your North Star", what is the story you're trying to tell? What are the themes of that story? What is important to that story? We're working on this game called Draw Steel, and it's a tactical, cinematic, heroic fantasy game. Whenever we do something, it's got to be in service of at least one of those four things. So, we're probably not going to make something that is about romance among the stars in a hard sci-fi world, because that doesn't really fit the things that we're trying to do with that game, and it is a similar thing to when you're crafting a narrative in television, you need to think about the things that you are doing. Are we telling a story in service to that, and not getting distracted or tempted to go off into the weeds?
>
> Often in television, you have a limited amount of time and are usually constrained by a budget to tell your story, and so you need to think about, how am I going to do this? How am I going to convey this idea in this many seconds? Most tabletop RPGs are a book-based medium. We're constantly talking about how many

pages something is going to take up. How many words is this? How many of those words fit on a page? Because you've only got 400 pages in this book, or if it's a smaller book, maybe you only have 32 or 16, whatever it may be. Those things are very similar, and actually writing for one really helps you with the other. When I had to write 10 and 15 second spots, or even 44-minute television episodes, you learn how to be economical with your words. You also want moments without words when you're crafting a narrative in video. Sometimes you want things to breathe, and so in books, it's the same way. You just want a cool piece of art that people get to take in and allows them to live in the world. You need to be really economical with your words and learn to tell a story in a restricted format. The parameters are there, and what's fascinating about RPGs is, if more people embraced eBooks, an RPG could be as long and as many words as the author wanted it to be, and I think that would be bad for the medium. Those restraints are good for both mediums, because it means that we need to be focused on this "North Star". We're not spending a lot of time wandering around, getting lost in unnecessary stories.

Besides your main characters, keep your reference materials for your secondary, tertiary, or otherwise "NPC" characters handy. Make sure that those characters are more than just cardboard stand-ins in your script. That doesn't mean you need to describe each one, but every character that your main characters interact with in the screenplay should mean something. Otherwise, what is the point of them speaking with that character in the first place? Is the interaction between your main characters (whether they are the protagonists or antagonists) moving the story forward in any way? Can you eliminate or move this interaction to be between the main characters? Can you merge two NPC characters into one to deliver information urgently or effectively?

Speaking about characters in TTRPGs for a moment, many people want to build a character for a game that has optimal stats so they can be prepared to take on any challenge. The checks and balances built into games like D&D and Pathfinder stop most character builds from being overtly overpowered, and the DM/GM can always raise the difficulty level of encounters, but if your character is an invincible tank, they won't be very interesting story-wise. Storyteller and GM Jennifer Kretchmer elaborates more on this:

> If you're the best at everything, there's nowhere for that story to go unless you lose. If you're perfect, if you're Achilles, you've got to have a heel, and if you don't, you're not interesting. There's nothing interesting about that character. It's cool. You hit really hard. No one ever hits you. You have no flaws. Great. Where's the story in that? You're the best at everything. Congratulations. You're also the prom king and the CEO of the company, and the chosen one. There's no story in this. The entirety of narrative is conflict. Story comes out of conflict, and if you are perfect, there is no conflict, unless that perfection is at odds with the world you're in, which most of the time, a person who brings a character that's like a super character to the table is not going to want to be at odds with the world.

Create flawed characters that have traits that relate to real people. Even if you're writing a story about an alien from a faraway world, you still need to give them at least one trait that a human perceiving them can see themselves in. Flaws don't always need to be a physical or mental impairment that could appear ableist or insensitive to people who are actually disabled. Instead, you can give them an attitude problem. Make them narcissistic, greedy, nerdy, or clumsy. If you're set on giving them an impairment, like making them deaf, consider collaborating with someone who is deaf to create an accurate picture of their lived experience to add realism to your story.

Update any maps or location information in your notes to reflect the changes that your characters are making to the world they inhabit. This also includes noting any changing relationships that characters have with each other. Does one character grow from loving to hating another? What about the other way around? Did your chief antagonist blow ten stories from the top of a skyscraper? Make sure you note that to ensure that your hero doesn't end up somewhere they shouldn't be.

These things might sound tedious, but they will save you time in the overall editing and perfecting of your script. If the story logic is there, if the character interactions are solid, and the dialog rings true, all the effort you're making will be worth it.

ANATOMY OF A SCREENPLAY

As previously stated in earlier chapters of this book, screenplays follow their own sets of rules, with formatting being the chief among them. If you spend any amount of time on social media following screenplay discussions, you would think that the largest cardinal sin you could commit with your script was not following one of these rules. The disappointing double standard is that the rules only matter when you're breaking into the industry. This is partially to gatekeep, but also because professional script readers (not necessarily those reading for paid coverage services) who are reading for reps or studios are doing it with speed as their primary driver, with the content being second. If you send out a script that is dubiously formatted, they will immediately flag it for the recycle bin as the work of an amateur. They won't spend the extra couple of minutes learning your formatting style and adapting to it. There are too many scripts in the pile and too few hours in the day. So how do you break through? What are the rules for proper script format?

The first piece of advice is not to really worry too much about it. If you are using screenwriting software like FadeIn or Final Draft, generally speaking, they will properly format your screenplay for you. If you can't afford these industry-standard programs, you can also use free software like Celtx, or even the Notepad app on your computer if you don't have Microsoft Word available to use. First off, scripts typically use a Courier 12-point font. You should format your top and right margins to one inch, with the other margins set the same (but some people will fiddle with orphaned one-liners on otherwise blank pages to get everything to fit neatly).

Your script's cover page should contain the script title, your name, the date the draft was completed, and your contact details.

Script pages contain Scene Headings (Sluglines) followed sometimes by action lines, for example:

```
EXT. CEMETERY—DUSK


It is an ordinary dusk of normal quiet and shadow. The
gray sky contains a soft glow from the recent sun, so
that trees and long blades of grass seem to shimmer in
the gathering night. There is a rasp of crickets, and
the rustle of leaves in an occasional whispering
breeze.
```

Character names and dialog, sometimes including parentheticals:

```
                    BARBARA
     They  ought  to  make  the  day  the  time  changes
     the  first  day  of  summer.  Then  two  good  things
     would  happen  all  at  once.
```

Transitions such as CUT TO, FADE IN, and FADE OUT generally go between scenes to indicate when one scene is over and another begins. FADE IN and FADE OUT specifically are seen mostly at the beginning and end of a script but aren't required as a rule. You can start and end your script however you want.

Your scene headings contain three elements: whether your scene takes place Interior or Exterior, the location of the scene, and the relative time of day (Day, Night, Dusk, etc.). It's a matter of debate whether your scene headings should be bold, but you can do either with little fear of it negatively affecting your script. If you're using software, you likely won't have to worry either way since it will do the "proper" formatting for you.

Your character names are always in all caps to make them easy to spot and the dialog is centered on the page. Any parentheticals should also be centered underneath the character names, while any off-screen (O.S.) or (CONT'D) mentions should be put next to the character name.

If you have any important props or sounds in your scene (a gun, or a honk of a car horn), insert them in your action lines in all caps as well. Your action lines should be formatted with no indentation of the first line (like the way you'd write a business letter).

The length of your script is going to be determined by a few different factors. The first thing being whether it is a short film, a feature film, a half-hour sitcom episode, or an hour-long television program. Most scripts run about a minute of screen time per page. So, if your script is 90 pages, you could reasonably expect the outcome to be roughly 90 minutes on the screen. Most comedy sitcom television shows run about 22–30 pages (depending on whether this is meant to be shot for a streaming service or a network television studio that needs to accommodate commercial breaks). A dramatic scripted television series would run 45–60 pages, again depending on commercial breaks or the intended destination.

Length is always something to consider when you're writing a feature film script. If you're writing something to shoot yourself, you can allow yourself to work within the bounds and budget of what you have available to you. If you have the budget and ability to make a three hour-long movie (179 minutes) like Abdellatif Kechiche's *Blue Is the Warmest Color*, then by all means do so, but also keep in mind that an audience member sitting down to watch a three hour-long independent feature film is a big commitment. Your film needs to earn that attention every minute. In a world where people have the internet in the palm of their hands every second of the day, keeping that attention is a tall order. Sometimes brevity is a better approach. If you are a known quantity in Hollywood like David Lynch, who is known for his off-beat and experimental film style, you can get away with making your three-hour *Inland Empire* with little fear of being castigated and thrown from the hallowed grounds of Hollywood. Lynch has earned the right to make the kinds of films he wants and has proved himself to be competent at creating mainstream successes like *Mulholland Drive*, which goes far when he goes to pitch his next films to executives and/or financiers.

The majority of your script is going to be dialog (unless your intention is to create a silent film), so you need to think about how you want your characters to speak in your story. One of the most common problems for new writers is that all of their characters sound the same (and often like the writer). Veteran screenwriter Dan Hernandez talks about his approach to dialog and finding character voices that are interesting and inform the story he's trying to tell:

> I think the way that I approach dialog is I usually find it helpful to have a North Star. Whether that is a person who I know and I have studied how they speak, or they speak in a specific way, or an interesting way, or they have lots of turns of phrase or malapropisms, or whatever the case may be, where you sort of say, oh, this is an interesting voice to bring into this script.
>
> So, then you start to think, well, what would Matthew Crawley from Downton Abbey have to say to the son of a plumber, Dusty Rhodes, the American Dream? That's an interesting thought experiment. Dialog is tension. Finding points of tension. This goes back to acting, and the intention behind why someone is speaking, what the person wants, what they're trying to accomplish, what they're trying to hide, what they're trying to bring forth. All of those things are really just a way of exploring different tensions

that you have in any conversation or in any scene. So, when you have a voice in mind that's very specific, it becomes a lot easier to figure out.

If I have an upper crust guy like Matthew Crawley talking to a very blue-collar kind of guy like Dusty Rhodes, maybe there are things that they're saying that they don't understand what they're talking about. Maybe there are words that someone is familiar with that they're not familiar with, or maybe Dusty Rhodes thinks that this guy's a snob, and so that makes his attitude be a little bit more standoffish than if he were talking to someone that he felt more philosophically aligned with. We're talking about a lot of things simultaneously happening. It's intention, it's status, it's desire, it's stakes, it's all of those things that kind of coalesce, and then you add on top of it, what is the actual situation that's occurring? So now let's pretend that Matthew Crawley is a Jedi and Dusty Rhodes is someone that just learned that they have the force. Okay? Now the content of what they're talking about, it's the same character dynamic. It's no different from all the things that I just talked about, about class and status, but now we've given it a spin that it's science fiction. It dictates how they speak to each other. It dictates the dialog.

I have my main Dungeons & Dragons character, a goblin chef named Tum Tum. So, Tum Tum was modeled after this incident on the original Japanese Iron Chef show that I always got such a kick out of. When Morimoto became Iron Chef, there was a faction called the Ōta Faction that did not believe in his Neo-Japanese cuisine. They only wanted him to cook in a classical Japanese style, and so they didn't like it when Morimoto would do things like use ketchup in a Japanese dish, or whatever thing that he felt was qualified as Neo-Japanese cuisine.

So I took that concept and applied it to this goblin chef, Tum Tum, who felt that he could bring Neo-Goblin cuisine to the world, that the full range of what goblins were capable of cooking was not understood, and that even though the ingredients were sort of gross to a human or elf palette, he could elevate it in such a way that you wouldn't mind eating purple worm anus or whatever the case may be. That was the concept, and as I played Tum Tum more and more, and as I sort of understood the things that

Tum Tum was interested in, the things that Tum Tum was not interested in, the things that Tum Tum would get mad about. It was a lot easier to improv dialog in the headspace of Tum, because I really understood him from the inside out.

This chapter covers a lot of different examples and concepts related to structuring your stories. It is encouraged that you play around with them and figure out what works best for your style of writing. Additionally, while it's important to understand the format of a screenplay, it's important that you don't allow formatting to get in the way of creativity. Software will do the heavy lifting of formatting, leaving you to concentrate on building your worlds and characters into something wondrous.

CHAPTER 3

Worldbuilding

TYING IN THE STORY

POINT OF INSPIRATION

"To make a conclusion really pop, to make it really sing, it needs to be the conclusion that was hidden from you, and you didn't see all the pieces until the end."—Jason Bulmahn

Worldbuilding is a skill that many writers struggle to master. Not because they lack the ability to express what physical objects are in a room or create a pantheon of deities that inhabit the afterlife or lord over their mortal realms, but because the sheer breadth of what it takes to create a living world, once you stop to look around you and take in all the details, is enough to give anyone pause. When asked about his lore creation process and whether you can add too much lore to a story, famed author and world builder Ed Greenwood commented thus:

> It can bog down a researcher's process. It can cause dungeon masters who are novices or have imposter syndrome to get it in spades, because they just stopped dead, overwhelmed. I'm from the other school. I don't think it's possible to have too much lore. It is possible to overwhelm yourself if you want to follow it all religiously and not deviate, but if you just view it in the same way

DOI: 10.1201/9781003538202-3

that when we were little kids, if you read through the encyclopedia and you just sort of page through stuff at random, you'd find all sorts of fascinating things. If you tried to read it cover to cover. Yeah, it'd be too much. But if you just sort of use it to dip into and find stuff, and don't feel bound by the stuff next door. That's the way I do lore.

Do not procrastinate. Once you find yourself writing timelines for a kingdom or a dynasty past three generations….It's one thing if you want to know who's on the throne now, who his father was, and who knows, his father may still be around, deposed or lurking or is undead or whatever, and who his grandfather was, and if he had a famous founding ancestor who founded the kingdom, and is known for lopping orc's, heads off, one handed as he strode out to the battlefield with his breakfast tea or whatever, then he would be recorded. If you're writing anything else past that, you're procrastinating, you're getting away from writing the story that you should be writing, because what humans want is to be told stories, and everything else you're doing should support the storytelling. If you go through the history of the kingdom and write these huge, long timelines, you are procrastinating so you don't have to write the story. I would say, at that point, there is too much lore, because you're allowing the lore to take control of you, not the other way around.

Sometimes the story comes to you, and you work the script around an existing idea you've had knocking around in your brain or one of your cohorts brings an idea to the table. Filmmaker and author Jamie Nash has written for a variety of projects in different genres. He's done everything from horror to family films. Jamie is the writer of "Save the Cat! Writes for TV" and "Save the Cat! Beat-Sheet Workbook." He discussed the unique way his latest film, *Last Night at Terrace Lanes* came together on the independent film podcast FilmSnobbery Live! and how collaboration was the key component in finding the right people to bring his film to life:

Terrace Lanes was an interesting one because it was made locally. I live in Maryland, by the way, and it was made in Frederick, Maryland. A producer, Carlo Glorioso, who I've known for years, and the first project we worked on together was V/H/S/2. In

V/H/S/2, we did a short called A RIDE IN THE PARK. It was, if you remember V/H/S/2, the zombie one shot with a GoPro. We shot that in Frederick as well, in a place called The Watershed. So, Carlo, who I went to high school with, actually, but this was the first project we worked on together. He had basically three things when he called me up. Carlo had a one-page synopsis, a lead, the elite actress, Francesca Capaldi, who wanted to do horror movies now that she was an adult (after being in Disney shows as a kid such as Dog With A Blog). He had her, and he had a bowling alley. He took that to me, and he said, hey, you think you can come up with something for this? And by the way, they're closing the bowling alley in eight weeks or something. They're tearing the bowling alley down in like eight weeks.

So, no script yet, really, eight weeks to go and a one-page synopsis, which he pitched to another writer that used to be local, Jenna St John, and she wrote a pitch to show to Epic Pictures to get the money. Epic said, okay, we like this, but we'll have to see a script. So, I brought in a co-writer of mine, Adam Cesare, who I had been working with for a few years prior to this, and he was able to rip out the first draft of a script. I was the boots on the ground. I could go to the bowling alley and stuff like that. So, as he was writing, we were modifying the script to the actual location, to actors, to stunts we could do, all that stuff. It was definitely a fun collaborative thing. Adam was able to fire up a script in a week or two while he was on his vacation. Then, of course, we kept writing it up to the last minute with Adam, and then we shot the movie. It was a 12-day shoot. They were pretty full days. That's the long story of how the movie came about, and how I came to be on the movie.

Writing a script in a piecemeal fashion like Jamie and his friends allows you to write for the resources you have, building the world your characters experience around your ability to execute. To put it in TTRPG terms, if your character's backpack only has a certain set of items in it, and you aren't in a town with any shops to buy new weapons or potions, then you need to use what you've got and make the best of it. That's what many independent filmmakers do when they're making movies outside of the Hollywood studio system. This is where your creativity can really shine in a collaborative situation. When you know that all you've got in your "backpack" is a bowling alley, an actress, and an idea, you take those things and create magic with them.

Sometimes you're telling the story on the fly with only a few key points fleshed out at first. TTRPG GM, podcast producer, and actor Sara Roberts (also known as TheHypeGoblin online) talks about her experience running sessions of Apocalypse Keys with her players, and how she relied on them to help her fill in the gaps in the larger elements of her storytelling:

> I ran a short campaign of Apocalypse Keys, and the way you structure a mystery for Apocalypse Keys is you essentially just have a list of clues, and then as things happen throughout the game, you're meant to ask players specific prompting questions that then further build out the world.
>
> So, I told them I was going to have an overarching storyline because we were playing all the pre-written adventures that came with the Apocalypse Keys Kickstarter, but I wanted to tie it all in into this overarching mystery that they would also have to solve at the end. They all brought to me these fantastically vibrant characters, and after we got towards the end of the first mystery, they gave me the BBEG (Big Bad Evil Guy) through their actions. I found the bad guy, and as their characters developed throughout the story, I dropped little tidbits of what the overarching plot was. The more they played, the more it fully formed in my head.
>
> We were probably halfway through the campaign when I knew what the endgame was for the big bad. It was very collaborative and got me really comfortable letting the players direct what's happening, while still knowing what my big bad wanted to do in the back of my mind.
>
> With my 5e campaign I'm currently running, I came up with what the BBEG in this game wants. I know what their goals are. I know the items that they're trying to get, and I can essentially move that information around wherever the players go. So, there's always going to be a way for them to discover it wherever they try to explore. But for how they are further tied into the main plot, that's just been something that I sat down with (the players) at the start of the game (and I didn't really have much of the world built when I brought them in). I knew what the first town was that they were going to start in, why they were there, and I had the little

fetch quests they were going to do as they team-built together for those first four levels.

I sat down with each of them for about an hour, and I said, okay, tell me who you are. Where is your character from in this world? What does your hometown look like? I am firmly of the belief that every player should be an expert in their character's hometown. Those shouldn't be questions that they have to look to me to be like, hey, would I know this about the place where I grew up and lived, and I'm an adult elf in my 50s with 50 years of experience on the material. You should know where to go to get the best deal on magical items. You're going to know who is likely to swindle you, who's the local politician that's currently in power. So, I sat down with them for about an hour, and we went through step by step, and we talked about those sorts of things, and I wrote them all their own little article. Then I made them do things like give me an NPC somewhere in town that you didn't like. Tell me why. Give me three NPCs that you're close with. Give me the NPC that you would go to if you needed really good advice. So, through those conversations, that's where I got the information that I needed. Outside of their backstories that they handed me to better tie them into the main plot, I've been able to pull items from their characters' past that have nothing to do with that backstory they gave me, but still support it, and will still be things to drive them instinctually forward through the narrative, because they're things they didn't even think about as players, that could potentially be a big deal to them, that mean a whole heck of a lot. I to let the players dictate main plot points outside of those key things that the BBEG has to do.

THE LOCATIONS

You have a fantastic plot and characters ready to go, but you still need a world for them to carry out their whims and machinations. Where your story takes place can be almost as important as any other component. The location informs the momentum of the characters in it. Locations provide atmosphere. The sun setting over the dunes of the desert outside of Dubai hits entirely differently than the same thing happening from the rooftop of a convenience store in New Jersey. Famed worldbuilder and author Ed Greenwood discusses how characters and story are informed by location:

What are my story needs? I'm not usually formalizing this in my mind. I'm just looking over the character's shoulder at the surroundings. What's the look and feel? Is this a creepy old street? Is it a street you would not want to be on after dark? I don't mean from thugs, though maybe there's that too, but because it's haunted, because things could come sidling out of the shadows that you don't want ever to touch you. What is the vibe here? What is the architecture? What do I smell? What do I see? I'm in the immediate surroundings. What are the surroundings doing? They're grounding the story. They're giving the reader, or they're giving the viewer, for movies, an idea of the stakes, which is why so many movies in the middle of a big or build up to a war scene will show a little kid crying or being pulled away by their parents. You're reminding the audience; this is what you're fighting for. This is what hangs in the balance here. These are the stakes. So, what you're doing is setting the stage by what's immediately around your protagonist, your on-screen characters. That's where you need to put your immediate work, and then afterwards you can world build to support that.

For example, I have built this billboard. What do I need to support it so it's at the right height that cars can see it driving past and will stay there for more than five minutes, or the next high wind? What do I need to build in underneath it? That's where the world building comes in. That's usually the way I do it. If I was answering a question in, say, a course where somebody was asking, well, the world building, what do you do first? I'd say, what do you want to use it for? Is this a one-shot story that's never going to have a sequel? Then you just need the immediate story needs. That's all. You can do more if you want to do more, if, like me, you love the world building.

If it's going to be a long-running series, if it's going to turn into a STAR WARS, you better have all that stuff worked out, because otherwise somebody else is going to work it out for you, and they're going to work it out 'wrong'. I don't mean that their stuff is going to be crappy, but they will not know where all the skeletons are buried. They're not going to know the cross linkages that you know, because you haven't yet put them into print. They're in your head. So, if you want to get there first, do that much, and then you can at least hand them a story bible. They can then ignore it, but you have done it. And if they ignore it, they're idiots. Now, there's no shortage of idiots in the world. The nice thing about a story bible is only fools ignore them, because if somebody has done all that work for you, that can be really handy, and it's all there for a reason. And the reason may just be because, oh, I put a dinosaur in, because I like dinosaurs or whatever. But usually, it is something that is story useful. There's a reason every single element is there. So, you can ignore something, and you can change something, but you should know why it was there in the first place.

If the person's still alive and handy to talk to, talk to them, okay, why'd you put that in there? What is that setting up? What is that bridging? Are there plans that I don't know about for a sequel? Is that where the big invasion is going to come from that's going to sweep away the kingdom? I start with the look, feel, and smell. I developed a shorthand years ago for the Forgotten Realms adventures. Name of the city. Population. Its nickname -- City of Spices, City of Golden Staves, or whatever it is. Who rules? Who really rules? What meets the eye, the imports and exports, because that's your lifeblood? That's what's flowing. That's where the business and the income come from, the salaries. So that tells you all you need to know about how to, say, starve out the city or ruin it, or whatever. So that's your wider story. If there's suddenly a shortage of this crop that fails, a potato famine. Now you have your huge story prompts and things that are going to change the world.

I'm almost a movie camera when I start, because it's what am I seeing all directly around me. Because if you're doing it for gaming, role-playing, that's what the Dungeon Master is going to have to describe at the table, first and foremost. So why not help the Dungeon Master by actually putting what they need right now, right there in front of them, and then, you can do all the airy-fairy stuff.

Everything Ed Greenwood says above is correct, and he should know, as the author of hundreds of books, including games and scripts, that filling out your locations is an essential aspect of worldbuilding. Not just knowing the cities and towns in relation to one another, but also understanding how changes in one affect the others. Wars change landscapes, economies, populations, birth rates, and more. Using another example straight from the not-so-distant past of the United States, there are many businesses like gas stations, hotels, and tourist destination spots that were built along long stretches of out-of-the-way roads on the promise that a major highway or railroad line might soon come through the area, creating an economic boom for the residents there. Only for politicians or gangsters to sway the vote for the highway or railroad to go in another direction, decimating the chances of a future for the towns affected by the decision. A scenario similar to this makes up a subplot of the movie *Psycho* and explains why the Bates Motel is sitting on a lonely stretch of road with few people taking up vacancies in the establishment. What can you take away from a setting like this?

The smell and heat from the surrounding desert give off an arid feeling. It's oppressive if you're out in it too long. There's no humidity there, but the sand and the sun penetrate and dehydrate you. The loneliness of the setting makes getting away feel difficult. There's nowhere to run to but it also gives the viewer/reader a sense of sympathy for Norman Bates' character, stuck all by himself (unless you count "Mrs. Bates") in a big empty motel and house. The furniture in the motel probably smells musty from lack of use, despite Norman's attendance and care for the property. Hitchcock does a wonderful job of setting the stage for his horror masterpiece.

FROM THE AUTHOR

Filmmaker Kevin Smith made his first film at the Quick Stop convenience store where he worked at. Doing this didn't just save him money on locations, but he was also intimately familiar with that store and its frequent customers. He took his day-to-day experiences and made an unforgettable piece of cinematic art that spawned two sequels and jumpstarted his career. He's not the only filmmaker to take a familiar place and set their stories there. Directors like Martin Scorsese, Spike Lee, Barry Jenkins, and Woody Allen have all captivated audiences by personifying their cities by immortalizing them on celluloid. This follows the "write what you know" principle of storytelling. It doesn't matter if you come from and still live in a small one-horse town. Small towns have secrets and intrigue too. Just look at how the Coen Brothers portray small towns in their films (if you've never seen *Raising Arizona* or *Fargo*, what are you waiting for?).

Professional GM, producer of the Luck & Chaos podcast, and improv actor Sara Roberts (also known as TheHypeGoblin online) goes over some tools she uses to create the worlds she and her players immerse themselves in. She also covers how she keeps track of all the different information that is essential to effective storytelling at the game table:

> I would love to use minis, but I play with people all over the world online. So unfortunately, that's never been something I've been able to do, but I try to bring that same experience to our VTT sessions. We use Foundry and I use Dungeon Alchemist to create 3D perspective and animated maps, trying to make it as immersive a visual experience for the players as I can, and I have added recently Syrinscape to that as well, so I can sound-scape environments a little more.
>
> As far as keeping it organized, I actually just started using World Anvil because I was already using the wiki-style features of the note taking journal in Foundry, but it was limiting. Only my players could see it, and I wanted to create something for the people who support our campaign to get a little more lore about the world or be able to go and look up the photo of an NPC. I do Hero Forge minis for all the NPCs that I give a name to, and I also have some in my back pocket that don't have names yet. I don't always go into detail about what the NPCs look like, because I'm a big believer in people using their own imagination to fill in the gaps with storytelling, so I usually just give them enough that they can pick up on the personality and whether the person is like a gnome or a bugbear or whatever. But I created a wiki through World Anvil, and that has been, for me, the best place to organize all my notes, because I only have to create an article entry once. Then, when I've started writing when I have to create a dungeon, or I have sessions where there's going to be lore drops, I can create myself a private adventure page or a private wiki page for that session, and I can hit the auto-link feature and everything I could possibly need that I have mentioned in that (adventure) is already linked within what I just created. I can also just do a keyword search for anything that I need to find. It also lets me reveal things to the players. So, as they find things, the articles get added to their view. Then they can go in and they can keyword search, and

they can look at the city, and when you're on the city page, it lists all the NPCs that are there and all the different shop names that are there. I have all the maps there with different points of interest pins, so they can see where they are in relation to the other items in town.

It's been a large undertaking, because I didn't start it when I started the campaign. I started it when we hit level six, so I had a backlog of things to get in there, but it's been one of the best ways to interlink pieces of information in ways that are digestible for people and for myself. There's even a relationship tracker on there, so I can track family trees and stuff, and I can instantly pull up the family tree for an NPC.

Map-Making

Many popular franchises have released maps related to the places their characters have visited. If you want to place the Shire in Middle Earth in relation to the Eye of Sauron, you can do so easily. When Luke Skywalker describes Tatooine as the planet farthest from the bright center of the universe in *Star Wars*, you can jump online and find dozens of official and unofficial representations of the galaxy far, far away.

TTRPGs, in the past, have been played in the "theater of the mind," but even the oldest editions of D&D have seen Dungeon Masters taking out graph paper and drawing scale representations of the caverns and castles their players have traversed. Times have changed, and there are many tools available to people looking to make their games more visual. VTTs (Virtual Table Tops) have maps built into some of the adventure paths you can load into them. Many rule and adventure books come with fold-out maps you can put on your tables or walls. There's even a community of mapmakers that you can commission to bring the worlds in your head to life.

Want to create your own maps? Try online services like Inkarnate or RPG Map, or other online map-making platforms. Roll20 is a virtual table tops (VTT) that has its own built-in map-making feature. There are also some great YouTube videos that you can watch and try to emulate what the experts there suggest. If you want to have a bit of fun while you're doing some map-making, have a go at some cartography and drawing-based RPGs like D100 Dungeon: World Builder or Cozy Town. Having a clear description available to you of the world your characters are inhabiting has many advantages. If you're explaining that the journey your characters are on will take a week, then it's advantageous to track that journey to ensure that it makes sense to the rest of the story that fills in the gaps between point A and point B.

Understanding how your world is put together will give you a clearer sense of the ecology of the world, how nations communicate with each other and share (or go to war) various resources available to them. Knowing the regions of your world will aid you in knowing the kinds of crops that grow there and the animals that farmers use to work on their farms or keep as pets. Dash Kwiatkowski, who has worked on the Pathfinder Tian Xia Lost Omens World Guide, elaborates on this and gives an example they've used in the past that they found fun and helpful:

> There's a game called A Quiet Year. It's a DM-less game you play with a couple people, and basically, it's a deck of cards, and each card has a little prompt. You are not role-playing as an individual character. Everyone around the table is role-playing in the same community. It's a lot of drawing. You have this big blank piece of paper, and together you draw a map on it, and then the prompts affect the society that you're building and how that map fills out and how you decide this society. The entire premise is, you're a society, or some community that has escaped destruction or the apocalypse, and you're founding a new community.
>
> There are some games that are really focused on just the character-building thing, that maybe go more in depth on character stuff than a D&D character builder. If you want to do just map building, world building, setting building. If you're a person who struggles to make a map that is consistent, that you can keep in your brain to say where are things located, stuff like that, this game is what you're looking for.

Interiors

Everything has a place. If you were to close your eyes right now, could you picture everything in your bedroom? Do you know how many steps it is from your bedroom door to your closet? From your closet to your bed? Not everyone has the ability to comprehend the scale of a space, so having a representation of any room a scene takes place in can be very helpful to players, or anyone else who might need to know that there's a secret passage leading to the villain's lair behind the bookcase at the far end of the library.

You might not need to know this as a screenwriter per se, but the clearer you can communicate your settings to the other people involved in bringing your vision to life, the happier you'll be (especially if you're dealing with any pre-viz people or location scouts).

Exteriors

Sometimes overlooked and as important as interiors, exterior locations can be more than just passing establishing shots between scenes. Think of iconic scenes in film that take place outdoors, like the reveal of the DeLorean time machine at the Twin Pines Mall in *Back to the Future*, or the Art Museum Steps in Philadelphia, made famous in the movie *Rocky* during the iconic training scene. Writing exteriors can open up your film, expanding the scope of a series of scenes that might otherwise feel claustrophobic or limiting to the characters' motivations or story.

Novice writers can sometimes feel like they're writing large exterior scenes irresponsibly of the movie's budget. This might be true if you're an independent filmmaker responsible for every dime that gets put on the screen, then consider writing toward the resources you have and exteriors that you can film cheaply, without expensive permits, or in places you can get permission from. When you are writing and submitting scripts to your reps, studios, contests, and other avenues, don't hold yourself back from giving your story the breathing room it deserves. If you need to set an emotional scene at the Grand Canyon or the top of the Empire State Building, just do it. The people writing the check for it can decide whether your scene needs to be rewritten for their budget.

History, Politics, and Society

Your story takes place in a living, breathing world. It's up to you to fill that world with people—complicated, messy people. This aspect of humanity gives you so much to play with when you're writing. Giving your people a history and heritage, good or bad, makes them relatable. Showing off the good and the bad of how their societies are set up adds essential flavor and backstory to how people perceive the tale you're telling. It can tell them who or what to root for, or who to despise, just as much as outright telling them who the antagonist is.

The Godfather series is one example of how a movie that includes complicated ties between family, the politics of leadership within a strictly coded ethnocentric world full of guile and violence. If you were to strip away any one element of that film, the rest of the worldbuilding would fall apart. Take away the family aspect of the Corleones and you wouldn't be able to connect to and humanize them. Take away the historical vendetta of the organized crime scenes and you would lose character motivation, and it would just be people murdering each other for territory and clout. If you were to take away the violence, then the movie would lose some of its most iconic scenes. The violence isn't necessarily what makes those scenes iconic, but the way the scenes are executed and how the people involved in them behave is why we're so drawn to them. We see the chain reaction of violence within the family and within the mob community portrayed in the movie.

TENSION, DRAMA, AND SOMETIMES COMEDY

POINT OF INSPIRATION

"We want to have something ridiculous and something fun, but something unsettling throughout all of it."—Grant Howitt

Professional GM, actor, and gamer Jeff Cannata (The Dungeon Run, The Totally Rad Show, We Have Concerns) talks about the challenges of creating tension in games and balancing the audience's and player's expectations of success:

I think that's one of the biggest challenges of using role-playing games as a storytelling device, especially for an audience is the tension, because what works in storytelling is act two, you got to fail for act three to feel good, but players never want to fail. They want to have all wins, and that tension of the player inside the character, playing the character, wants to always do the best possible thing they can do in that moment. But as a screenwriter, the characters have to screw up. They have to get it wrong. They have to fail and be miserable for the audience to become invested in their eventual success, and that tension is the hardest thing to manage. I have found in doing an AP in front of an audience, because part of me as the facilitator of fun wants to give my players wins, wants them to feel good, wants the session to end on them to be like, that was awesome, but also I understand the audience needs them to fail and needs it to be hard and needs them to do the wrong thing. But it doesn't feel good for the players for that to happen. To navigate that is a real, real challenge.

It's not even winning. It's doing the best possible thing in the situation. Players want to feel smart. They want to feel like they did it. They played the game the best possible way and supported their fellow players like you're part of a team. So, nobody wants to be the one that screws up. Nobody wants to roll the natural one. Nobody wants to be the one that had the spell that would have worked, but they did a different spell, or whatever it is, but, man, that's so satisfying to an audience. The natural ones are way more fun than the natural 20s, most times.

Canadian tabletop role-player and co-creator of the Malevolent and Dice Shame podcasts, Harlan Guthrie, speaks to one aspect of what makes comedy work within the scope of TTRPGs:

The secret to good comedy, and Leslie Nielsen is the master of this, and all comedians, actors like Vince Vaughn, take the world seriously. No matter how wacky AIRPLANE is, Leslie Nielsen believes he's a doctor and believes that he can help these people. Comedy is played straight, and that's how good comedy works. You don't break that character because the characters have to feel authentic to the world. And there's, to me, there's too many RPGs that miss that. They're joking outside of it, and they're not really taking it seriously, because then it just makes me feel disconnected from it. And it's this interesting wave of, like, having comedians on your D&D show and your D&D podcast, not someone who loves role-playing, really, not someone who's a friend of the player, but just somebody who's really funny. It's always a weird perspective.

As we'll discuss later in this book, when we talk about writing for specific genres, comedy relies on many factors to work effectively for the audience.

One factor is timing, which is crucial, and the other is chemistry with the other actors in the scene. This is why the majority of famous AP players, currently, have backgrounds in comedy improv acting. They understand and trust their scene partners, or, with tabletop gaming, their fellow players, and to some extent the Game Master, to keep pushing the rock up the hill until they fulfill the premise of the joke.

Comedy can have many uses in your story. Sometimes after your characters have gone through a rough patch, a moment of levity can give them the energy to move forward. It can be a morale booster. Other times, it can act to close out a scene (also called a button). Another effective method of using comedy in your story is as a callback to something that happened earlier in the tale. This can be expressed multiple times over the course of your story but works most effectively in 3s.

The "rule of three" is something that is used in stories all the time. For example, the story of "Goldilocks and the Three Bears." There are three beds, three bowls of porridge, three chairs, and of course, the three titular bears. The technique is used to reinforce the theme and make the story more memorable and persuasive (consider that the story of the three bears is a parable about not entering someone's property or using their things without permission). In comedy, the "rule of three" uses the first example to set up the joke's premise, the second is to reinforce and telegraph the joke, and the third instance is the payoff and/or punchline of the bit.

Consider that a large portion of screenplays and stories are told in three acts. There is a correlation between the number three and how we perceive a satisfying story arc. In advertising and marketing, they use the "rule of three" all the time. Look around you at billboards, watch commercials on TV or on the internet, and observe how often most taglines and sayings are made up of three words or short statements.

EXERCISE 3.1

Find and document three examples of the rule of three from three separate pieces of media. Why are they effective (as comedy, as prose, or as marketing/advertising tools)?

Jeff Cannata continues, discussing how he would structure his episodes of The Dungeon Run and how aware he was of the ebb and flow of the episodes as he was both GM'ing in front of the camera and working on the edit after the fact. He also briefly talks about the grueling pace at which most APs are produced, with many shows not having any breaks for their cast and crew because of the need to keep up with audience demand and not wanting to lose their attention amidst the sea of other content creator:

> It was a very difficult thing. It was hard on me and on my family. That we went for three and a half years without a real break. I mean, we had like one or two weeks off for the holidays, that was it, and I was coming up with four hours of new content every single week. It's intense.
>
> One thing we were reacting against in creating The Dungeon Run was just putting the video camera on a bunch of friends playing a game, which is a perfectly viable way to do it, and very entertaining, and a lot of people do it to great effect. I have nothing against that, but we didn't want to do that. We brought together people that weren't friends ahead of time. We cast the show with people that didn't know each other at all, but were very highly skilled and committed, and wanted to create episodes modeled after episodic television. I was extremely disciplined with myself about moving things along when they got stagnant, allowing the players to have room to improvise and RP and dig into their characters and have these lovely moments where I just shut up and let them do it for long stretches. But also, they were great at recognizing when things needed to move on. They were great at self-editing. This is something that improv actors know very well; when to edit a scene, how to get out of a scene, and how to help other actors get out of a scene. Our players were excellent at that, and I prided myself on that as well.
>
> In my prep, I would structure episodes very technically. We had an intermission in our show, and I knew I needed to have a crescendo before intermission and a crescendo after intermission. So sometimes things got shifted around, and you definitely are spinning plates and coming up with stuff on the fly, and things don't go where you want them to go. But I had that (prep to) be able to hang my hat on pre-show, knowing that there was going to be a satisfying A-part and B-part, and what the audience was going to come away with that episode, thinking we've done something, and it was important (to the story and characters). That

honestly isn't always the case with some APs that I watch, where sometimes, in a whole episode, hours of your time, and there's been no progression of the story.

That's not what we wanted to do. We wanted to have an episode be about something, and then the next episode be about something, all adding up to something even greater, and I really think, with only a few exceptions, we accomplished that over 150 episodes (of the show).

DEATH, DYING, DISEASE, AND DISABILITY

Like novels and movies, TTRPGs are trying to tell a story. Sometimes the less fun parts of life become part of that story. In reality, if you come down with a disease, you might be in for a tough fight for your life. In films, disease can become a central part of the plot, either acting as a storytelling MacGuffin or a metaphor for larger themes. It doesn't come with real-world consequences. In games, you can cure a disease with a potion, or by seeing a shaman or alchemist. Disease becomes a token or badge on your character sheet. So, how do you make things like death and disease mean anything in the fictional worlds you're creating?

Writer and director Harlan Guthrie, who created the Lovecraftian audio drama Malevolent as well as the sci-fi/horror podcast Deviser, talks about death and dying in his games and podcasts:

I don't do character death unless it goes back to the story. To me, a character death needs to be deserved. If you can cross a plateau of lava rocks and roll a one and everything you've built towards with that character is gone. Is it indicative of reality? Yeah, people can fall, and they can die, but we're not telling RPGs to be real. We're not telling RPGs to be a reflection of reality (unless you are, then fair enough). I think death should be as random as it is in reality. Your character should roll for strokes and heart attacks and all that kind of shit that people get.

Similarly, Brogan Kelley, who goes by the moniker NoNat1s on social media and his YouTube channel, speaks about his experiences at the table handling character death as both a player and as a GM:

I am a firm believer that death should mean something. You should never die for no reason, unless it's session one. Session one, death is fully on the table, and it's fucking hilarious. Session one of one of my first Pathfinder 2e campaigns. I wasn't GM'ing. We were being chased after a prison break. We were being chased by the guards, and the investigator fell into a pit trap. The investigator had an eight strength and no athletics training, and it was 20 feet down, so we couldn't get him out, and we didn't have any equipment, because we just escaped from jail. So, we didn't have any rope or anything, and so we just had to be like, 'sorry' and keep running. And even the player was just like, 'No, no, no, you're fine. You're fine'. I think he was suffering bleed damage too from the fall, so he was just bleeding out in the pit, and we couldn't help him.

When I'm a player, yeah, I'm totally fine. Kill me. Make it matter. If it's past session one and a kobold from a random encounter in the woods critically hit me. It would suck to die there. It wouldn't be satisfying from a story perspective. I understand some people are like, well, it's realistic, and I'm like, "cool, there's also dragons", it's not exactly realistic.

As a GM, I will, especially after session one; if somebody were to die, I will always take them aside, either during the session or after the session, and say, "hey, how attached are you to this character? How much do you really want to see their story conclude and proceed and progress"? Depending on their answer, I'll change things. I'll leave their fate ambiguous. If we're in the dead middle of a session and they're about to bleed out and die, if they want to stay with that character, I'm going to have them suffer a major permanent injury of some kind, or some kind of consequence.

In a movie script, consequences can be a powerful storytelling mechanic. Decisions made early in the story can have a significant impact on the characters and their ability to succeed later, with death being the ultimate consequence for a main character or their loved ones. One of the more popular examples of this is the film *The Godfather*. Al Pacino's character Michael tries so hard to stay out of his family's business, start a family of his own, and live a life free from the decisions and influence of his father, Don Vito Corleone. A large part of the film is Michael exploring "civilian" life outside of the criminal enterprise that the Don has surrounded himself with. Each decision erodes the morality of Michael's character, culminating in his joining his father and then succeeding him after his death. The parting shot of *The Godfather* is a meeting in Michael's office, with two men paying their respects to Michael as the new Don Corleone. Michael's wife is looking on from the next room, with the door to the office being closed to symbolize the separation of the life Michael wanted from the one he ultimately chose.

Acclaimed writer and GM B. Dave Walters speaks more about how consequences affect the story, especially when your characters are extremely powerful and almost godlike:

> My big niche is 'level 20'. That's the stories I tell. Those are stories I love. People are concerned about party balance. At level 20, that's not a thing. Everybody can do everything, and that's not the point. The point isn't about whether you have the power to do a thing, because you all most certainly do. The question now becomes, what are the consequences of that application of power? You can show up and you can destroy a kingdom with Meteor Swarm pretty easily.
>
> In D&D 3.5, there was Tidal Wave. A character did it once and wiped out a kingdom. Now you got a refugee crisis because you didn't kill them all, or did you? Did you want to kill them all, because that country had allies, their allies are now marching against you, and you're like, "Well, we're going to kill them too". Okay, but they're going to send 10,000 soldiers, and statistically speaking, 2,000 of them are going to get natural 20s on their Longbow shots, and you're going to get shot out of the sky. Everything continues to the next and next and next and next and next. My philosophy with the Wish spell, I use the old Twilight Zone monkey paw version, where you can do absolutely anything, but it is going to do exactly what you say, as twisted as possible.

A sometimes-touchy subject in TTRPGs is how the players and game companies handle disability in their sessions and rulebooks. Representation matters. If you are someone with a disability, whether it's prominent or imperceptible, you deserve to see yourself represented in the world. This is true in fictional worlds as much as it is in the real one. Having a diverse population filled with people of all abilities, ages, races, ancestries, religions, and heritages makes a world interesting, and full, and contributes to the growth of all peoples.

Jennifer Kretchmer, a seasoned film and TV professional, discusses her transition to tabletop gaming and her role as a disability consultant in media:

> Regardless of what type of media you're talking about, it's a vastly underrepresented community in the real world. It's more than 26% of the population. In media, it's an infinitesimally small portion of the characters we see represented and the performers we see represented. And of those, there are certain types of depictions that are much more common than others. There's not a lot of understanding about the nuance of disability and that often things are a spectrum. They're not binary. Things aren't on-off switches. A lot of my work is individualized to the project. Sometimes I'll be working with writers rooms teams, talking from the inception of a project. Ideally, I come in from the very beginning and can work with the team on creating inclusive worlds, accurate characters, authentic representation. Often, I get brought in at the last minute, and then we're trying to go back and course correct things (which are often more expensive for projects when they decide to do that), but making those changes is better than not making those changes.
>
> It can be looking at art and evaluating the art and working with a design team, evaluating text, looking at mechanics, discussing how certain things would work in a world, talking about, especially when you're talking about speculative fiction. What does that mean in terms of disability? Too often people think that having magic or high-tech options means there's an erasure of disability, and because I have a background in the academic work around disability, in disability studies, and a lot of work in Disability Justice spaces, I get to introduce people to understandings about the frameworks around disability and the models around disability that change how you can think about how you know what disability means in terms of a society, what access means, what inclusion means, because it can mean different things in different places and different ways.

I worked on Starfinder's Ciravel character, who's an Iconic Precog and an ambulatory wheelchair user. Part of what we thought about was, you're in space, and I have Ehlers-Danlos Syndrome (EDS), which is a connective tissue disorder, and thinking about what gravity would mean to my body in different places, and my ability to move around, and whether I'd be able to walk around or if I'd need my cane, if I'd need a wheelchair, and how that would apply to a character like Ciravel. Getting to think about that in terms of speculative fiction, how does that change how your body moves around a space in space?

They've actually found that often, deaf people are some of the best astronauts because they are less susceptible, because of inner ear imbalances, to a lot of the motion sickness and several other issues that are challenges for non-disabled people. It's really interesting when you scratch the surface. My favorite moment when I'm consulting, especially with writing teams and worldbuilding teams, is that moment where I can see the light bulb go on and people realize that there's creative potential in acknowledging these communities, in discovering that these stories have value to add to these worlds.

It's commonplace to play a TTRPG game, read, or watch a story about a character with a disability that is defined by that disability and usually comes with a tragic backstory to explain it. Jennifer Kretchmer outlines why that way of thinking, despite putting a disabled person into a position of being seen, isn't a healthy representation for that person.

Getting away from the idea of tragedy or needing to cure or fix people, or infantilizing people, or that a disability is a narrative tool for a lesson someone has to learn. That's Narrative Prosthesis. There are these tropes that so often people who haven't been exposed to these ideas fall into and when you sit down with the team, and they're discovering that actually there are these really rich, beautiful stories about community interdependence and the strength of that, the creativity and creative problem solving of the disabled community. These are all things that are so important, the snark of the disabled community. We often say snark is a disabled cultural value. This is so much of who we are and bringing that to the fore within the stories that we're telling is such an incredible part of what I get to do. I love it when people discover that. I've had several people come to me and say, I've never felt comfortable talking about being disabled before, or I've never felt proud about it, like I've never felt like this is something that I can bring to the things I write and having these conversations has changed that. Those are the things that are so amazing about doing the work that I get to do.

Helping people make their games more accessible, making how people play their games more inclusive, to find ways for communities that haven't had access in the past to get involved with tabletop gaming or watching shows or taking part is so exciting. We had one of, if not the first, bilingual ASL English, spoken English tables in a show I was in called Galesong: Dragons' Convergence, which was an all-disabled cast, and that was so exciting, and so many people were really excited to see a show that had sign language, spoken English, and captions. It created this new way for people to access and engage with the material and also to discover how ASL really enhanced storytelling. It's a language, and Deaf culture is so beautifully built. Rogan Shannon talks a lot about this. They describe how ASL is a language perfectly grammatically designed to work with tabletop storytelling and descriptive storytelling. It's an incredible, phenomenal way they describe it.

TROPES, AND WHEN TO LEAN INTO THEM

Tropes in movies are loosely defined as dialog and situations that appear commonly across multiple films, mostly within the same genre. For instance, in a horror movie, the trope would be that after the protagonist (sometimes, in another example of a trope, called a "final girl") defeats the villain, the villain pops back up one last time to take a final swipe at the protagonist before they are dispatched for good. There are two tropes within Disney movies that get brought up often. The first is that a parent is going to die, acting as the catalyst for the protagonist's journey to become their best self. The second is that the villain is likely to die from a fall, plummeting to their demise.

Producer and star of the television show Encounter Party, Ned Donovan, talks about his perspective on how tropes factor into telling a story:

Tropes give us the ability to get to a common language faster. So, I think it really just depends on "what's our purpose here"? If I need to spend 45 minutes setting up something that will allow you to understand what I'm doing, or I could just introduce a trope that does something similar in five minutes and know that I've got you on the right brain length. I would rather get to the point. Let's say I've written this massive world, if I need you to understand the interconnected political whatever, between three factions that you're now going up against. If I can do that in a modern-day example, I'd much rather do that than have to give you all the history that I've written separately. So, in my mind, when I play tabletop games, and when I DM things that I've written, I use tropes wherever it can shortcut me to a common language.

Tropes aren't inherently good or bad. It just depends on how creative the writer is when using them. *Scream* is a wonderful and often-used horror movie that deliberately leans into very specific horror tropes as part of the meta aspect of the story the film is trying to tell, with the conceit being that the villains (spoiler alert) at the end of the movie know and understand horror films well enough to think that they can commit multiple murders and get away with it.

In TTRPGs, tropes are story points that GMs can lean against to give their players a familiar handhold in the story they are creating together without having to come up with more elaborate and separate scenarios for each player. This is especially important in stories that take the reader or viewer out of their normal worlds and thrust them into spectacular science fiction or fantasy realms similar to what you'd encounter in a D&D/Spelljammer, Pathfinder/Starfinder, or Alien TTRPG scenario.

Popular GM and YouTuber Brogan Kelley (NoNat1s) has this to say about the trope of starting players off in a tavern, arguably the most over-used beginning location in a TTRPG:

The most popular start to an adventure is you meet in a tavern. There is a reason that is a meme. There's a reason that is a trope. It's because it works. A lot of tropes are like that. You're all in a tavern, which is a very safe place to role-play and experience each other's characters and get introduced to each other without an immediate threat or a reason to leave. Everybody's in that tavern for a reason. That could be because they stayed the night there, because they're getting a drink, because they're getting dinner, because they're a rogue and they're sitting in the corner by themselves asking someone to tell them about their daddy issues. They all have a reason to be there, and that is why it's such a great starting point for an adventure. The trope is a trope because it works.

EXERCISE 3.2

Make a list of five popular tropes from movies, games, or literature. Explain the trope and then write a one or two paragraph scenario of your own incorporating that trope.

Producer of The Heart Is A Dungeon podcast, performer, and poet RahRah talks about their experiences with tropes and how they deal with incorporating them into their stories:

If I don't feel like I can pull it off in a unique way, I try not to touch the tropes because tropes make things more commonly noticed, but also harder to stand out compared against every other story. But I also see it as a fair challenge. I enjoy telling unique stories. A trope I go back to is surrealism. A lot of 'dream reveals' is a trope I go back to. Trauma would probably be a consistent one, whether that's emotional or physical. We have a home game where I run combat every other session, but for storytelling that someone's just listening to, it's not the thing I put a lot of energy into, because it's hard to follow. I also think there's worse monsters than violence out there, and most of them are the choices we make. So those (choices) tend to be the bosses in my campaigns.

Author Ed Greenwood adds his two cents on how to make an old trope feel different, and another trope to avoid altogether if possible:

In the fantasy role-playing genre, the trope that has been done to death is you have to rescue the princess. And of course, that's done to death for two reasons. The first one is everybody's done it. It's been overused. It's like ho-hum. We're off to rescue the princess again. And then the other one is—tell me exactly why this princess can't rescue herself, you know, and I have rung the changes on that particular trope when I did my Kingless Land books. These two soldiers on the losing side in the war come home, and they're living off whatever they can steal and cooking it in the wilderness. They're thinking, we'd like the high life, and they've heard about this famous baron's daughter who has a wardrobe of gowns made of gems. So, they figure, okay, we'll just swim in the river—she's alone in her tower. I mean, what problem can one woman be for us? One girl at that, a young woman. We'll just steal a couple of her dresses out the window and our fortunes made because we're going to break them up. We can't sell a gown made of gems, but we can sell all the individual gems. So of course, the first thing that happens, they get in and she is delighted to see them, because she is, in effect, her father's prisoner, and she wants to break out, and they are going to be her means. And by the way, she's a powerful sorceress, so she can mop the floor with them. That was how I was going to ring the changes on that trope that I otherwise would never touch, because it's been done to death. And yes, why can't women protect themselves? Now that we are changing, and society is changing, this is the most interesting and relevant story to tell right now. But that would be one trope to leave alone.

The attraction of fantasy, it's the fatal attraction. The good guys can really be good guys with shining teeth, and they can look nice, and they can be beautiful, and they are really the good guys, and the bad guys are really evil, mustaches twirling and dark. There's a loaded thing right there, and you can differentiate them, and it's the same sort of clear delineation that we so seldom get in real life. There's something satisfying about being able to know that these are the good guys and those are the bad guys. That is in itself a trope that should be avoided because it's too lazy, too easy. Everybody should be shades of gray.

Putting a story together is no easy feat. Being inclusive with your characters, understanding, integrating, or avoiding tropes becomes a matter of taste, and a risky endeavor to pursue if you don't fully understand your characters and the story you're attempting to tell with them. Using your locations to prop up your characters and their intentions can become a crucial part of worldbuilding. Making your locations feel real to your audience goes a long way in getting them to buy into your characters' actions and motivations. As you move forward in your own storytelling adventures, take care to use all the tools and knowledge available to you. If you have difficulty visualizing a place, create it, and then place your characters in it. If you don't know whether you are doing right by your disabled main character, consult with someone with the same disability or an expert to make sure you're portraying them accurately. And if you're going to use a trope, either get it right or be really funny.

CHAPTER 4

Characters

THE MAIN PLAYERS

Character creation is often the first step for players when they join a table-top game. Whether a one-shot or a campaign, their character is their first viewpoint into the world they're about to enter. While there is no real wrong way to create a character (absence of following the mechanical rules of the character's powers and abilities as set in the player's guide), there are ways to make your characters feel more complete, real, and interesting.

Award-winning writer and narrative designer Ashley Warren, who has worked on TTRPG properties such as Dungeons & Dragons, explains her character creation method, whether she is writing a narrative story or a character for a TTRPG campaign:

> I think the characters that we all like to celebrate the most in pop culture canon are those characters that have a really specific goal and problem to solve. Especially in narrative design, I'm always thinking about motivation and an objective for everyone; players and NPCs. When I'm fleshing out NPCs, I find that to be really helpful, because even if they're a major NPC or even if they're the villain, they need to have a clear goal, and then sub goals within that, and they need to have a clear motivation. Just with those two concepts, you can come up with a pretty rich backstory, because sometimes they are related. Their motivation is what leads to their goal. If someone has wronged them, then their goal is to

DOI: 10.1201/9781003538202-4

take down that person. Those are linked. But sometimes they're separate. They don't always have to be overlapping things. When I start with that, that's a good place for me to kind of start fleshing out a character so that they are believable.

In D&D, there's a nice framework where you think of your character's traits, bonds, and flaws. I always like that as a checklist for things to think about when you're creating your own character, but also when you're writing new characters. What's their physicality? How are they perceived? The characters that we think of as iconic such as Harry Potter. He has a scar, and that's his motif throughout the entire series. Everyone knows that. While I don't think resting on physical traits is very interesting storytelling, it is part of the character equation.

Thinking about physicality and aesthetics. Drizzt, who is a dark elf in D&D, there's a lot of history and lore. He has white hair. That's an easy starting point. What does that say about where they're from, or what they've experienced? If they have a scar, it's because they've gone through something kind of traumatic. But then it has to always go deeper than that, and that's when you come up with the really compelling backstory, breaking down their bonds. What are they? Who are they loyal to? What are they connected to? Whether that's like a faction or a person or a thing or a place, and it could be even more figurative than that, like their faith. Then their flaws. What are their tics? How can you tell when they're lying? Those little things really break down and become a pretty cohesive character template.

Then, as you're actually incorporating NPCs into a story, that's when you bring in some of that world building. How do they act when they go to a restaurant? There's a lot you can learn about a character through those kinds of things. It's fun to place characters with that framework in these different scenarios and build out more from there.

I remember thinking when I was writing my early D&D work that the bonds, traits, and flaws were such a helpful way to summarize an NPC, because also in adventure writing, you don't necessarily want to write 10 pages about one NPC, because you don't even know if people are going to meet that NPC, they could totally bypass that whole character. You just never know what they're going to do. But you need enough there for the DM to bring them to life at the table. Using archetypes, I think, is really powerful. I love using the classic archetypes that are in classic literature, and mythology is always a good starting point. It's fun to take like an archetype and then put a put like a twist on it. I feel that's something I do a lot in D&D. Use what already exists and then change it up a little.

At this point in human history, a lot of stories have been told. I don't think any of us is doing anything 100% original. We're always spinning something that's already exists. But I also view writing and storytelling as this great ongoing conversation, and so it's okay to borrow and then make it your own. It's helpful to have that foundational knowledge.

EXERCISE 4.1

Take a character from a popular movie or television show and create a list of their traits, flaws, and bonds. How would this character be different if these were changed? Can you improve upon this character by changing these attributes? How would this change the film or television show they're in?

What's the secret to creating a great hero? An undeniable villain? World builder and author Ed Greenwood has some great tips and tricks to share:

They don't think they're the villain. They think they're in the right and they think they're doing the right thing, because then you have a clash of values or a clash of ideologies, or just thinking, what is the best way forward? You are choosing a different path for the future, hopefully choosing between various visions of the future. I want my antagonists to not be out-and-out villains. What you can do is make a choice and show the reader the moral choice you've made. Does the end justify the means? To put this in Star Trek terms, the Kobayashi Maru—Kirk won in that training exercise by breaking the rules, because winning mattered more than anything else, but does it? That's the choice you put in front of the reader in your story, and it's far more interesting in the Forgotten Realms. Khelben Blackstaff is very much James T.

Kirk of the starship Enterprise, and he was very much an ends guy. The ends justify the means. Elminster is far more of an "if you do that, you're as bad as the people we're fighting". You cannot stoop to that thing to win. It's the clash between those approaches, and those make for really interesting stories.

Captain Kirk's character growth is clear as his journey in the chair on the bridge of the Enterprise progresses. He maintains his cavalier attitude toward norms and rules but eventually learns the meaning of personal sacrifice and the weight of being in the captain's chair. In some ways, when viewed through a fantasy lens, Kirk and Spock have a squire/knight relationship at the beginning of their journeys together. As Kirk grows as a captain, learning from Spock (and the other main characters that make up his core crew), the role becomes reversed in some ways, graduating Kirk to the full role he was meant to take as the captain, more than just in name and rank. That's when they become equals and friends.

Screenwriter and producer Margaret Borchert has her own take on what makes a great villain:

The most fun is coming up with the villain, coming up with the big bad, evil guy, the person that everything is working against. It's about finding the thing that they are doing and why they are doing it. No one really wants to go up against a super, cartoonishly evil villain who's being evil for the sake of being evil, rather than for a tangible reason or if their plan doesn't make any like logical sense for why they're doing what they're doing. It's about building a character that has a good reason for doing what they're doing but has taken it a step too far and is making it other people's problem. I think one way that you can do that interestingly is to take the characters that your players have given you and go—these are the themes that you guys have brought to the table. These are the things that you're playing with here. How can I take those and take advantage of them and make this plot something that your character is going to care about, and make the villain someone that you are going to care about, someone that you almost like and understand why they're doing what they're doing?

When you GM a lot, you notice your own patterns in the stories and the characters that you keep coming back to, and the villain characters I keep going back to are women who have been wronged, but now they're taking their revenge too far. I think there is a joy in getting to come up with a great adversary.

Often in TTRPGs, characters are defined by their tragic backstories. This is common in a lot of media. Comic books are a major offender with this trope. Whether you are writing Batman and having his origin story rooted in the violent death of his parents, or the Kyle Rayner version of Green Lantern having his girlfriend Alex DeWitt "fridged" by one of his villains, Major Force.

Poet, GM, and creator of the Heart is a Dungeon podcast Rah Rah discusses their approach to conflict in stories, especially those they used to create as a child with toys in their backyard:

I loved very large casts, and I hated the ending. If there were folks that lived in the mountains, the forests, the rivers, or the unwanted, and one of them kidnapped the girlfriend of someone from the other side, they're all going to fight. A Battle of Five Armies situation, I'd get them all set up, and after a week-long game, I'd just nod and pick them up. I was never very interested in who won. I just wanted the story leading up to that point.

In a lot of the Heart is a Dungeon series, people will notice it's going to be very slice of life. There's not a 'big bad' they're trying to defeat. The only thing they're trying to be is better than themselves. It's an ongoing theme. At its hardest, it's a slice-of-life, kind of sad, melancholy, cozy story.

I got surreal with writing more in my 20s. I got way too into Samuel Beckett's prose and some of those things. I have a few poetry books out, and wrote a few, very prosaic, short novellas and things like that, but with Heart is a Dungeon, I'm trying to be more specific in making every story important. My style tends to be melancholy, but I have a few guest DMs coming up next year who I've asked to come DM a smaller series, and I'll just do all the sound stuff for it, and they're like, oh, I don't really do sad. I was like, well, it doesn't necessarily have to be sad, but it has to be important.

In many TTRPGs, people might create their characters as "lone wolves" whose parents were killed in front of them when they were children, and now, they are on an adventure filled with revenge and angst. While there's nothing inherently wrong with this, it's also common and boring.

We've discussed what makes a compelling villain or antagonist, but what makes for an interesting protagonist or hero? The answer to that can be complicated, and often the difference between a hero and a villain comes down to perspective and/or one wrong choice. Professional DM and writer B. Dave Walters gives his take on the differences between heroes and villains:

> I'm a huge adherent of the fact that the villain is the hero of their story. I always want the villain's motivation to make sense. Sometimes you can have the locusts, or the all-consuming Horde, but the all-consuming horde should have a reason for why they're all-consuming. Why are they doing this? It's the difference between the Joker and Mr. Freeze (I'm oversimplifying the Joker). There is more nuance to the character, but it's the difference between the characters that is like, I'm going to blow up the Statue of Liberty because I felt like it, versus someone like Mr. Freeze is doing all this because he's trying to save his wife Nora. And that has pushed him to a place where he does some terrible things and inflicts the same harm on others that he's so resentful of having been inflicted on him. Heroes and villains have the same origin. The origin is pain, but a hero feels pain and says, I'm going to make sure no one else feels this way. If the villain feels pain, they say, I'm going to get even with the world for having hurt me.

NPC'S (NON-PLAYABLE CHARACTERS)

POINT OF INSPIRATION

"I would advise GMs to get out of the mindset that the NPC is aware of the story or gives a shit about the story."—Justin Miller

Non-player characters, or NPCs, are the people and sentient things that your characters interact with throughout their journey or quest. In a script, this would be the person loading and unloading crates on the docks that the police detective needs to question about the murder or suspect they're investigating. Sometimes these people are just nice citizens that populate the planet your characters are living on, and other times they carry essential information and puzzle pieces that move the story along. In a TTRPG game, the Game Master controls these characters.

How do you create NPC characters that feel real? Screenwriter and Game Master Carlos Cisco speaks about his approach to creating an NPC that feels like more than just a body his characters interact with:

> There are a couple of questions that you need to answer for your NPC. The first is, what culture were they born into, and do they reject or embrace it? I think that is ultimately the crux of a person. If you were born into evangelical Christianity and you full throat embrace it, that is a very different thing than someone who fully rejects it. That tells me very different things about a person who came from the same origin, right?
>
> I think that's the first step that will give you their reason for being where they are. It will help guide you towards their core philosophy and core wound. If they've rejected their culture, it's probably something tied to that. But then I think you need to for NPCs, you need to answer, what do they know, and then what do they not want to reveal? It's important for people to have secrets, whether it is world shattering or innocuous. People have to have things they don't want others to know about, whether it comes into play. Especially if you're writing it for someone else you know, knowing that they don't want to reveal this thing that instantly tells that GM how to run that character a little more without saying you have to address this in the game, you know? It's just like, oh, they're going to maybe be a little cagey about this, and then if my players clue into that, then we can reveal this information, if need be. So, I think that those are, at base level, the things that I try to answer.

Not every person or thing in your tabletop game needs to have a rich backstory. Sometimes they're just filling in the world the main characters are walking through. This can have funny repercussions for the players and Game Master when the GM hasn't prepared for an NPC interaction.

Game Master and screenwriter Margaret Borchert speaks about an NPC encounter her tabletop players experienced and she needed to improvise:

> In my home game, we had the players going on a fetch quest to go do something for an NPC, and I set up, not quite a random encounter, but like a mini little boss battle situation where there were bugbears on the side of the road who had set up a fake toll booth, where they expected you to pay money to cross the road, and if you didn't pay them, they would attack you, and they'd drop you. So, they pull up to this log that's laid across the road, and the bugbears are all there being like, 'pay the toll', and the bard rolls a NAT 20 on persuasion, and you got to honor the NAT 20 my guy, and convinces the chief bugbear to let them pass without paying.
>
> She gives him a kiss on the cheek, and they drive away. Okay, so the next logical step here for this creature is because they have to come back along this road now to get home, is that now the bugbear chief, who I, off the cuff, named Chief Bugaboo, because I didn't think that this character was going to be important, didn't give them a name, and then she asked for the name, and so Chief Bugaboo was going to be waiting for her coming back. So, they're like, engaged now.

In film and television, the analog to NPCs would be extras (or supporting artists and background talent). Extras are the actors you see in the background of each scene to make the locations feel alive. If that extra is more than just a face in the crowd, they're considered a featured extra. If they have a line in the show or movie, then they get bumped up to co-star. For the most part, screenwriters don't need to be concerned with most background people in their scripts. If the scene takes place in a busy arena during a boxing match, it's enough to say as much. But once you zoom into the ring and the boxers, who in this case would be considered main characters in this hypothetical situation. The people in the boxer's corners, and the referee, however, might be considered co-stars or background actors, depending on their involvement in the scene. The referee most certainly will have lines if they need to count down a fallen combatant. How can you make that referee character stand out even more?

Screenwriter and TTRPG notable Game Master B. Dave Walters shares his method of fleshing out the background characters his players meet during their adventures:

> What I like to do, especially when developing NPCs in particular, is I make sure they always have at least one adjective. It is never the Dwarven barkeep. It's the itchy Dwarven barkeep that I will describe. I know he's got psoriasis, but I will describe his red, irritated skin flaking over the bar as he's asking you what you want. They're never going to forget that guy, ever. They'll run into 100 Dwarven bar keeps, but will always remember the itchy, flaky Dwarven Barkeep, the agoraphobic kobold, the kleptomaniac half elf. Give them a determining characteristic. After that, I like to play with their assumptions. I'll have the kobold have the 20 strength. The Goliath is the intellectual, the orc is the pacifist.

Being specific about your background character descriptions can have other benefits as well. If you describe your boxing ring referee as only having one arm, that might give the people in casting an opportunity to give a part to a person with one arm. The same goes with BIPOC, LGBTQIA+, and other marginalized people. More diversity in your screenplay and story will result in better representation of the reality of the world around your characters. The caveat to this being if your script takes place on an alien world, or if you are making a specific point by having your main and background characters be all one race, gender, or physical type.

If you are writing characters outside of your race or lived experience, you might choose to have a sensitivity reader look at your script to make sure you are representing those characters properly. You may also want to reflect and ask yourself if you are the right person to tell this story in the first place. It might be wise, in that case, to take on a co-writer or consult with someone from the point of view and background you are trying to capture in your script.

LETTING YOUR CHARACTERS OFF THE CHAIN

Not every character can be the Indiana Jones of their party, and when you're writing your screenplay, ultimately there's going to be one person who stands above the rest and who steals the spotlight from the others. It could be the wisecracking sidekick, the love interest, or even the villain. These characters are going to be the ones that sit with people once they finish reading your screenplay, and if you're lucky, once the lights come up in the theater.

DM, educator, and TTRPG player Cate Osborn explains her approach to finding the moments to let her characters shine, using her theater and improv training to find the right moments to bring her characters to the forefront to lift the scenario she's playing to the next level:

> It's not unique. A lot of TTRPG players do this, but I have a habit of figuring out the most bassackwards, broken way to do something, and I've had the luxury of playing with DMs who usually support that. What I have found is that if we're doing it like a recorded series, the timing is different. I have found that usually my (character's) moment seems to fit in somewhere around the two-thirds mark, and it usually has something to do with moving the story forward in a way that people weren't expecting. That's something I take a bit of pride in.
>
> For RealmSmith, when I did their Tales of the Wasted West, Kobold Press wanted us to use their spells and their third-party stuff, and they have a spell that's like, interact with object or speak with object, basically. You can talk to a chair. We were solving a murder mystery, and we were like, all right, who killed the sheriff? My character was being questioned in court, and so I had them bring in the table that the victim had died on, and then I spoke with the table, and then I spoke with his blood, and we solved the mystery and cleared our innocence. It was great, it gets clipped a lot.
>
> I haven't spent a lot of time ruminating on it, but I think a lot of that pattern of that sort of, like, two-thirds of the way through whatever…I think a lot of that's just theater training. I think a lot of it comes from improv training and wanting to ask, "where are we going next, where are we"?
>
> In Actual Plays when you're maybe not playing with people that you've played a lot with, or you've just met them for the first time like in a charity stream, or on stage and you're like, "all right, we got to make something happen". It's not about me getting my moment, but about how do we get a satisfying wrap-up or

conclusion to this, where people are going to go away feeling like they got a good show? It's less about what cool thing I am going to do.

Educators and internet experts on social media are obsessed with structure. They will preach how many acts a script should have, how many beats, and with comedy scripts, there is even a metric given for jokes-per-minute. When you are creating for a company or in a writers room, it's understandable for people to fall back on tried-and-true structures and methods to expedite the end product. The Hollywood studio system is couched in fear and predictability. The fear of losing money, status, or face with one's colleagues is the driving force for most decision-making at that level. For the people who watch movies and television, however, they don't think in those same constructs or constraints. They just want to be entertained. They want poignant and powerful moments that are going to move them and make them laugh, cry, or cover their eyes. That is what you should strive for in your script.

Writing is a time to let yourself be free to create the stories and characters that speak to you from your heart. But that doesn't mean you need to be rude, crass, or unethical in your story creation process. You can describe a sexual act with grace and dignity for the characters while still maintaining an erotic undertone. Likewise, you can create characters that might fall into tropes or stereotypes that may fall into or skirt the lines of good taste. You might think you're being edgy by creating racist archetypes, but are they serving the story? Or do they just exist to serve your own bigoted interests (which could be completely subliminal on your part)?

Sensitivity reader and consultant Rue Dickey defines what their job is and how it affects the stories they consult with:

> Sensitivity reading and consulting are terms that people use interchangeably. I say consulting usually means that I've been brought onto a project before it's done. So, if a project is going to focus on a Romani cultural analog, like the Vistani in D&D. They're a Romani cultural analog. Or if you have actual Romani people in your game, like in Vampire the Masquerade, because it takes place in the real world and I'm brought on to give a presentation about a particular cultural element, or breakdown stereotypes, that's consulting.

If they're like, hey, we already wrote this thing. Here you go. We want to make sure that we're not hitting any terrible stereotypes or doing anything off base. I would call that reading because it's already done.

What I love most about sensitivity reading/consulting is that it allows you to go wider with your worldbuilding, because if you bring on someone who understands the culture that you're referencing, or understands the very complex disabilities or mental health concerns that you're addressing in your piece, you can actually dive into that, as opposed to just having it be an off-mention where you might think, I don't feel comfortable exploring the Holocaust, but I have to reference it in my game about World War Two, so I'll just kind of vaguely reference that it's happening over there, and hope that no one asks questions.

I think in terms of censorship, that's never something that I want to be doing in the work that I do. I have worked not only with tabletop companies, but I do sensitivity for video games, as well as for Penguin, Random House and Macmillan and the biggest thing, for me, is never changing what an author or a game designer or whoever's vision for the project is.

It's informing them when that vision crosses lines, and sometimes it'll be like, hey, this could be read as sexual harassment. Do you want it to be that way? If you do, that's fine. I'm just letting you know that this is how that will read to someone who has experienced sexual harassment. Sometimes the author's like, oh, no, I didn't want that at all. Thank you.

I think a lot of what I do when I'm doing the reading side is go through and flag things that could be triggering or upsetting to certain readers or which falls into ethnic stereotypes or transphobic or homophobic stereotypes, etc. I will offer either suggestions if it's not something that the author wants, or I'll be like, hey, if you want to tackle transphobia in this game and have it be a topic, totally cool. Just make sure that in your opening statement you give content warnings for that kind of thing, because not everyone's going to be ready to open your book and have to deal with that.

Sensitivity consulting is about expanding the worlds that are existing in tabletop to include topics that otherwise your bog-standard person who doesn't have experience with those things would not feel comfortable writing, but also to make sure that when those topics are being handled, they're being handled safely, and how the author intends them to be. Because I think sometimes people with the best of intentions will write something that they think is good representation and wind up having touched a stereotype they didn't even know existed.

CHARACTER CONSISTENCY AND GROWTH

POINT OF INSPIRATION

"You can't write defensively. You just have to tell the story that you want to tell, and trust that the majority of people will get it. If you have a clarity of vision, they'll get it."—Jonathan Wilder

Failure is inevitable. But failure doesn't have to be the end of the game. Just like in a movie or a television show, when the protagonist loses, the show isn't over. Game designer Banana Chan talks about the idea of "failing forward" as a method of character advancement rather than as a punishment:

When you fail, you gain experience, because that's what happens in real life, right? You learn from growth. You learn from your mistakes, and so at the end, you can spend that experience to do cool things, like tanking on a move, or being able to add plus one to one of your stats.

I like the idea of what you do between when you first start and when you end the session. All the stuff that happens in between is like facing adversity through failure and learning from that. So that way, by the end of the scenario, you're probably ready to take on the big bad. If I'm building a campaign, how do I break it down into something more episodic? What if every single time you fail, you're learning? So that way, once we ramp it up to the last episode, you are ready to take on that big bad? Thinking about that way has been really helpful for me to create different stories within a longer campaign.

The concept of "failing forward" is something to keep in mind if you find yourself in an act two slump. Look at what the main character(s) are trying to achieve and actively try to make them fail. Work backward from the act three goals and try to put roadblocks in place to make them stumble and fall. But also give them the tools necessary to pick themselves back up and persevere. This can be in the metaphorical sense, like in the movie *Rocky*, where his scrappiness and determination are at the heart of his under-dog story. Even when he loses, he feels like a winner. He's learned some-thing. He's gained experience, and in the next film, he wins in his rematch with Apollo Creed. This perseverance through failure also gains him the respect of his rival, who eventually becomes a good friend and confidant through parts three and four of the franchise.

American pulp-fiction writer Lester Dent, who created the adventurer hero Doc Savage, had his own method with his heroes fighting through failure in his roughly 6,000-word stories. Each beat/point comes at each 1,500-word milestone. The following was excerpted from Marilyn Cannaday's biography of Lester Dent, *Bigger than Life: The Creator of Doc Savage* (Bowling Green State University Popular Press, c1990), transcribed by Jason A. Wolcott, 1995.

FIRST 1,500 WORDS

1. In the first line, or as near thereto as possible, introduce the hero and swat him with a fistful of trouble. Hint at a mystery, a menace, or a problem to be solved—something the hero has to cope with.

2. The hero pitches in to cope with his fistful of trouble (He tries to fathom the mystery, defeat the menace, or solve the problem).

3. Introduce all the other characters as soon as possible. Bring them on in action.

4. Hero's endeavors land him in an actual physical conflict near the end of the first 1,500 words.

5. Near the end of the first 1,500 words, there is a complete surprise twist in the plot development.

SO FAR: Does it have SUSPENSE?
Is there a MENACE to the hero?

Does everything happen logically?

At this point, it might help to recall that action should do something besides advance the hero over the scenery. Suppose the hero has learned the dastards of villains have seized somebody named Eloise, who can explain the secret of what is behind all these sinister events. The hero corners the villains, they fight, and the villains get away. Not so hot.

Hero should accomplish something with his tearing around, if only to rescue Eloise, and surprise! Eloise is a ring-tailed monkey. The hero counts the rings on Eloise's tail, if nothing better comes to mind.

They're not real. The rings are painted there. Why?

SECOND 1,500 WORDS

1. Shovel more grief onto the hero.

2. Hero, being heroic, struggles, and his struggles lead up to:

3. Another physical conflict.

4. A surprising plot twist to end the 1,500 words.

NOW: Does the second part have SUSPENSE?

Does the MENACE grow like a black cloud?

Is the hero getting it in the neck?

Is the second part logical?

DON'T TELL ABOUT IT***Show how the thing looked. This is one of the secrets of writing; never tell the reader—show him (he trembles, roving eyes, slackened jaw, and such). MAKE THE READER SEE HIM.

When writing, it helps to get at least one minor surprise onto the printed page. It is reasonable to expect these minor surprises to sort of inveigle the reader into keeping on. They need not be such profound efforts. One method of accomplishing one now and then is to be gently misleading. The hero is examining the murder room. The door behind him begins slowly to open. He does not see it. He conducts his examination blissfully. The door eases open, wider and wider, until—surprise! The glass pane falls out of the big window across the room. It must have fallen slowly, and air blowing into the room caused the door to open. Then what the heck made the pane fall so slowly? More mystery.

Characterizing a story actor consists of giving him some traits which make him stick in the reader's mind. TAG HIM.

BUILD YOUR PLOTS SO THAT ACTION CAN BE CONTINUOUS.

THIRD 1,500 WORDS

1. Shovel the grief onto the hero.

2. The hero makes some headway and corners the villain or somebody in:

3. A physical conflict.

4. A surprising plot twist in which the hero preferably gets it in the neck bad to end the 1,500 words.

DOES: It still have SUSPENSE?

The MENACE getting blacker?

The hero finds himself in a hell of a fix.

It all happens logically.

These outlines or master formulas are only something to make you certain of inserting some physical conflict and some genuine plot twists, with a little suspense and menace thrown in. Without them, there is no pulp story.

These physical conflicts in each part might be DIFFERENT too. If one fight is with fists, that can take care of the pugilism until the next yarn. The same goes for poison gas and swords. There may, naturally, be exceptions. A hero with a peculiar punch, or a quick draw, might use it more than once.

The idea is to avoid monotony.

ACTION:

Vivid, swift, no words wasted. Create suspense, make the reader see and feel the action.

ATMOSPHERE:

Hear, smell, see, feel, and taste.

DESCRIPTION:

Trees, wind, scenery, and water.

THE SECRET OF ALL WRITING IS TO MAKE EVERY WORD COUNT.

FOURTH 1,500 WORDS

1. Shovel the difficulties more thickly upon the hero.

2. Get the hero almost buried in his troubles (figuratively, the villain has him as a prisoner and has framed him for a murder rap; the girl is presumably dead, everything is lost, and the DIFFERENT murder method is about to dispose of the suffering protagonist).

3. The hero extricates himself using HIS OWN SKILL, training or brawn.

4. The mysteries remaining—one big one held over to this point will help grip interest—are cleared up in the course of final conflict as the hero takes the situation in hand.

5. Final twist, a big surprise (this can be the villain turning out to be an unexpected person, having the "Treasure" be a dud, etc.).

6. The snapper, the punchline to end it.

HAS: The SUSPENSE held out to the last line?
The MENACE held out to the last?
Everything been explained?
It all happened logically?
Is the punch line enough to leave the reader with that WARM FEELING?
Did God kill the villain, or the hero?

There are aspects to this that mirror Joseph Campbell's Hero's Journey, especially at the "all is lost" parts in the third act (or around the fourth 1,500 words in the above example). It should be noted that for all the credit Campbell gets for "Hero with A Thousand Faces," arguably, it was never meant to be used as a method for creative writing or screenwriting, but was his take on how myths were constructed based on his background as a professor of literature and his work in comparative mythology and comparative religion.

Meghan Cross, a TTRPG designer who specializes in GM-less and solo TTRPGs for Siren Song Games, speaks about using music as a way to get inside a character's head or emotional state:

As somebody with a theater background, a lot of it is a character study and letting myself exist and answer things and react to things organically. Another huge thing for me, especially on longer campaigns, is music. I always make playlists for all of my characters. I'll start off with a set of songs when I'm creating my character, songs that are tied to their backstory and their goals and dreams and wants. Then as the campaign goes on, if something happens, I'll add more to that. You can track character development through the playlist as you go. I would always listen to my character playlist before playing, just to get into that mindset.

Because an AP, as opposed to a home game, is a performance. You want to give an excellent performance, so you want to make sure that you're doing it right, for lack of a better term. If I'm playing at home, I'm a little less concerned if I do something that's a little out of character from something that's been established in the past.

Great characters don't always need to be out saving the world from evil. Sometimes they're just hometown heroes winning the big game. They might be down-on-their-luck street urchins that happen upon riches beyond their wildest dreams but still struggle with their own happiness. Sometimes a character's BBEG is just the fear they keep inside themselves and can't let go of. These characters can be the backbone of powerful stories that will move audiences to tears and cheers, and you to box office success. Focus on the characters, build a rich world around them, and walk them through their journey, however you've decided to structure it. Follow these steps and you'll be well on your way to telling stories that will stand the test of time.

CHAPTER 5

Actual Plays, Table Reads, and Next Steps (the Business)

PLAYING WITH YOUR STORY

Now that you've gotten the hang of your story, locations, and characters, it is time to consider the less fun aspects of being a storyteller. Whether you are a screenwriter, novelist, actor, podcaster, or any other discipline within the entertainment industry, if you want to survive and thrive working in this business, there are a few things you need to know first.

The entertainment industry is unlike any other. The things that made you happy in your childhood could become the things that you make a living with as an adult. As a child, you could make a mess with your toys and the only consequence might be a stern talking to your parents about the importance of playing responsibly. As an adult, you probably have more things to keep in mind, like keeping a roof over your head and food in your belly.

That doesn't mean you can't have a blast working in the entertainment industry, but you need to learn the ins and outs of the business and set expectations for yourself professionally before diving in headfirst. Screenwriter and TTRPG enthusiast Dan Hernandez speaks of his experience working on projects involving his own childhood heroes:

DOI: 10.1201/9781003538202-5

It's funny that the things that I was passionate about as a kid are actually the things that have given me a career, or at least been the fuel to build the foundation of a career, are those same things that I was still interested in and I've been really fortunate to get to play in a lot of the worlds that I really loved growing up and that has been a real gift, but also not a coincidence, in the sense that when I go into these situations to talk about, hey, I want to write Ninja Turtles. I want to write STAR WARS. I want to write *Pokémon* or whatever. Yeah, there's a real enthusiasm and a real passion, a fan's passion, on my end, toward what my version of those things could be, and I think it served me really well.

It's important to keep that child-like sense of wonder and passion in the entertainment industry. You almost need to be of two minds about it. One mind dwells deep in your subconscious, pulling out the creative stories that fueled your childhood playtimes. The other mind is focused on the business of storytelling, and how to get those stories you've created in front of audiences and people with the money to make them a reality.

Sometimes you need to hear your work out loud. It's not enough to recite it back to yourself. You need outside feedback. Maybe your dialog doesn't sound authentic. Your action lines might not be hitting correctly. There might even be misspellings and mistakes that you missed because you're too close to what you've written. Great news! There are ways within both the TTRPG world and the screenwriting world that, while having some differences, can contribute mightily to helping course correct your scripts. These methods are actual plays and table reads.

The first method, actual play (AP), refers to a recorded or live-streamed game of a TTRPG system that is performed specifically for the camera and/or audience. It is not player-focused, but character-focused, and story-forward. APs like Critical Role and Dimension 20 have become popular for their fun characters, dramatic scenes, and chaotic actors.

The second is to set up a table read. This is a more straightforward reading, word for word, of your screenplay by a group of actors, folks from your writing group, or other industry professionals with the goal of listening to the dialog and structure of the script.

Both ways are effective tools to help you improve your script by being able to view your work from other people's perspectives. The major difference between the AP method and the table read way of getting feedback on your script is that the AP method, as this book will use it, uses the script as more of a guideline than a strict tome to be read verbatim. The people you choose to perform your script AP will inhabit the characters in the world you've built and will use the scenes and scenarios in the script as a basis for their organic performances. This is to give you more off-the-cuff dialog that may or may not sound more organic to the character. You might even hear that the performer is giving a completely different take or perspective on your character than you might have originally thought. This exercise is to open up the possibilities of your story and make your world and characters breathe with a life of their own.

The idea is to get from the start of your script to the end, allowing the characters to flow from scene to scene while you act in the role of Game Master, guiding the performers through each scene. You might even perhaps giving them cues or prompts that aren't in the script to open up more story and character pathways. If it helps, think of it a bit like the old-school "choose your own adventure" books. Try to get the characters into different situations to find the best outcome for the story. Don't force the story to be what you want it to be, and try not to force the performers into playing their characters the way you distinctly see them.

At the end, compile any notes you've gotten from your performers. Take any recordings you've made and use your materials to rewrite your screenplay until it feels right. It's not as important, when planning an AP version of your script reading, to have an audience present, as you are the intended recipient of the feedback in this case. The key to AP-style readings is to be open to exploring new options for your story, not examining the story for plot holes, grammatical or formatting errors, or trying to cut/add pages. This is an active participation method to get you deeper into the world you've created.

EXERCISE 5.1

Reach out to a group of friends, your writing group, or performers you know and set up an AP-style reading of a short script or half-hour television screenplay. Record this AP on video and use the information to rewrite the script you just performed. How did the performances impact your understanding of the characters? Did the story change at all from the improvisation of some scenes? Did the script go completely off the rails? If so, how did you course correct and get back on track?

Writing, by itself, doesn't cost a lot of money to do. It takes time. Creating something from your writing, whether it's an indie film or an AP from a TTRPG, is something else entirely. Zachary Vaudo discusses his experiences entering into the AP space and how it compares with the film industry:

> The barrier of entry dropped dramatically, and I actually attribute that to Covid and us all realizing that we had to do a lot of stuff from home, because there were people that were still doing this (APs), but our examples at the time were Critical Role, Adventure Zone and LA By Night, and that's why ATL (Atlanta) wound up doing it in-studio to begin with. But I think that because of Covid, the barrier of entry dropped. More people realized they could do this virtually, and it costs a hell of a lot less than it does to even do an indie film like this, because you need a web camera, a microphone and an internet connection. That's the bare bones that you need to do this.
>
> At that point, in terms of genre marketing, it really boils down to if you are good at your own marketing, and what game you're playing. If you're running D&D, you're in a saturated market, people will find you because they just have to type D&D into Twitch, and there's so many streams that pop up. The marketing is almost done for you at that point. If you're playing a smaller game, then you actually push that. But that's where this community, that's where this industry-building has come up, like on Twitter and threads and whatnot, to really push that within the community and cross-promote within that arena.
>
> We're seeing an influx above and beyond even the film industry, because of how many people realized, oh, I have less to worry about on the money side of things, and there is no film school for actual play, so I just have to play the game and make people watch the game. That's so many fewer things than what goes into a film. Many people now know how to do this because of that.

Table reads are also an excellent way to get feedback for your script, though this is a far more passive experience for the writer than running an AP-style run-through of your work. It is a more direct way to get reactions from an audience. It relies on the screenwriter being more of a fly on the wall than the AP method. You should be listening and accepting feedback rather than interjecting or adding to the reading as a direct participant. The screenwriter should pay less attention to the reading of their script and more to the audience's reactions to specific beats, moments, jokes, or reveals as they occur during the reading. Doing this will give the writer a better understanding of where audiences are falling off and losing the plot, and what material might hit the way the writer intended.

EXERCISE 5.2

Reach out to a group of friends or your writing group, and set up a script reading for a short film or half-hour television script. Have an audience, either online or in-person, of at least ten people to provide feedback at the end of the reading. Supervise the reading and take notes of the audience's reactions. Use that information and other feedback you receive to rewrite the script. How did the audience's reactions change your plot structure or story beats? Did hearing the script being read out loud make you change any of the dialog to improve how the words sound or flow?

The business of writing is full of stressful meetings with executives looking to get your work (and more than likely at the lowest possible price). You'll face complicated contracts, and you'll be doing math for the rest of your life, making sure your paychecks add up to the right amounts after paying off your reps, lawyers, guild dues, and taxes. With all the hard work that goes into writing, give yourself the grace to have fun with the actual process of writing. Once you've sold your script or manuscript, the "work" part of being a working writer begins. Take a breath and approach your storytelling the way you did as a child. Explore every corner of your imagination and allow yourself to write the silliest, stupidest, most messed-up stuff you can think of. Once you've got most of your story together, you can refine it into what you need the result to be.

MCDM game designer and writer James Introcaso talks about how TTRPGs and writers rooms are similar:

> RPGs are giving you the framework to create a writer's room for a television show. Groups of players, not as actors, but as writers in a writer's room, and the person running the game is the head writer, and everybody else controls one character, which would

be a really weird way to write a television show, but I think that's the fun.

Inviting this type of collaboration for a feature film might result in some murky rights issues, as all the people involved might see their participation as some sort of ownership. However, this model works perfectly for television writers rooms where everyone is responsible for creating all the characters and situations for an entire series.

When you invite other people into your sandbox to play in the worlds you've created, give them the same breathing room you gave yourself while writing your work for them to interpret it. Take notes on their body movements and other physical indicators. These can become good additional descriptive words for your character and their actions in your revisions. Listen to the tone your collaborators are choosing. Do they understand your intentions correctly? Is their interpretation of your work different or even better, than what you have on the page? Don't feel intimidated or upset. Writing is usually a solo endeavor (unless you're working in a writers room), so getting feedback early, especially before your intended audience gets a peek at it, is a vital part of the process that you should embrace wholeheartedly. Hearing other people out doesn't mean you need to incorporate all of their opinions, but you should be open and willing to consider them. Being collaborative doesn't make you any less of a writer. It doesn't insult your talent. Working well with others is something that only has upsides and will serve you well as you move forward in your writing career.

HANDLING FEEDBACK

POINT OF INSPIRATION

"In a writers room, it's important to balance 'yes and' with 'nah,' and to be prepared with alternative ideas."—Carlos Cisco

Feedback can be a touchy subject with creators, not only because of the potential for bruised egos but also because feedback is entirely subjective and also goal-oriented. For instance, while you may not be able to control the feedback someone is giving you, you can at least specify some criteria and parameters for that feedback. Some feedback might be completely valid for one use case, but the same feedback might be detrimental in another circumstance because it doesn't speak to the end goal of what the creative is doing. For instance, streamer, composer, and narrative play podcast creator Patrick Perini talks about his experiences and advice in handling feedback from a YouTube streamer perspective, which might differ completely from someone looking for feedback from a table read of their script:

> I'll speak first to the audience side of it, because we have some content creators on the show where that's their full-time job, they're full time YouTubers. We have a lot of friends who are in this space, and one thing that we've all collectively been learning over the course of our respective entertainment careers is you have to be very cautious about listening to audience feedback, because you're going to get a lot of "your most popular thing" which has a lot of comments of people saying, do something different. But hey, actually, these are comments on my most popular thing. Maybe I'm doing something right. So, what we try to do is we try to remember that we should look to behavior, and we should look to positive reinforcement, and feedback.
>
> What is getting people to click, view, like, subscribe, or share? We want to be aware of what's working, and part of that is also listening to what do people say positively about the show. "I love this NPC", or "I love it when you guys do this", because that's something that we can reflect upon and say, "that's a strength that we might build on". It doesn't mean we need to do more of it. It just means that we need to be aware of the fact that it resonates with at least some subset of people.
>
> Where people might say, "I don't like the way you did this". You just got to ignore them. You just got to ignore them because they're not your audience, and it doesn't matter, because at the end of the day, they're one voice in a sea of you know, for us, 10s of 1000s, and for other shows, I'm sure much more. So, that's kind of how we feel about the audience.
>
> What we do really try to pay attention to is feedback to each other, and again, I'll talk on positivity, because the end of every session we do a kind of lightly structured feedback process that I think in a lot of games is called something like stars and wishes,

which is really focused on, 'how do I highlight what someone else at the table did really well'? I think that's really valuable.

One thing that we enforce is that you have to give yourself a star. What did I do that I thought was really good? That's always the hardest one for everybody, because they're so immediately self-critical. It helps break people out of that imposter syndrome. It also reinforces what we are doing well so that we can build on it, because chances are, we just need to be doing more of the stuff that we do well, not less of the stuff that we do badly. That'll come from practice, that'll come from leaning into the good stuff.

When I don't like how something is handled, we maintain a really active off-mic set of conversations, and I will reach out to every single one of my players, usually once or twice a month, to ask them, "where do you want your character to go from here? How do you feel like things are going so far? What feedback do you have about our process?" I'll also do that, albeit a little less frequently, to people who work in our crew, to people who are just friends of ours that are listening to the show and ask "how are things going for you? If you dropped off, what made you drop off?"

It's like any other art. You try to keep an open mind to what they're saying, but also not keep your head in the sand so that you're not hearing how people are genuinely feeling, both positively or negatively, about what you're doing. So, kind of maintaining that balance.

Getting feedback from the people involved in your project is hard. They'll know whether you've incorporated their feedback into the project (whether that's a script, audio drama, novel, or other creative endeavor). You may be afraid of offending them. In the event you take their advice, you might think that giving someone the power to change your art might compromise the integrity of what you're trying to do, and it might tug on your ego. The thing that makes movies great isn't just the script, but also the director, the cast, the editor, and all the people who work behind the scenes to bring the script to life. All of them leave their mark on the movie, which affects the final output the audience sees. There is feedback given at each stage of production, sometimes by people who will never visit the set (studio executives and focus groups). All of this feedback contributes to the story being collectively told.

Fortunate Horse podcast studio founder Taylor Moore talks about his experiences getting feedback from consensus:

> One thing I did learn as a union organizer was how to make decisions in a group by consensus, and when I started Fortunate Horse, I took those practices in to work with the groups that I work with, and it has been a defining aspect of my personal and professional life ever since then, where feedback is not a reaction to something that's happened, it is intimately tied up in the process to where you are really trying to get multiple people to create a group mind, which is also something that comes from improv training, where everyone is there, and everyone is contributing. We are all becoming an organ of a greater being than ourselves.
>
> I've been very intentional with who I've worked with and how I've worked with them since those days. I don't give a ton of feedback either way, because the process is so open, and there's so much discussion everywhere all the time, everyone feels very much on the same page. I much prefer to put consensus and feedback and temperature taking in the early stages than in the later stages.

Getting feedback from strangers is equally hard but easier to ignore. You might do yourself a disservice by ignoring that feedback, though, as sometimes a fresh set of eyes on your project might be just the thing you need. Being too close to your art makes it precious. You don't want to be told your baby is ugly. A stranger breaching that sacred space between them and your creative process is difficult. Your first instinct might be to make excuses like "it's not finished yet" or to go on the defensive to the person giving notes, alluding to them not knowing what they're talking about. "They just don't understand" can be a misused phrase. Sometimes people know exactly what they're talking about, but you aren't ready to hear it. Other times, people don't understand what you're trying to tell them, but their feelings on the matter are strong. This type of gut instinct on their part can also be valid, although taken with much more of a grain of salt.

Professional board game developer Banana Chan discusses their process for getting feedback from other developers and GMs:

I prefer playing games with game designers. They can give very direct feedback and very specific feedback too. Whereas sometimes when I'm playtesting with a group that probably doesn't know as much about systems design or game design, they might give feedback where it's like, this is fun, or this is not fun, but why? Why was it fun? What did you enjoy about it? I got to play with my friends. That's not really feedback. Trying to play with people who will give direct, honest, and specific feedback is something that I prefer over playing with folks who might give general feedback.

I think that in the beginning and the end stages of playtesting, I end up just grabbing whoever I can and being like, okay, I need to just know if this works, right? That's helpful information for me. Then in the middle stage where it's like, okay, I need more specific feedback, I would go to game designers, because now that I have a bit of a network of people that I can trust and talk to, I would try to get game designers to look over my game. Closer to the final stages of playtesting are usually when you want to do marketing and get the word out there. So going to conventions, going to games-on-demand, running your game there that gets a lot of eyes and ears on the game, and also gives you feedback on what to improve upon.

Dimension 20 Executive Producer and frequent guest GM on Critical Role, Brennan Lee Mulligan, talks about getting feedback from his fellow GMs:

There's a really funny conversation I've had with a Aabria (Iyengar) about specifically this, and I had it with Aabria, and also with our pal Matt Mercer over at *Critical Role*, which is this art form is so new that you have to receive feedback from your peers, right? This happened to me too, when I was doing stuff at UCB. UCB, like a lot of improv theaters, had this cardinal rule of, like, do not "note" each other. Do not "note" your teammates. Have a coach or have someone in that position of experience and wisdom that's "noting" you, because it will corrode your trust. It'll corrode your trust if you "note" each other. And I remember being on a team at UCB, and it was this thing where it was like, guys, the only best coaches at the theater are our former teammates from other teams. There is no Phil Jackson.

I think with actual play, I depend on people like Aabria and Matt. Even though we are pals, I depend on their feedback and input. I depend on Taylor's (Moore) feedback and input. I depend on the feedback and input of Lou (Wilson) and Erica (Ishii), because there's no actual play "Academy" with 1000-year grand tradition where I can go find some who's the fucking Uta Hagen of actual play that can straighten me out. There is none. So, I think that in a weird way, I've had to divest from some of those tendencies to not want peer-to-peer feedback, because the people I trust most in this space are my contemporaries, and I depend on them. There is not this ancient tradition of received wisdom. I depend on them to clarify and point out and help me shore up my weak spots and try to try to advance as an artist.

Receiving feedback after your project is already in front of the audience's eyes is another thing entirely. Once it's public, it's (unless you're George Lucas) hard to go back and fix the mistakes (or even acknowledge there are any) in your work. In the world of film, websites like Rotten Tomatoes bring to bear the full weight of criticism from both audiences and professional critics down upon the casts and crews of dozens of movies per week. Some of these movies are big-budget Hollywood blockbusters with a seemingly unending budget, while others are smaller, personal stories making the rounds through the film festival circuit. Both are treated with an equal amount of praise or disdain, depending on the person or outlets viewing them.

FROM THE AUTHOR

As someone who has made a living as a film critic for a long time, I can tell you that one of the most frustrating parts of my profession is that I can only give a filmmaker my two cents about their work after it's too late to fix it. I see it generally around the same time an audience sees it. It frustrates me because I know that I could help if I was involved earlier in the process. I've seen enough movies at this point in my career to know what audiences, film festival directors, programmers, and distributors are looking for at that particular time in the marketplace. Do filmmakers necessarily want to hear that opinion? Not always. Sometimes they just want to create the art that's in their heart. But feedback can save a lot of stories from being pushed aside, thrown in the "slush pile," or panned critically. Please take

> this advice to heart: get feedback throughout your process from people you trust and respect. They don't have to all be industry pros, just people you know have your back and want to see you succeed (and will be brutally, and I mean brutally honest with you).

The language we use to talk about movies has developed over the last one hundred plus years since its inception. Movies have gone through many iterations, from the silent era to the "talkies," colorization, CGI, 3D, film, tape, digital, and more. Each leap in technology or technique has allowed us to better explain the process. Unfortunately, the main discourse over film has been reduced to opening weekend box office numbers and social media hot takes. There are still many film critics and enthusiasts who dig deep into movies and how they're made, and they create essays and videos that show off their passion and expertise in their field.

Gaming, as an entire genre, of which TTRPGs are a part of, has gone through its own iterations over human history. Most people would discount TTRPGs as being new, and while filming a game session or campaign is certainly something that's only been occurring within the last couple of decades with 2003, and a live stream from the Bradford University Gaming Society's (BURPS) Paul Maclean claiming the spot as the first live-streamed actual play. Earlier than that, in the 1980s, the company TSR, which owned the rights to the Dungeons & Dragons IP prior to Wizards of the Coast, created a D&D (more accurately Advanced Dungeons & Dragons) radio show pilot that was a story set up similar to an actual play and could be considered a spiritual precursor to streamed actual play games.

The language used to talk about devised theater, actual plays, narrative play, etc., is still being developed and takes cues from film and literary criticism as a basis of description and review.

THE BUSINESS OF SCREENWRITING

FROM THE AUTHOR

I actually went to great lengths to keep the "business" part of screenwriting out of this book. I wanted the book to be purely from the creative standpoint, but as I came closer to the end of this book and needing to pad my word count slightly (just kidding), I realized that there is really no way to speak completely about being a screenwriter, or a professional storyteller for that matter, without addressing the capitalistic elephant in the room.

Truthfully, this will either be the most boring section of this book, or it might be the one that causes you to be giddy with excitement. The business of screenwriting and being a professional creative is one of the most difficult things a person can do. Sure, it isn't building bridges or skyscrapers from wrought iron and cement with your bare hands, but mentally and emotionally, it can pack a wallop.

Before we get into the nitty-gritty of it all, do this first and foremost. Establish an LLC. Use a service like LegalZoom or one like it and get your federal EIN number and file your paperwork to start your business. Did you do it? Great, now you have some legal protection for yourself and your work, as well as a legitimate means to write off any expenses you'll incur during your tax year. This includes the money you spent on incorporating as well as your tax preparer's fees.

Is this required? No. Is it considered a best practice? Yes.

Now that you're all legit and everything, let's talk about what you do after your script, story, podcast, audio drama, novel, etc., is complete. The main thing about being a creative in the entertainment industry is exposure.

FROM THE AUTHOR (AGAIN)

A quick note about "exposure." Many people will try to get you to work for free (especially writers and performers) with the guarantee that you'll get exposure. Don't do these gigs. It's never worth it, and you'll be taken advantage of every time. Two things can buy you exposure: money and time. Money is the obvious thing because you can buy ads, or social media verification (getting you higher post views, sometimes) and things like that. Time, because if you spend the time to create and implement a powerful marketing strategy, you'll see a return on your exposure from it.

You can't talk about exposure without also bringing up the concept of impostor syndrome. Those two little words can kill your career before you've even started if you let them get the best of you, take root in your brain, and allow them to paralyze you.

Brennan Lee Mulligan, the creator of the hit Dropout.tv show *Dimension 20* and the popular AP podcast *Worlds Beyond Number,* talks about his ideation surrounding impostor syndrome, and how he handled his fears and doubts at his recent sold-out show at Madison Square Garden:

> This is going to sound like a bit, but it's not. It's dissociation and compartmentalization, which get a bad rap. They are incredible psychological tools. A little bit of denial is great, amazing. A lot of religious texts talk about, like, the watcher who watches you watching. I am the seer, and I am the seeing, and I am the seeing of the seer. That third part you gotta let that guy out of the cockpit if you're gonna walk on stage at Madison Square Garden. It really is something where it's like, don't perceive yourself doing this. Just go do this. Don't be aware of doing it while you're doing it. My God, you'll collapse, you'll have an aneurysm, you'll vomit. Just do it and don't have the awareness of doing it.
>
> To give insight into the Madison Square Garden thing. I walked backstage after the show ended, confetti in my bag. I had my, my little computer bag with me, and I put it down, and I was also part of the (production) team. Any *Dimension 20* thing I do, I'm also part of the team producing the show. So, I wasn't even as nervous as the cast, because you're doing a million things. We gotta talk to the security people and our people others. At the end of the show, I put my bag down, and I went, Okay, what's next? And there was nothing to do next. And I burst into tears. And it was literally like, if you stay in 'shark mode' of just what's the next thing you have to do? That's that is the psychological key I've found into avoiding imposter syndrome, which is that imposter syndrome requires you to regard yourself in order to do its nefarious thing. So just don't regard yourself. That's the key.

Worlds Beyond Number's producer Taylor Moore chimes in on this as well:

> Here's a great way to avoid imposter syndrome…it's okay to suck. It's okay to suck, but you have to mean it, and you have to have tried really hard. That is my philosophy. As a musician goes, I am really bad. I cannot stand toe to toe in any regard with people, even at the bottom of the media composer world, I can't, but I can

do just enough to make the show I hear in my head or get close to making the show that I hear in my head, and I'll sweat and I'll bleed to do it. So even if you hear it and it's not very good, there is something. There's blood in it, like it's real, you know?

Soul Operator's Tatiana Gefter speaks about their experience in the audio drama space trying to reach an audience, how APs have their own strengths in marketing, and how screenwriters can benefit from what works in these spaces:

It's been a huge conversation, I would say, in the audio drama space in particular. I think APs are slowly getting brought into this conversation, just because so many APs are primarily video versus audio. There is really no platform that is podcast forward. I know most of my listenership for my show is on Spotify, and Spotify has horrible monetization for its creators. Unless you're literally racking in millions of listens, you will not make any money, and it's also not built to categorize shows. It's very difficult if you like something, but you can't explicitly search for podcasts that have this, this and this, right? There is a platform called Apollo where they're trying to do this. It's still very much early days for the platform, and not many people use it yet.

How do we get this audience that's found their preferred listening platform? How do we get them to change to a completely different platform? I just don't see that being really feasible. Bringing it back to the marketing aspect of it with the whole Twitter blowout. People kind of escaped to the edges of social media. So now there's people on BlueSky and on Mastodon and Tumblr and wherever. If you want to get listenership, you as a producer have to have all these different social media platforms, and you have to be advertising on every single one. That costs money. Even if it doesn't cost money, it will cost you time. I don't pay anyone to advertise for me. A huge source of ads in the audio drama space is ad swaps, where one show will reach out to another show and be like, hey, I'll put your trailer in front of one of my episodes, if you put our trailer in front of yours. It is like a perfectly legitimate way to advertise something.

Something that the AP space does well that the audio drama space has yet to catch up on is paid advertising, sponsorships, that sort of thing. When Knave of Cups asked me, hey, what's the rate that you're wanting to charge us for having one of our ad reads at the end of your episode? I had no idea. I asked my audio drama friends, and none of them had ever sold ad space in their life. (I spoke with) Connie Chang from Transplaner, and they walked me through it, and they gave me excellent advice on how to price myself and my show and how to sell that ad space. There's just so many little elements.

But I think what I was circling back to before with that Twitter thread when someone was asking, hey, is there any short (audio dramas)? No one had any recommendations until someone recommended my show. Soul Operator is between 15 to 25 minutes, and that was exciting for the original poster. Like, yes, this is what I'm looking for, episodic content that actually is the length of an episode. It's very difficult to do that in the standard AP format, where you have a lot of improv moments, and you don't want to cut off the time, because what if this is a great moment, and all that stuff is really natural and happens in that sort of show. But I think having scripted content that exists in the world of APs and TTRPGs makes you more marketable.

Screenwriters on social media tend to have their own little corners within the various apps, usually defined by hashtags like #screenwriting, #amwriting, #writingcommunity, #scriptsky, #filmtwitter, or something similar. These are wonderful places to find writing partners, talk about the difficulties of being a screenwriter, and find out information about upcoming deadlines for fellowships and contests that might be worth entering your work into.

These spaces can also be populated by people looking to prey on novice screenwriters with promises of future fame and fortune if you hand over your script (and probably a few thousand dollars too). Don't fall for these scams. If you have a question about a particular person or entity, run it by some of your peers first. They'll have your back.

While promoting yourself and your work via social media, you might be tempted to share your first pages, plot, etc. with other people, especially when folks are following a hashtag like #firstpagefridays. Don't make a habit of sharing your work outside of professional settings.

Copyright your work when you're done writing your first draft. There are a few different ways to do this. Some people recommend mailing your manuscript to yourself, with the date it was sent to you from the post office serving as the copyright date. There are also online services like WriteVault that allow you to securely upload your manuscript to their site to preserve the copyright date (you'll even get a PDF certificate that you can download from them with the date/timestamp of your manuscript upload).

There is also a method of using the Electronic Copyright Office (eCO) website. You create an account with them, register your work, pay your filing fee, and submit a copy of your script. If you are a Writer's Guild of America (WGA) member, they also have a way to register screenplays with them, but it is not always considered a replacement for a valid copyright method by some people in the industry.

You've written your script, but how do you get it to the studio head honchos that can greenlight your work? That's a tough one considering you can't just submit an unsolicited script. You can't even submit an unsolicited screenplay to another working writer. If you try this method to "break in," you'll not only be wasting your shot at success, but you'll probably burn a few bridges in the process. Unsolicited scripts go immediately into the garbage, and most writers and studio employees will block whoever sent it. The issue at hand isn't gatekeeping, but legally speaking, they don't want to take your script and then be held legally accountable if the studio does something similar in the future. It's nothing personal; they just don't want to get sued.

So, what then? You'll need to get a manager or an agent to send your scripts to the studios on your behalf. This is also easier said than done, and there are many conversations online, in books, and at industry events occurring throughout the year that try to shed light on this mysterious process. The short answer is: get lucky. The long answer is that the luck you need is made by being a decent person within your writing community, being seen at the right places, by the right people, and ultimately, being talented and having a good product (script) that's ready to go into production.

When everything lines up. The right opportunity, the right script, the planets, whatever. Then you'll have a shot at getting your script to someone who can actually do something with it.

Your other option is to go the indie film route. Find a filmmaker who's looking to produce or direct a script like the one you've written and set up a pitch date with them. Pitching is an art all on its own and there's a plethora of information in the world about how to do it effectively that we won't cover here. If you put the same amount of passion into your pitch that you do into your stories, you'll have a good chance of getting someone to option your screenplay.

Speaking of optioning, you don't have to get a lawyer to sign an option contract (a contract where a director or producer has the exclusive rights to make your script for a certain period of time, for an amount of money), but it probably won't hurt. The main takeaways from an option contract are:

1. How you are to be credited in the movie?

2. How long is the option for?

3. How much money are you being paid, and when?

Credits in the entertainment industry are more than just words on a screen. Guild members and leaders fight for these, and they mean something in terms of dollar value in the industry. "Created by," "written by," "teleplay by," and "story by" all mean different things and can carry different weights depending on how they're used. Don't get screwed into a co-writing credit just because the producer's nephew did a spell check on your script.

Screenplay options run for different lengths of time, depending on how the option agreement is written. Sometimes it's written longer as a shopping agreement with a producer who intends to package the script with a director and actors to raise money for production. This means that they might need up to a year or longer to get everything together before the trigger is pulled and the film is greenlit. Until then, your script is effectively off the market and will sit in limbo until the option agreement lapses.

The option agreement might only be for six months, which is a suitable length if you're working directly with an independent film director who intends to make the movie soon. Six months with an option to renew is a good way of not letting too much time pass with your script off the market while still giving the filmmaker a chance to re-up (for a fee) for another six months if they're having trouble getting all their ducks in a row.

The question of payment can be a tricky one. Some people have trouble asking for what they're worth. The good news is that the WGA, and other screenwriters online, have a rate sheet available with guild minimums for various types of scripts and agreements. If you are hesitant about using a rate you made up in your head, use those instead. You'll also want to make certain you are getting some sort of payment upfront, payment for rewrites and second drafts, and a conversation regarding residuals if the film gets formal distribution.

The entertainment industry can be a blast. You'll rub elbows with celebrities, have your picture taken on red carpets, watch your words being said by actors on the screen, and there will be days when your heart will swell with all the support from people around you.

There will also be days when everyone seems to say "no" to you. The phone isn't ringing, the words aren't coming naturally onto the page, and the bills are due with not enough money in the account to cover them.

This is normal.

This is temporary (if you stick with it and make good choices).

Not everyone will get the golden ticket to get through the gates to consistent work in Hollywood, but there's a lot of work to be had at the indie level, in other forms of media outside of Hollywood, and more. Patience and perseverance are the two most valuable attributes, outside of talent, that a person can have who is pursuing screenwriting as a vocation.

CHAPTER 6

Finishing

THE VOMIT DRAFT

Writing is hard, and the words don't always come easily. A bad but completed script is still better than no script at all. Sometimes you just need to get the words out, even if they make little sense, don't further the plot, or contradict themselves. Getting from Fade In to the End is the first goal of many. Don't worry about things like formatting, spelling, or grammar at this stage. The vomit draft is about one thing and one thing only: getting to the end and, ultimately, overcoming any potential fears that may prevent you from completing your script if you dwell on them for too long.

The key to the vomit draft is momentum. It's not about accuracy or even about the story making sense. It's about flow and consistency. Sitting down to write is a commitment that, as a professional storyteller, you need to make with yourself. The words won't always come easily, but you have control over when and where you're going to write. Game designer, screenwriter, and transmedia storyteller Christian Nommay, who created the Titan Effect TTRPG, shares his method of getting in the zone:

> I use automatic writing. I have a lot of notebooks, even in this age of computers and all this kind of geeky stuff. You know, for me, I have all kinds of notebooks everywhere in the house. It drives my girlfriend crazy, but I have one dedicated to what I call automatic creative writing, where I blog. I sit for 15 to 30 minutes, I start a timer, and I write anything that comes through my mind, and I

DOI: 10.1201/9781003538202-6

mean, anything, and I don't care about how I write it. If it's full of typos, I don't care. It's not the goal to show it to someone. It's just for me to grease the wheels.

The vomit draft is about looking forward, not behind. You are a train barreling down the tracks toward the next scene, chapter, etc., and you aren't stopping until the last piece of coal in your brain burns up and turns to smoke. Only then, when the gears have ground to a halt, do you look back and survey the damage you've wreaked on the page. You are trying to get past the point of self-judgment and move into the flow of the story. You're not trying to make bad art, but you're giving yourself the space and grace to fail forward (if you can even call it failing, as you're actually moving closer to your end goal of having a complete draft).

For some neuro-spicy people, the idea of proceeding forward without a plan can seem shocking and untenable. But that doesn't mean you can't take advantage of this process. You'll just need to outline first so you can understand the direction you want to take your draft. You can outline the entire piece at once, or you can do it in stages, breaking down the acts, scenes, or chapters into bite-sized chunks that will allow you to narrow down the topics, settings, or themes of your draft. Your vomit draft session doesn't even have to be actual words on a page, but can be charts, character sheets, histories of your story world, arcs for each scene or the entire story. It can be on notecards that you lay out in front of you or tack up on a corkboard, or on a dry-erase board (take a picture afterward in case everything gets erased).

EXERCISE 6.1

Sit down and set a timer for 15 minutes. Write whatever comes into your mind in your notebook. At the end, look at the things that you've written and see if you can connect the dots between your thoughts. Do they connect? Are they random? Is there a story to be told here?

Another method of vomit drafting that might also suit creative folks is the Talking Draft Method, which is basically an improvisational exercise where you record yourself doing all the scene dialog and then transcribing it after and then formatting it into your chosen storytelling format (script, prose, etc.).

For many writers, staring at a blinking cursor on a blank page is one of the most daunting visuals they come across. Marring that sea of untouched, virgin territory with your words can be like being asked to perform surgery with no training. You don't want to mess up. But it's okay to mess up. In fact, you now have permission to mess up. Be as messy as you need to be to get to the end of your story. If you're going to make a mess of things, do it with gusto, intention, and audacity.

Actor, singer, producer, and TTRPG enthusiast Ned Donovan, who is a multi-hyphenate both in front of and behind the camera of the show Encounter Party, speaks about his vomit draft process:

> I have this sort of life mantra in that I have 1000 ideas a year, but only four of them are any good. But I don't want to focus on having only good ideas, because that's a lose/lose, zero-sum game. So, what I do is I have a pretty specific process that is maybe just how my brain works. I'm pretty good at knowing when ideas are not good, or, more specifically, not produce-able, or not produce-able quickly. I know I can't produce something I need $30 million to make. I'm not going to get $30 million, so why spend any time on that idea in that same vein? I'm pretty good at knowing which ideas have promise, but I don't take them out of the brain. I just let them percolate for a while. Every once in a while, I think of a thing, and I go, oh, that would help this, and I file it away, and then someday I hit a point where I go, ah, that idea is ready for development, and that's when I get it out of my brain. That's when I get it on to a piece of paper.
>
> I use Notion pretty religiously, and Notion's pretty useful for drafting, tracking, and understanding. Then when I'm sort of ready to move on, I go into whatever scripting platform I'm planning on using, historically, it was Celtx, but right now I'm probably just going to use Highland because it seems really easy for word vomit, and that's how my brain is currently working, and I bang out anything I can think of, scenes, whole script, who cares? I let it be bad. I let it be miserable. Then it's time to sort of refine, and I say Oh, when I was in the ideation phase, I had this idea for this. I didn't incorporate that in my word vomit. How do I get that in? I sort of refine from there. But for me, when I take something out

of the ideation phase in my brain, I try to never take something out and spend time on it where that time doesn't feel well spent.

Ultimately, being a writer is about actually writing. The vomit and talking draft methods are just more tools in your arsenal to give you the excuse to do the work, even when the goal is not for the work to be exceptional. One great thing about writing is that it doesn't cost a dime (and yes, this might be a bit of a privileged statement as it's much easier to write when you don't have to think about money, keeping a roof over your head, or other basic necessities that we need to survive). It only costs time, and if you're not on some crazy deadline, there's time to clean things up and rewrite when you come to that next stage in your project's development.

There is no wrong way to write, as long as you're writing.

REFINING

This is the part of the book where we cover the least fun part of writing and editing. It is the part of the process where we take the story, themes, characters, locations, and everything else that goes into telling our tales and make them palatable and salable to the masses. It's the part where we agonize over every sentence, word, and letter. It's where we take a ruler to our margins and analyze whether there's too much white space on the page. Or we don't worry about any of that and just focus on making sure what we've written makes sense and is entertaining.

There was life before Final Draft!

Before the digital age, screenplays were hastily written and rewritten on any scrap of paper that was lying around and then typed up into something resembling today's screenplay structure before they were inevitably rewritten again by someone on the set. Don't focus so much on formatting and don't sweat over the details. You'll hear from people on various social media channels who will ardently tell you what you absolutely cannot do, and what you definitely need to do, to write and sell your script. Some people will tell you that only a pro screenwriter can get away with certain things and that amateurs or up-and-comers should stay in their own lanes and not take the same risks.

Take all of that advice with a grain of salt.

Refining your work can be stressful. It's the opportunity to fix all your mistakes, but first, you'll see all your mistakes, and that can be demoralizing, causing you to get down on yourself. This is why it's recommended to refine after you've reached the end of your story or script. That way, you at least have the advantage of a completed draft in your hands before you start looking for all the problems.

AP podcast producer, composer, and founder of Fortunate Horse (which produces the hit AP *Worlds Beyond Number*), Taylor Moore discusses his approach to the age-old "kill your darlings" method of editing:

> We are not we are not forced into a 24 minute or a 40-minute block on network television. We are not doing season orders for a production studio, and we don't have to worry about a network or anyone like that. So, we don't have to kill *any* darlings if we wanted to. We could publish every utterance, every squeak of the chair, every dropped dice, every pee break and lunch break that happens on the mics. Most people are editing to fit a format, and our format is, there's no format. Our format is whatever makes the most compelling experience for the listener, and whatever we think makes the best narrative, as far as what gets cut and what stays in. I mean, comedy is easy, because Brennan (Lee Mulligan) and I have spent many, many years in the trenches as friends and as professional people, publishing work on the internet, making things funny and exciting for people. I trust my gut. I trust my gut more than anything else, as far as editing comedy, as far as everything else. I think it's very simple.
>
> It's very, very rare that there is a hard editing decision, because I work with people who are extremely experienced. They are the top of the field of people improvising compelling narrative. I have worked with people who have, and do not have experience doing this. I have another show called *Fun City*, where we intentionally cast outside of the world of performers and podcasts and actual play, and your editing process is different for every group, but with *Worlds Beyond Number*, there's very, very rarely a hard editing decision.
>
> There was one time where there was a big moment where our character is getting these new abilities and sort of going through this big character catharsis. But the way it was played at the table was, to understand the mechanics of that important moment, you would have to understand very particular mechanics of the Paladin class of Dungeons & Dragons, 5e. You would have to

know that this ability only comes at this level because it was not explained. It's happening in the game. But of course, a lot of listeners, even if they're fans of D&D, might not know that at this level, this thing comes, and that means an extra d8 so when this player says, put an extra d8 on. If you know all that stuff, it's a big emotional moment, because you understand what's happening. But if you don't know that particular rule, there's no emotional electricity to that scene at all. So that was rearranged and reordered in the edit to bring out the actual fiction action and the character's reactions and things like that, using music and sound design to tell the story in fiction about this big, transformative act of heroism.

The editing process can be a very stressful time. You're both finished and far from finished all at once. Charity TTRPG content creator Jes Wade discusses their insecurities during the review and refining process:

I get really nervous about sharing. Sharing my stuff with other people, and so I had it completely formatted and everything before I wanted to see another set of eyes on it, just because I don't take criticism super well. I'm not bad at it, but it hurts. It hurts me, the person, not necessarily the work. So, I wanted it to be as perfect as possible before other people looked at it and before I had people playtest it.

Tactics that work for some people won't work for others. Remember that even the most seasoned screenwriters and showrunners started out exactly where you are now. Success doesn't happen overnight. Until someone else is paying you to write their vision, focus on perfecting your vision.

There are things you do for yourself because you love them; hopefully, writing is one of those things. Sometimes we get to do those things and share them with other people. Sometimes we get to earn a living doing those things. There is no one road or real trick to it. Keep doing it as long as you're able to.

Editing your work can feel almost as hard as writing it in the first place. So, start with the low-hanging fruit first. Run your work through a spelling and grammar filter. These aren't 100% accurate, especially when you're writing genres like science fiction or fantasy that contain a lot of made-up words. Below are ten examples of spelling/grammar checking tools:

Microsoft Word

Google Docs

ProWritingAid

Grammarly

LanguageTool

Quillbot/Scribbr

GrammarCheck

WordTune

Linguix

AutoCrit

Some of these tools work with writing software like Final Draft, Fade In, or Scrivener and others rely on you importing or copy/pasting your work into their systems in order to check them. Ultimately, do what works and feels best for you.

EXERCISE 6.2

Take a small sample of your work and put it through a minimum of three different spelling/grammar checkers. Did they catch any/all of your errors? Which one seemed to work the best for you?

Now that you've done a spelling/grammar pass on your work, you can start the next steps. From here, I would recommend looking at the feedback you've received from other people for your work and examining what advice you want to incorporate from their perspectives. You might not agree with everything the folks who gave you feedback said, and you're under no obligation to use any of their advice, but it still warrants a hard look, from a non-emotional position, to see if anything has merit.

Break the work down into smaller pieces. Editing a whole book is a huge process, and so is a script (the average script being between 90 and

120 pages). Take it act by act, scene by scene, or in the case of a novel, chapter by chapter. Take time in between your edits to step back and view your changes with fresh eyes.

Hemingway is credited with saying, "the only kind of writing is rewriting." Find the points in your story or script that breathe a little too long and squeeze them until you can't cut one more word. A screenplay's themes often become clearer during the rewriting process. While the first draft might hint at overarching ideas, subsequent drafts allow the writer to weave these themes more deliberately into the narrative. This could involve adjusting character arcs to reflect the theme more profoundly or incorporating visual motifs that reinforce the story's message. Ask yourself, did my characters accomplish everything I needed them to in this scene?

For example, if a script explores themes of redemption, a rewrite might emphasize moments where the protagonist confronts their past mistakes or faces moral dilemmas. Ensuring that these thematic elements are consistent throughout the script enhances its emotional impact and resonance with the audience.

Look at your dialog. Does it sound natural? Are your characters conveying their dialog in ways that sound authentic to them, or do all the characters sound alike?

Natural and engaging dialog is one hallmark of a great screenplay. Writers often read their scripts aloud or workshop scenes with actors or other writers to identify lines that sound awkward or unnatural.

Subtext is another area where dialog benefits from rewriting. The best lines often imply more than they state outright, allowing the audience to read between the lines. Rewriting can help strip away unnecessary exposition and replace it with dialog that conveys meaning through subtlety and nuance.

Rewriting isn't just about fixing problems; it's also about maintaining momentum and energy throughout the script. Scenes that drag or feel redundant can be reworked or cut entirely. Conversely, moments that feel rushed might be expanded to give the audience time to absorb key developments.

A well-paced script keeps the audience invested in the story. During the rewriting process, writers often use tools like scene cards or beat sheets to visualize the script's pacing and identify areas that need change. This helps ensure each scene contributes meaningfully to the narrative.

It's not uncommon for a script to undergo dozens of drafts before it reaches its final form. Each rewrite brings the story closer to its potential, whether by addressing structural issues, enhancing characters, or refining dialog. While the process can be time-consuming and sometimes frustrating, it's also deeply rewarding.

The evolution of a script through rewriting highlights the iterative nature of storytelling. Ideas that seemed brilliant in the first draft might be discarded in favor of better ones. Conversely, insignificant details added during a rewrite can become pivotal elements of the story. This constant refinement transforms a rough concept into a polished screenplay.

Make backups as you progress using a file-saving method that makes sense to you! Don't just back up the final copy, but make sure you have separate backups as you progress in case you ever need to revert to a previous copy.

FROM THE AUTHOR

On the subject of industry pros (in whatever medium you're writing for), don't fall for the scams. If you're going to pay for things like script coverage or writing advice, do your due diligence first. There are many people in all walks of the arts who make a living preying on novice writers. If you're submitting your screenplay to a contest, look at their history, previous award winners, etc. Are they online only? That's a red flag right there. There are only a few places I personally would recommend submitting your scripts to. These all have track records of doing something for a screenwriter's career after they've won. Whether it means getting repped, getting optioned, or getting to pitch their work in front of studio execs, these at least live up to their promise of being an accelerator and/or incubator for new talent. The Academy Nicholl Fellowship, Sundance Writer's Lab, the Austin Film Festival, ISA Fast Track Fellowship, the PAGE International Screenwriting Awards, and the Stowe Story Labs.

Just like filmmakers submitting to film festivals, you can go broke if you're not careful when submitting to all the contests out there. You need to be careful how you approach these. Take your time. Make sure your script is ready to go (I hesitate to use the word perfect because that doesn't exist and will only give you false expectations that you'll never meet). Don't worry if you submit a script to a fellowship and find a spelling error afterward. One misspelled word isn't going to make or break your career. You got this!

AFTERCARE

POINT OF INSPIRATION

"giving them a safe space to feel dangerous, or a safe space to experiment and push the boundaries and overstep the mark, and have the tools to have someone say, I don't want that…if you want to have emotional impact, then you have to provide a safe space to do that."—Grant Howitt

The topic of aftercare is something that is basically unheard of in the writing world but has gained in popularity in the TTRPG space. It's also something not uncommon with actors who go through emotional scenes and need time to process the emotions that come up during their acting process.

TTRPG players, especially ones who have training in improv or acting, can get so deeply involved in their characters that the feelings they are expressing affect their real life. In the TTRPG space, this is called bleed. Writers can sometimes experience this same phenomenon when writing intense scenes that include love, loss, and especially scenes that the writer is pulling directly from their own lives.

TTRPG producer, player, and patron of the polyhedral, Katie Downey, talks about her experiences in handling character death in a game she was playing in, and how open communication is the key to making sure that everyone's needs at the table, and beyond, are being addressed:

> I have had one permanent character death, and it was on one shot charity game. I was really irritated because it was a great character, and I'm of the opinion (that if) the character is dead, I can't play him again. I've had some very close calls, both in LARPs and tabletop games.
>
> There's a rules expansion that was written for the D4 game by Dustin Fletcher and Devin Henderson, who were the co-DMs. They ran simultaneously, so we had two DMs every night. They wrote an expansion to the rules for resurrection, and gave it the possibility of failure, or you could have a flawed resurrection, so your character could come back with a really big flaw. I think I lost two from my wisdom score when I resurrected, because I got a flaw and that had a big impact on the character.

It's anxiety invoking if you've played that character for a long time, or even if you just really like the character. Aftercare, talking after the game, I think is an important thing to do if you've had a major emotional event or there is something that has happened that there's a potential for bleed or something like that. It's important for the whole table to come together and talk to each other, make sure everybody's okay, because it can be really emotionally impactful if you lose something that you've grown to love.

The important thing is just communicating. If there's something wrong with how your character went out, talk to your DM after the game. Talk to your storyteller, Game Master, whatever you call them, whatever term is appropriate for the game but talk to them. They may see your perspective and come up with a solution that your character returns, because maybe the rules as followed weren't quite accurate, or something like that. Just communicate.

Some people might balk at the thought of giving credence to feelings, citing "it's just a game," but some of these games go on for years, and the storytelling in relation to the characters the players role-play can make them deeply invested, no more so than any character you might watch on television or in a movie that you as an audience member would get attached to.

TTRPG players and GMs have introduced a series of safety tools that they can choose to implement in their games to protect players from bleed and from topics that might lead to instances of PTSD or other trauma. Unbalanced Encounters' Patrick Perini discusses an instance of safety tool used in his games and goes into detail about how safety tools were not created just to neuter GMs and players:

We used safety tools to nail a moment of emotional hurt and then got nominated for a Crit Award for that moment. I think that in general, because this is something that is really prominent in Unbalanced Encounters, it's almost like a meme, that we hit these emotional moments, these absolutely devastating emotional moments, really, really, really hard, and sometimes purely interpersonal. Sometimes they are trauma connected, sometimes they are just visceral, just gore. It's just like somebody loses like a limb, and we sit in that space really aggressively, and the way that we manage it is twofold. One, we make sure to do the necessary content warnings on top of the show, just because we respect the audience, and as somebody who has a long history of medical trauma, I am very sensitive to and can't watch horror stuff where agency is taken away by a doctor, that really fucks with me. I'm a big fan of, right at the top, just let me know what we're talking about, and I can make that call for myself.

From a player's perspective, it all comes down to consent, because safety tools are not there to make every moment soft. They're not there to make every moment without sharp edges. They are there to ensure that players are, and the GM is able to consent to what's happening at the table. So, if we go into a conversation where we want to really hit a moment and we want to make that moment kind of fucked up or emphasize how aggressive or full of betrayal this instance is, whatever it is we have a conversation about, and we check in up front and we say, hey, is this cool? Are we going to do this?

There are lots of systems that people use to manage this. I think it gets a bit trickier when you can't edit when you're doing a live show. I know that some of my friends will use an X with their fists if they need to pull out of a scene. We don't have that complexity because we're in a fully edited medium. We just have a conversation, and we talk. Consent, consent, consent, and then we hit it. We also have broader conversations around that kind of stuff in between sessions where it's like, hey, I may end up taking this in a direction. Are you okay if I just floor it? The answer is almost always yes, but in some instances, and this is the moment that we got nominated for Crit Award for, the answer may become "no", we're going to go back to the Drake Warden, (this is heavy spoilers for season one) and the lizard. Emily Greymoore has spent all of arc two externalizing this rambunctious, flamboyant, inner-child character that steals the spotlight. He's the absolute star of the show. By the end of arc two, we use him as a mascot now, he has just absolutely run away with us, and the way that she played him, the little idiosyncrasies and the almost more animalistic tendencies that he had, were really heavily based on her cat that was back at (her) home in London. This is around the time that we are getting engaged, that she's moving to the United States, that she had to leave the cat at home, and the plan was to bring the cat over (later). We're headed into the end of arc two, and we're having discussions about, hey, the lizard is low on hit points. There's a chance that I'm going to land a hit and really take him out. If you feel like that's not what we want to do, let me know, and I can redirect, right? I have agency over where the enemies throw their punches.

We're having this kind of consent conversation, (Emily) says, no, it's fine, it's fine, and then the unthinkable happens, and the cat gets suddenly sick and has to be put down, and there's all this bleed and cross emotional association between the two. And it happens, I think, the night before we go into the final recording. I go back to her, and I'm like, hey, I want to have just another confirmation. This will not be worse art if I pull this punch, it'll be fine. We don't need this moment. We can find a different moment later She said, no, I think if it happens, it needs to happen, and I want to actually make it a moment. I want to, because the character doesn't know that she could just bring the lizard back. That's not a mechanic that the character knows yet, and so I want to really lean into it.

We started playing, and it happened, and I rolled the crit, and I took out the lizard, and Emily choked up and couldn't keep playing. She asked on-mic to step away, and we stopped playing. We're an edited medium. We could just cut this or do it a different way, or we could just kill it. She takes about an hour. We reconvene, we have a conversation, and she makes the decision that we are going to keep it in because we want to demonstrate to players that safety tools are about continuous consent, and no amount of conversation can change how, A, a player is feeling at the table, and B, that they don't need to take away the sharp edges. We leave it in, and I will be damned if everyone I've seen or heard who has listened to that episode didn't break down in tears.

The thing that cinched it was the crack in Emily's voice when she asked to step away from the table. We go get nominated for a Crit Award because of how this is such a great example of how safety tools aren't interruptive to play. They can actually be additive to play, and they're important because everyone needs that space, and everyone needs to manage the character bleed and whatnot that's happening at the table.

That is an incredibly roundabout way of saying that I think safety tools are rarely in the way of hitting those moments, if you're having open conversations, if you are genuinely managing consent, and if you play them right, they can actually elevate (those moments) because they underscore the real feelings that are happening at the table.

When you think about safety tools, consider the MPA rating system for movies. It might not have been enacted for all the right reasons (do some research on the old Motion Picture Producers and Distributors of America (MPPDA), which then became the Motion Picture Association of America in 1945, and which was re-branded in 2019 to the MPA that we know today. While you're at it, research the Hays Code as well), but it is used as a guide to warn people of the content they are about to view, giving them the agency to make another choice if the content of that film or television program has something that might bother them or is something they want to shield their children from.

What does this mean for your story or screenplay? Be aware of the audience you want for your work, and tailor your work to that audience. For instance, adding mature themes to children's stories might make parents think twice about letting their kids consume their entertainment. This might also help you in dealing with studio notes or other voices that might try to interfere with your vision for your story and allow you to get ahead of any feedback about the content of your script before it happens on set, where you might not have as much control over the end result.

CHAPTER 7

Dealing with Writer's Block

LET THE DICE DECIDE

If you're a TTRPG player, then you probably have at least one set of dice hanging around. If you're an avid TTRPG player, you might have gone full dice goblin and have sacks full of dice. Some of your dice might be in "jail" for giving you bad rolls, others might be your "go to" dice for all your games, while still others you might change out each session you play.

Either way, dice are an important mediator in the outcomes of decisions made during your games and can be just as helpful to you as a writer. If you feel stuck in your story, make a small list of potential choices your character might make, or directions your story could take. Then throw the dice and accept the outcome.

You can simplify this even more if you need your character to make simple decisions, like whether they need to go left or right. Take a D20 and choose high or low. A 1–10 on the die is low, and an 11–20 is high. There's also the option of choosing odds or evens depending on your need.

Some decisions are bigger than a D20 can provide, though, and sometimes writer's block can become so severe that no amount of thought can bring forth the story resolution you're satisfied with. What do you do in those situations?

DOI: 10.1201/9781003538202-7

Writer, content creator, educator, and Game Master Cate Osborn has her own way of overcoming writer's block:

> Getting over writer's block, for me, has been a combination of three very specific things. One is just writing it badly. A lot of what I turn in is just (insert better name here) in parentheses, just so I can get through a paper. The second thing is working on other projects at the same time which, I have ADHD, so I get a pass on that.
>
> Currently I'm writing a column for Playboy magazine, which is fucking wild to say out loud. It's a very personal column, and it's been really nice because on one side of my day, I'm writing rules and lore and pretend and fiction, and then I go home and I work on this Playboy column, which is very intimate and very much my experience. I found that's actually been really helpful in clearing my brain and just being like, okay, now I have a clean slate.
>
> The last thing is just, and this is going to sound so fucking trite, but I really mean it. I think inspiration is everywhere, and you have to just be able to sort of look at it and go, okay, what can I make this? What can this turn into? How can this fit into the story? Sometimes the answer is, it can't. I think being able to look and say, well, how could this be interesting or generative or horrific, or whatever you need it to be is helpful.

Writer's block is more akin to decision paralysis, or to the more neurospicy, they might recognize it as executive dysfunction, or the inability to do "the thing" even though you want/need to do "the thing," whatever that thing might be. Regarding storytelling, you might have so many things your characters could do that you just freeze. You aren't creatively bereft. There are too many choices for what to do, and you back yourself into a corner. This is where a roll of the dice comes in handy. You could even use a die roll with tools like the Dungeons & Dragons wild magic table, which contains both good and bad consequences to rolls, allowing you to create scenarios for your characters that incorporate whatever comes up on the dice into your story. The wild magic table is normally used in D&D by spellcasters (usually a Wild Magic Sorcerer) and suggests a chaotic magical effect that occurs when they cast a spell, which can result in something ranging from beneficial to horrible for the character and their party.

Need more help? There are more than a few companies out there that sell dice, cards, and other accessories specifically designed to help you tell your stories and/or break through writer's block. Two Tumbleweeds, a company started by two sisters, has its own version of "writing dice," a 9-dice set meant for story inspiration by creating new possibilities with every roll. Rowan Zeoli, journalist and one founder of Rascal News, the website at the forefront of reporting on the TTRPG industry, discusses some of the different choices you have when looking to make a decision using TTRPG tools:

> If a character has a choice that they can make, and they can go in any of these directions. I think (a D20) is really useful. Will they succeed or fail? You can use that mechanic to either exceedingly exceed, or they can kind of succeed. Or with a failure, they can really fail, but something good happens, or they can completely fail.
>
> Something I think is really useful, going back to the solo TTRPGs. There are a lot of different systems that don't just use dice, they also use things like tarot cards, or they use a 52-card deck, and they lead you towards different prompts like, what is this place that you're going to seem like? You pull out this card, and it gives you an adjective for what this place appears like to you, and you pull out a different card, and it shows you a specific landmark in that place.
>
> I know, in my brain, trying to create whole worlds, if I need to go bring this character to a bar, but I don't know what kind of bar I want to bring them to, or if they're going to go to a bar at all. You draw a card, and you go, oh, yeah, they're going to bring me to a dive bar that is tended to by a former WWE wrestler. Something like that. Finding those kinds of games for those specific purposes, there are tons of them out there, and I think leaning into those elements of chance, and sacrificing that control is also really useful, because you can also just feel that now you've discovered that you don't agree with the choice the dice have made for you, it feels wrong. Even if it doesn't point you in the right direction, it cuts off an avenue that you don't think is correct, which is just as valuable in writing stories.

Storymatic has a system that uses cards to deliver writing prompts. The system uses 540 cards to help break writer's block by using combinations of them to create stories based on the prompts that are revealed. This might not seem relevant to someone who writes fantasy for a living but gets dealt a card about a bus driver, but the point isn't to write your story but to just write something, anything, and to get back into the creative flow.

FROM THE AUTHOR

The concept of rolling dice to decide an outcome isn't new. Popular TikTok and media creator Jake (who goes by the moniker Adventures in Aardia) hosts Roll for Sandwich, a series of videos where he rolls dice for each component of a sandwich, from the bread to the condiments, and then eats whatever the result is. His videos make for some hilarious content while also showing that if you're feeling stuck in deciding, whether it's what to write or what to eat, the dice have your back (although the pickle sandwich video might be contrarian to this, I invite you to watch for a laugh).

GETTING FROM FADE IN TO THE END

Everyone is different, which means that everyone has an excuse for why they're not writing. You're reading this book right now instead of writing. Are you using it as a procrastination tool? Are you genuinely looking for answers to become a better writer? Only you can answer those questions yourself.

Writers like to talk about their ideal writing time/space. The internet is littered with photos of the author's private spaces where they create. Some are simple desks with picturesque windows in front of them to stare out of, with an old-school typewriter sitting square in the middle of it (often looking untouched, by the way). Sometimes you see a desk littered with papers and other detritus from multiple attempts at creation that just aren't meeting the mark. Other times, you see elaborate computer setups that reflect a neon glow across the writer's room.

However, you write, write. Prolific author Ed Greenwood shares his take on his ideal writing time, and how he overcame bad habits early on in his career that keep him on task now:

My ideal writing time these days is late, late in the wee hours when the house has gone to sleep and the number of interruptions from around the world has dwindled to the few people who know my phone numbers. I can ignore the internet, the stuff that's coming via email or Facebook or Twitter or whatever, I can just not open those and get my writing done. Whereas it's very hard when you're my age, we were brought up to answer the phone, because in those days it was dire news. It could be an ambulance. It could be you know, because I was raised by maiden aunties. Everything costs money. So, I'm just programmed to; the phone rings, you answer it.

It was training for being able to write under any conditions, which was really useful. I've made use of that ever since. But, given my druthers, it's when I can seize enough time to take the ideas that pop into my head all the time. Take the ideas that have occurred to you and work them up into something that captures you as a story, put a name and a face, a character, a gesture, a quip, anything with those so that you are thinking to yourself, oh, I've got a story here. Now, I just have to do the old thing about the sculptor taking the big block of stone and taking away the bits that shouldn't be there until he's got the sculpt. I just need to unearth the rest of the story. It's submerged right now. I need to get it out there into the world by just digging down around what's already been in my mind.

I took a journalism degree when I was like a teenager, not because I wanted to be a journalist, but because I wanted to break the incipient habit of, I can only write when the wind is in the east and my favorite music is on and I'm wearing my favorite fluffy pink slippers and I'm in the mood and the, you know, Vivaldi or whatever is on. I can't be like that. Journalism in those days was ringing telephones and pounding typewriters, and we had assignments at the university where the professors would come into the room bellowing about stuff. Car crash! President United States killed! Write the headline. I need it right now!

Game designer Banana Chan talks about her experiences dealing with getting stumped by mysteries in her game, and how creating can sometimes leave you blocked. They also talk about some of their methods for overcoming writer's block, creating, and solving their own mysteries and puzzles they're integrating into their games for players to solve.

So, with The Revenant Society, that's another game that Sen Foong-Lim and I created. It's a mystery game. It's basically about revenants who have been brought back to life, trying to figure out the mystery of their own deaths. If they solve that, they'll be able to move on. Then there's a shattering event, and it's related to this big scenario, and so when I was writing out one scenario for that, it sort of is like, okay, I have this big picture in my mind, but I want to make sure that the players can still make it their own. How do we make it so that it's not vague enough that the players can play with it, but specific enough that it's specific to the scenario, specific to the players, so that way they can tag in and go with it?

I think I got a bit of writer's block when I was writing clues. What are the sequences? What's the sequence of events that happen that would lead one player to another thing? Then, trying to create the NPCs that would guide them along. I think that what helped a lot was trying to just create (because the game functions in the time loop) the main timeline, and then as long as I have that main timeline, each individual place that they go to, having just a couple of lines on what they see, and then having a question at the end.

Questions are great. I think questions do two things really well. The first thing is that it gives players a sense of agency so they can build the story and the world around them. If you're asking them "what do you see"? What do you smell? What do you hear? That's where it gives them a way into the narrative, and they can just build on it. The other thing that questions really are great for is that it gives me an out in trying to figure out what else is going on, and it unblocks some stuff that way.

The question "what do you do" does a lot of heavy lifting in tabletop games, and it's one of the best questions a creative can ask themselves when they're writing. When you force yourself to make a decision, you are going to see progress.

Along those same lines, when the distance between the words in your mind and the words on the page seems too great to overcome, consider creating a challenge like an arbitrary deadline to force the creative juices to flow. There are also plenty of screenwriting and film competitions out there that challenge you to write and film a script in 48 hours. Often, when there are other people involved in a project, your first instinct is to not let those people down or look foolish. These competitions also put you in a creative space with other people (either remotely or in-person) and give you the ability to feed off of the creative energy of your team as everyone bounces ideas around.

There's no one "right way" to overcome writer's block. When your back is against the wall, try actress and writer Jennifer Kretchmer's method of breaking through a creative block.

> I go down research rabbit holes and hyper fixate following sites like Wikipedia wherever it may take me. I'm someone who always builds characters or worlds from a single thing that then sets everything else off. So, if I can find that one thing, then I'm set. But getting to find the one thing is the process I have to go through.

The next tip is a little more difficult for the neurodivergent folks out there who like to write linearly, as well as the "pantsers" who tend to not outline their work before they start, but you could consider beginning your script with the ending in mind first and writing that. Starting from that point and working your way backward can be especially effective when writing mystery or thriller scripts. Director of *The Godfather*, Francis Ford Coppola, is rumored to have written the endings to his stories first. Writing this way gives you the chance to provide a path for your characters by making the ending and emotional themes of the story the primary focus and serving as a waypoint for the rest of the script as you work backward. This allows you to ensure that all your narrative arcs serve that singular purpose.

CHAPTER 8

Tabletop Tools to Make Your Stories Come to Life

HARDWARE (MINIS AND MORE)

Unlike traditional board games, where your representation is based on what comes in the box, TTRPGs allow you to customize every aspect of the character you play. There are many ways that your character can be represented. The first is on paper (or a digital character sheet if you're using a third-party character builder or VTT (Virtual Tabletop) software), and another is by purchasing a mini figure to represent your character. If you're a little more adventurous, you can use a 3D printer to completely customize your character's look.

Going the 3D printer route can be expensive, time-consuming, and there is a substantial amount of learning curve if you're not already familiar with the concept (it's more than just a Star Trek-like replicator). But if you can take the time to master your 3D printer, you'll find that it can be useful around your household to make just about anything your mind can conjure. For your TTRPG, you can also make terrain for your maps, castle walls, or entire villages or cities. You can print dragons to menace your players, or you can create a "little guy" creature for your players to fall in love with.

DOI: 10.1201/9781003538202-8

Being able to visualize your adventures in an actual space that you can manipulate is the same concept you used to tell stories with your action figures or dolls when you were a kid. Make them fight, make them kiss; the world is yours to play God in. Using these tools to act out your stories, create dialog, and inhabit the characters in your stories will help you strengthen the realism and work out the flow of the scenes as you translate these playful actions into your screenplays or other creative art forms.

If you are lucky enough to have a spare flat-screen TV hanging around your home, and are handy with a saw, you can take things one step further by making an interactive table for you and your friends to play on. If you use a VTT like Foundry, you can load your TTRPG game of choice from your computer onto the table's display and load up whatever pre-visualized adventure you own or create your own based on your script's settings using homemade maps and settings you've done yourself.

Here is a list of digital mini-figure websites where you can create characters based on their pre-generated models (caveat: some sites may list STL files for download or sale that may not be owned by the site listing the model. Take care to do your own due diligence when using any website):

Hero Forge

Eldritch Foundry

TitanCraft

ANVL.Co

MyMiniFactory

WizKids

Hero MiniMaker

GamBody

Thingiverse

Cults3D

Yeggi

POINT OF INSPIRATION

"Yes, the minis are really cool, and the production value is really cool, but at the end of the day, it's a group of people that enjoy being around each other, enjoying playing a game together, and just have such good chemistry, and that's what leads everything that happens at the table, and that's what makes them so engaging and fun to watch. When I'm looking to consume an AP, if I sit down to watch it, or I turn on a podcast to listen to it, or something. If I can't tell that the people who are playing enjoy playing together, why do I want to keep listening? There's a spark that you find in groups that genuinely love playing a game, sharing a game together, that you can't fake, that no amount of cool game mechanics, no amount of interesting character backstories or worldbuilding lore can make up for that. That is the secret sauce to what makes successful APs. People who enjoy telling stories together, coming together to tell a story, and everything else just flows from there."—Meghan Cross

If you're not inclined to use one of the sites listed above, you could also contact a creator on Etsy or Patreon who specializes in making 3D miniatures for TTRPGs.

When choosing a VTT to use, you have many options to choose from as well. Here is a short list of popular VTTs that you might experiment with:

Foundry

Roll20

AboveVTT

Alchemy RPG

Beyond Tabletop

D&D Beyond

Fablecraft

Fantasy Grounds

Owlbear Rodeo

Quest Portal

Role

Tableplop

Tabletop Simulator (TTS)

TaleSpire

Dropout.tv's *Dimension 20* is known for its wonderfully detailed battle maps and sets lovingly crafted by Rick Perry and his dedicated team of artists, sculptors, and fabricators. Dungeon Master Brennan Lee Mulligan speaks to the pluses and minuses of having all these tools at his disposal for his adventures with his intrepid heroes, and the difference between running adventures that take place exclusively in the "theater of the mind":

> There are pros and cons. Having an exquisite battle map that is a gorgeous work of art to appreciate in and of itself, but when you have a large-scale battle with multiple enemies it is easier to run on a battle map. People talk about battle maps being a hassle, nothing is as much of a hassle as running a complicated theater of the mind encounter with multiple types of bad guys, and you need to remember who took what amount of damage. And by the way, I love theater of the mind, but there are certain classes that struggle in theater of the mind, Cunning Action and its utility is severely reduced by not having a battle map. Rogues are useless in theater of the mind. It's like, okay, what does it mean that I can move that extra couple of feet exactly? How many feet away am I? What is it I'm disengaging? How many people am I in melee with, right? The mobile feat and a lot of other things like that are really cool but require that kind of tactical battle grid.
>
> Now, that being said, getting to an expensive battle set and needing to get to it by a certain time is the hardest part of running *Dimension 20*, the idea of rail-less rails; of honoring player choice and being like the world is at your fingertips.
>
> "I swear to God, if we don't get to this dusty gulch, I'm gonna be so fucking pissed! We spent so much money on the gulch! Please go to the gulch!"
>
> Right like that, there is that constant push and pull with *Dimension 20* and with *Worlds Beyond Number*, there is a degree, there's an ease, and I think that running complex battles is not harder, but you have to have an agreement at the table about

what is going to be elided and abstracted. So, you're going to say, like, hey, we're going to move into initiative, but we might have a period of this combat that gets narrated through, like a cut-scene in a Final Fantasy game, right, which is very much a combat game. But there are moments where it's like, oh, this. You can't fight your way through this, so we gotta move past this and describe it and get back into another changing point and then *Worlds Beyond Number* also has the flexibility of not having a set place you have to get to. It means that in some ways, we can honor the pacing and storytelling of this long-form narrative in a way that, to me, feels a lot more effortless as a DM, where it's like, the more masters you're serving, the more stretched you become. I think *Worlds Beyond Number*, by having this really clear, definitive hierarchy where it's like combat is here to be a tool amongst a set of tools to serve this storytelling is adds a lot of ease as a dungeon master, I would say.

Throughout the course of his career, Brennan has seen the pros and cons of having all these fancy tools at his disposal to tell a story and also having to just rely on his own ability, and the imaginations of his players, to do the heavy lifting in their collaborative storytelling. The story always comes first, and as a screenwriter and storyteller yourself, you shouldn't allow yourself to be held hostage by the limitations of your material storytelling tools. Use what you need to tell the best story you can.

Of course, no TTRPG experience would be complete without one of its defining pieces of gameplay, dice. Dice can be immensely versatile as an arbiter for decision-making, as a type of fidget device, perhaps even a weapon (errant D4 caltrops are almost as damaging as Legos to step on).

Sometimes TTRPGs don't use a traditional D20 system. Some eschew dice altogether in lieu of playing cards or a tarot deck. Sometimes they use a coin, and some use nothing other than a journal and a pen/pencil. Don't feel like you need to be tied down to any one system or set of rules. You can create or use anything that helps you get from one page to the next in your writing adventure.

SOFTWARE (ONLINE AND OTHER RESOURCES)

The first screenwriting software was Scriptor, which debuted in 1983. Before that, scripts were written by hand or on a typewriter and format-ted manually into what is now considered the industry standard. For any detractors out there that believe that screenplays can be formatted any way they see fit, consider that a low-level industry reader is going to be responsible for going through hundreds of scripts per week and that something that doesn't conform to industry standards might strike them as a sign of a non-professional or amateur writer, and immediately put it in the "pass" pile. While a large part of this book is about breaking the rules, it's also important to know when to follow them. There are a lot of programs out there that can make writing your screenplay easier by doing the heavy lifting for you, formatting-wise. Below are some examples:

Final Draft

FadeIn

Celtx

Scrivener

Movie Magic Screenwriter

Arc Studio Screenwriting

WriterDuet

Trelby

Highland

Microsoft Word

Storyist

StudioBinder

KIT Scenarist

Squibler

ScriptBuilder

Slugline

Causality

Scriptation

Storyline Creator

TinkerList

Prewrite

WriterSolo

Sophocles

Writing your script is important, but sometimes it's hard to organize your thoughts. There are many other tools to get the creative juices flowing. Mind mapping tools and apps like Notion and Obsidian are very popular among TTRPG Dungeon and Game Masters for keeping track of the character and story arcs in the campaigns they're running. If you're not familiar with the concept of mind mapping, in a nutshell, it's a visual way to create structures around your ideas. It allows you to put your ideas down and create relationships between them, visually showing the connections between each idea and letting you manage them in a hierarchical manner. Below is a list of some mind mapping apps/software that you may find helpful (some of these may use AI as a means of helping you organize and categorize your information. If you're not interested in using AI in any part of your work, even at a research level, then feel free to ignore these suggestions):

Notion

Obsidian

Mem

Slite

Scrintal

Microsoft Loop

Nuclino

Trello

Evernote

xTiles

Bublup

Some scriptwriting software, like Final Draft, has outlining tools built into its features but are limited in its overall execution. It's not really built for free-thought exploration without trying to tie those ideas to a character or scene. Scrivener is an excellent piece of software that allows you the freedom to capture notes while not attaching them to the rest of your screenplay or manuscript.

Bringing everything back to TTRPGs for a moment, you should also consider joining a campaign or a one-shot to help get your mojo running. Websites like StartPlaying.games allow you to find games on demand and join them for a relatively inexpensive price point. Many of these games are helmed by experienced professional Game Masters and provide an immersive experience using VTT (Virtual Tabletop) software like Foundry or Roll20 where you can control and visualize your character, their actions, and the environments that the story takes place in. Sitting in another world for a few hours a week is a great way to get ideas for your own stories and allows you to watch how other people embody characters and solve puzzles that might be similar in theme to what you're writing about. Screenwriting at a professional level, like anything else, is a lot of work, but there's nothing saying that work can't be fun at the same time. Remember to reflect often about what brought you to screenwriting and continue to find the joy in that as much as you can. The entertainment industry is tough and full of "no." You need to find the wherewithal to keep going, even when it seems like you're not making any progress or seeing any forward momentum.

CHAPTER 9

Television Screenwriting and TTRPGs

SPEC SCRIPTS AND PILOTS (ONE-SHOTS)

Television is an ever-evolving medium that's about half as old as the film industry. If you were a screenwriter in the film industry, you'd worry about getting your scripts into the hands of producers and directors. Television does things very differently. For instance, while you might be able to sell a pilot via your agent or manager to a studio, there is a strong chance that you might not even be on the writing team that develops that pilot into what audiences see on their screens when it debuts.

Television scripts are written in what is referred to as a writers room (yes, that's spelled correctly). Each writers room is staffed in a hierarchical manner, with the Showrunner and/or Executive Producer being the top dog in the room. Showrunners are usually industry veterans with many credits under their belt and understand how to bring new scripts to life and lead their staff to deliver those pages on time to production. The Showrunner has a lot of responsibility and either controls or delegates everything from staff hiring, casting, schedules, and budgets to other staff positions such as Story Editors, Script Coordinators, and Staff Writers.

Under the Showrunner is a small horde of other Co-Executive Producers, Supervising Producers, Producers, Co-Producers, and Associate Producers. Under these people are the Story Editors, who help

DOI: 10.1201/9781003538202-9

manage the writers room under the direction of the Showrunner. They're ambitious Staff Writers with a better WGA credit and rate.

The Staff Writers and Writers' Assistants are the real workhorses in the room. They are responsible for "breaking story" (another name for plotting out each episode of the script beat by story beat) and actually writing the scripts. Writers' Assistants handle the proofreading and integrating any notes that are given from the Showrunner or any of the above-named Producers. They may also handle any research needed to make the scripts make sense.

Last, and 100% not least, are the Writers' PAs. This is more of a learning position, and they serve at the pleasure of everyone else in the writers room. They answer the phones, get coffee, order lunch, etc. They are the eyes and ears of the office and are an invaluable cog in the wheels of creativity that is necessary to make everything work like a well-oiled machine. While a Writers PA is an entry-level position, it is a great opportunity to learn and can often lead to a promotion to a Writers Assistant if they network with the right people and show they can be dependable and reliable in the room.

Television scripts are formatted similarly to feature film scripts but are generally shorter to accommodate for traditional television broadcast times (37–42 minutes depending on the type of series and excluding advertisements). Writing television (including streaming) scripts is a great way to practice telling stories with revolving plots, characters, and situations.

Kelly (thekellhop) talks about her love of one-shots as a means to test out new systems and characters, even though preferring longer campaigns for the emotional experience they can deliver.

I love a one-shot for trying out a new game to see if I have a good feeling for the system because sometimes you don't want to commit to it, not that you can't switch a game mid campaign if the if the game or the mechanics aren't working for you. But it's nice to test the waters just to see. Is this for me? Is this something I would want to do a campaign for?

I very much enjoy entertaining people. So that's when I get to take out my silly characters and have fun. I love the more serious, emotional characters that I approach. They have a special place in my heart, but sometimes it's fun to shake that off and get a little silly with it, and I just bust out whatever voice is on the front of my brain, and then I just commit to that for two and a half hours. And people just look at me like, what is she doing? Where did this come from? Like, you invited me to a one-shot. This is what's happening.

If you're not already familiar with the industry term spec script, it is a type of screenplay that is unsolicited, usually done as an example workpiece to illustrate your abilities and give you something to sell should opportunities arise. The first instance of a spec script being sold in Hollywood is believed to have been by Preston Sturges back in 1933 with his story *The Power and the Glory*, which was purchased by Fox.

Depending on what is happening in the industry, spec scripts for original stories might not be the best option to put forth when you're looking to sell your scripts or find representation, which is another use for spec scripts. Often a spec is used in television to get a writer staffed, usually at an assistant level first, and then as a regular writer. If you're very lucky, you might hit it out of the park and get to become an executive producer or showrunner of the work you sell, but veteran writers who have earned their stripes usually hold those positions after working on other successful series.

If you already have representation, your agent or manager takes your script out into the marketplace to producers who can get your script optioned by a studio. Optioning is nothing more than a fancy term for a screenplay being bought and the writer being put under contract for a finite period, giving the person, optioning the script, the ability to either produce it with a studio they are already involved with (sometimes producers will be under contract with studios on a first-look basis. This means that the producer works exclusively with one studio and must give that studio the right of first refusal on any projects they bring in-house), develop it with a studio in mind, or take the script and option agreement "shopping." A shopping agreement is used when a screenwriter options their screenplay to a producer who is then going to take their screenplay to potential buyers before giving up any creative rights or making any commitments. This is useful when a producer is trying to create momentum with a script by packaging it with a well-known director, actor, or other key talent. By packaging and shopping a screenplay around to different studios, a producer might create a bidding war for the script, leading to a larger sale.

There are many ways to make your spec script stand out in the market-place. One screenwriter, Meg Turner, posted the logline for their screen-play on X (formerly Twitter). Their script, *Organ Trail* was optioned and released in 2023. This isn't the norm, but it illustrates the luck that is needed when putting your work into the world. Luck doesn't preclude tal-ent. In an industry where the word "no" is the norm, it's important to get your work in front of as many eyes as possible.

Websites like Coverfly allow screenwriters a place to create a portfolio of their screenplays, apply for screenwriting competitions, and see current industry "mandates," or listings from industry partners looking for very specific types of scripts. Having this repository for your scripts is key to giving yourself the visibility needed to get your work seen by the right people at the right time.

Pilots are completely different. While a spec script can be episodic, and it's often encouraged that writers have several spec episodes in their arse-nal to show the range in their writing, or to show strength in a particular genre, writers need to be cautious that the episodic spec scripts they are writing are timely to what is hot in the industry. For instance, it wouldn't do a writer much good to write a *Married…With Children* spec script right now, since that show hasn't aired a new episode in decades. Even shows that are still on the air like *South Park* or *It's Always Sunny in Philadelphia* might not be worth the time to create spec scripts for since their writers rooms are smaller and usually filled with the same people season after season. The only reason to write a spec for either of these shows would be to show off your original ideas for these characters, showcase your writing style within the comedy genre, and your ability to write for a half-hour sitcom.

Pilots are the first episodes of new television shows. They introduce the main characters of the show, key supporting characters, establish the primary locations where the show takes place and the ongoing narrative themes while teasing future episode arcs for the rest of the season.

Television pilots often require more than just a fantastic screenplay. They are often accompanied by a story bible, which covers much more information than what is provided in the pilot script. A story/series bible will give a detailed background of the main characters and explain all the worldbuilding associated with the larger narratives for not just the first season, but the entire series. It breaks down each season (at least the first season) into a description of each episode. The story bible can be a hefty document, used in addition to your pilot script in the pitching process. To be clear, you will not go into a pitch and hand this large document to the person(s) you're pitching to. You should have it summarized to one or two pages as a takeaway item.

Your pitch is NOT the time to be coy about the intentions you have with your pilot script and series ideas. You need to make it very clear what storylines and surprises are in store for your audience. The pitch process is as much about how you say something as it is about what you say. You might only have 10–15 minutes to make your pitch, so make every second count.

To hear a "breaking-in" experience straight from someone who's been there, look no further than The Party's Margaret Borchert, who shares their experience going from school to Hollywood:

> I randomly took a creative writing class that was writing for short films. It was one of the few creative writing classes being offered that semester, and so I was like, I'll take this one. It'll be good for my creative writing major. I just absolutely fell in love with the form, and I love puzzles. The puzzle of all the rules that you have to follow in writing a script and the beats that you have to hit, and the certain things that have to happen, and then finding the creativity within those restrictions was something that I immediately loved and continue to love to this day. I love sitcoms because the formula of a sitcom is the same every single episode. It doesn't matter what series you're watching or from what era you're watching, you're hitting these beats at these times, and yet there is infinite story and character possibility that we have watched over the years as it has morphed and changed, but it still also remained exactly the same.
>
> I was immediately drawn to filmmaking, and then double-majored in film and creative writing, and then minored in theater. I only ever did directing and scenic design and stuff. I never acted, but I finished school and was like, well, I guess I'm going to Hollywood, because I don't have any other applicable skills. So,

I moved back to LA and started working in Hollywood, doing internships and taking any writing job I could, and I had the chance to be a writer's PA on The Bold Type, which was great, and I worked as a writer/researcher on An Oral History of The Office, which was a podcast with Brian Baumgartner. I got to see that from concept to completion, which was such a great experience, and got to watch how a project can be born and done, which I think is a relatively rare experience in this town. So often you get in the middle, or more often a project dies very early or very late. So, getting to watch that entire thing happen was really cool. Being in the pitch meetings with Spotify, trying to do this entire thing, and working with the editors to come up with how the story was going to be told, working with Brian to come up with the interview questions and do the research and all that stuff. It was really a spectacular experience.

Then the pandemic hit, and everything shut down, and I started working as an assistant to a writer who's a television and film writer, and she taught me a lot about the craft that I'm really grateful for, and basically my job with her was going to end because she got a job at Netflix in France, and she was going to move to France. So, I was like, Okay, what's next?

This led Margaret back to D&D, which then led to the creation of the Party later, an experience that Margaret described as:

the fastest, easiest pilot that we've ever written. It just came so naturally to us, and we were done with our third draft by the end of the year. Mind you, we both had full-time jobs. Tori (Chancellor) was there reading every version of that draft and giving us feedback, and so by January 2021, we had this lovely sitcom pilot, and it was like Cool, and it went into our pile of scripts. You know, every TV writer knows this one, your pile of samples. Hopefully, someday someone will want to read this thing. I luckily was in a financial position when my job ended where I didn't have to find another job immediately. We thought, was this the opportunity that we take to make something ourselves? We had this very filmable pilot, and so we're like, okay, let's talk about The Party.

COLLABORATION AND WRITING FOR SERIES (CAMPAIGNS)

POINT OF INSPIRATION

"Being able to put your own ego aside for the sake of the project is important, especially in franchise television."—Carlos Cisco

If you plan on having a career in Hollywood as a feature scriptwriter or an episodic television writer, you're going to need to get comfortable working with other writers. You might already be familiar with the concept of a writers room when writing for television or streaming series, but if you intend on working on big-budget Hollywood blockbusters, get used to other people playing in your sandbox.

While you might not be working with other writers directly, if you're writing a feature script, you might get thrust into a situation where your work is being rewritten or "punched up" by other writers, or you might have to provide those notes or re-writes yourself on other people's work. There is a big part of the Hollywood writing experience (and good money to be made) in rewriting. Often a film will go through several stages of development, and it's not uncommon for a new script to be requested each time a new stage of development kicks off. Sometimes this is because a new producer comes on board a project, or a director leaves and a new one gets hired. Acclaimed filmmaker Kevin Smith has told his account of working on the defunct *Superman Lives* screenplay for producer Jon Peters and director Tim Burton (*Batman, Batman Returns*) in which Kevin (who wrote the original outline at Peters' request), Wesley Strick (who wrote the *A Nightmare on Elm Street* 2010 reboot), and Dan Gilroy (*Nightcrawler*) all worked on screenplays for a movie that was to star Nicolas Cage as the titular hero but was scrapped in 1998 after production hassles. For anyone interested in the full story of the development hell this film went through, check out Jon Schnepp's definitive documentary *The Death of "Superman Lives."* While not every movie goes through this kind of disjointed process, it also isn't completely unheard of either.

Ed Greenwood speaks about his experience in collaborating on various types of work (scripts, books, and games), and why being a flexible and amiable collaborator is key to his career success:

I've been writing for so long; half the fun is doing a new project completely differently. So, if I'm collaborating with somebody, they'll say, well, so how do you usually work? And my answer is, how do you want to do this book? Then that's what we'll do. For me, it's new that way, or more different from what it would be otherwise. And that keeps it from becoming stale. Which is a very long-winded way of saying you write things differently all the time to fit the venue you're writing for and the way they do things. And that's okay. People who think that they are brilliant, and their way is the best, are the most dangerous people in the world.

What happens is, these days, if I'm collaborating with somebody else, and it's their project, as in, they have suggested it to me. They want to do it. I typically say, okay, you plot it. You make sure it has all the beats, all the things you want in the book. The best way to do that is for you to plot it, because then you can put them there, and then, if they're not there, you have nobody to blame but yourself, because I can't read your mind. You know that we've covered the bases you wanted to cover. Beyond that, it's literally, how do you want to do this? And everybody wants to do it differently.

I collaborated with two gentlemen on some large gaming rule books. One gentleman wants very much to do the adventure that's included in the book. So that's what he does. Another of the gentlemen really enjoys doing subclasses and new monsters. So that's what he does. I enjoy providing the tour of the world, the setting, and typing up recipes; stuff you'll eat in the taverns, and where are the taverns, and the inn in this town, and so on. I love doing that, so that's what I do. And we've sort of divvied it up because we're all getting to do what we want, and we're all doing it for fun. This is the reward when you've been slaving, toiling in these mines for low these many centuries. Your reward is you can do projects just for fun.

Being a writer who can create stories in multiple genres is just half the battle if your intention is to work with other people, either immediately or down the road. You need to be a versatile and willing partner to your collaborators. This is especially true if you want to work as a writer in television, where you'll be seated alongside a room full of other professionals developing entire seasons or series of episodic programing on deadlines. Understanding how the people you're collaborating with work best ensures that you'll be a person who others can count on, a team player. Just like you should pick up the tab for a pizza for your D&D adventuring party (and especially your DM), occasionally, you should also be willing to do the same for your compatriots in your writers room. A little kindness goes a long way to building strong and authentic relationships in any career.

Tabletop game designer and content creator Joshua M. Simons speaks about his experiences collaborating on his new game Paragons and how working with other people who shared the same passion and vision as he did for his game helped him create something that he was proud of putting into the marketplace without the help of a major publisher or game company:

> There are two, I would say, contributors who really helped significantly to shape the flavor of the game and the direction of the game, and Eugenio Vargas is one of them. He wrote a lot of our setting for the game. I basically went to him and said, hey, I have an idea of what I think this game could be in terms of setting and what's going on in the world's organizations. You think of superheroes, you think of the Justice League, you think of the Avengers, right? I want an organization like that, but I want it to feel distinctly original to this setting. I want original villains and evil organizations. I don't want this to be a rip-off of some other universe. Help me take these ideas and make them real, and he did a phenomenal job. The entire setting chapter is like 99% him. I've gone in and added some things, and may add a couple more things, but it's all additive to what he did. I really liked what he came up with. He took my superhero veneer and solidified it into this world that feels interesting and has stakes for these player characters that you're playing.
>
> The other person who I think really contributed significantly to the shape of the game itself is my editor. Taylor Navarro has been a phenomenal not just Content Editor, but Developmental Editor. Sometimes we've hopped on a call and talked for like 30 minutes about how specifically a mechanic works because I kind of picture it like this, but the text doesn't seem to convey it like

that, and we've made some pretty significant changes that I think are ultimately stronger. In a couple of cases, I'd written mechanics for things that weren't really necessary because he made me realize we already have a framework for how these rules are going to work out. The GM can just read that and understand. They can intuit based on what's here. This is how that scene plays out. You can give them a couple of bullet points about how to run that scene well, but you don't need to write a detailed guide on how to do this thing that you know exists in your brain. There are a couple places where we cut some mechanics too, that I was just over-detailing things that didn't need to be explained.

I think we landed in this beautiful spot, and we're still doing a little (bit) of polishing, a bit of tweaking, but I think the game feels like it's doing what it's supposed to do. It is not overly rigorous. It definitely leans slightly rules-light. But there's some crunch in terms of how your character's level up over time and grows. There's some crunch in how you piece together different abilities in order to make your hero and then how they get those abilities. How do they use them? You have flame control. How do you control those flames? Is that a thing that you do with your hands, with your feet, with your mind? So, there're all kinds of flexibility in terms of how the system works. But ultimately, I think it's really powerful, and it tries to balance super crunchy games, where it's all just about rebuilding existing heroes and making them all very strong and very rules-light games about telling a fun story and trying to do both in a somewhat elegant way. The heart of the game system is something that we'll continue to use as a company, and hopefully, other people will like it and want to keep using it as well.

Speaking more broadly about the collaborative process. As soon as we were like, hey, we're making a superhero game. I said, Great. Who are the writers I know who love superheroes, and how can I bring them in the process and supplement areas where I don't have as much expertise, or just bring their enthusiasm to bear on the project? We've assembled a really awesome team. When we said, hey, we want a piece kind of like X, Y, and Z, thing, they said, Actually, I would love to do this, and it was far better than we could have ever possibly imagined, because they're much more creative, and better at taking ideas and putting them into art on the page than we are. Finding people who were passionate about what we were doing and letting them do the things that they are best at, instead of us trying to dictate to them that they should do, wound up being very beneficial.

There is such a thing as too many cooks in the kitchen as well regarding collaborative storytelling. Audio drama producer and TTRPG player Harlan Guthrie discusses one of his experiences working with a company out of Hollywood trying to produce an audio drama without really understanding the medium while simultaneously creating chaos on the creative side:

> They hired me to be a writer on one of their audio dramas, which was produced by one of the producers of LORD OF THE RINGS. I can't remember his name. I even hired a writing partner to work with me because they wanted a female perspective. We wrote a 10-episode season. We were looking at four producers, and it was so funny to see. The notes were just ridiculous and overwhelming and constantly counter to each other. One person would say, well, you know, why do we need this? The other person says, well, this is the whole heart of this episode. My writing partner and I just got out of it as soon as possible. There are way too many cooks that do not know how to make an audio drama. They have made very successful projects on their own, but they have no idea what this is. They totally lost the plot, and we stepped away, and the show went on, and it's trash, the show that they did. It's because (after we left) they hired someone who is a Hollywood screenwriter who knew nothing about audio dramas and how to incorporate audio into the work.
>
> People write scripts for audio dramas knowing nothing about audio dramas and I look at them, and (ask) how you going to communicate this, and it's entirely visual. They'll say, well, he's crawling along the ground. Yeah, but he's not going to be saying, "I'm crawling around along the ground", and you can only do so much with crunches and dirt sound effects before people are just like, What the fuck is going on? That is why so many audio dramas have a disembodied narrator.

The entertainment industry is one where you need to be constantly listening to your gut. If you feel like a project is probably going sideways or has been misrepresented from what you were initially pitched, you are probably justified in finding a way out. When you're negotiating contracts, make sure you consult with your attorney to ensure that you have a clause where you can exit without taking a financial hit or leaving yourself open to litigation.

Writing for television offers you the chance to work in a room with other writers, form relationships within the industry, grow your network, and gain valuable insight into the inner workings of the studios. Keep in mind that not everything in Hollywood is merit-based, and that's not just referring to nepotism. Many opportunities you'll get in the industry are relationship-based. This is mostly because of how transient people can be as they phase in and out of the industry, and of course, there's a level of duplicity and "fake-ness" you'll find as well from people that feel that undermining or sabotaging others is the path to fame and fortune (they don't last as long in the industry as you think. Or they just become Producers). Getting to work in a writers room is extremely competitive, and there are only certain times of the year, often called pilot season, when most shows do their hiring. Ultimately, people want to work with people they like and trust, so if you've got that nailed down along with even a modicum of talent, you'll do fine. As you've read throughout this chapter, there are many different ways to approach the industry, and each avenue represents a chance to impress someone you might work with again in the future, or who might offer you your next job.

CHAPTER 10

Short and Feature Films

SMALL FILMS AND BIG THINKING

There's a contingent of people out there that will dismiss short films out of hand as flights of fancy from amateur filmmakers or a waste of money that could otherwise go toward a freshman feature debut.

Short films have a lot of value in the film marketplace if you understand how the business around them works, where to screen them, and set your expectations upfront for what you hope to get out of your experience making one.

Making a movie is a labor of love that involves collaboration with people. Even if you only have a few people helping you out physically on set, there are still hundreds more who are eager and willing to help you bring your short film to the waiting masses. PR folks, film critics, film festival directors and programmers, managers, agents, lawyers, accountants, dentists, and more are standing by waiting for your film to pass across their periphery.

Some will say that making short films is a waste of time, delaying your burgeoning career while you should be working on a feature film instead. While a feature film can garner attention if it hits at the right time with the right people, short films have the ability to fly under the radar, building their popularity and garnering their own prestige through a more roundabout route through the film festival, press, and awards circuits.

You might not believe this, but you can actually win an Oscar with a short film. As a matter of fact, short films are the only category of films

DOI: 10.1201/9781003538202-10

eligible to win Oscars through the film festival system. Even if a feature film wins the coveted Palme d'Or at Cannes or screens at Sundance, it still needs to go through the Academy nomination process, where it is put up against the biggest feature film blockbusters that Hollywood has churned out that year.

Short films have a different path. If they win a top award at a qualifying film festival (there are currently 181 of them as of this writing), they can submit to the Academy under the Animated Short Film and Live Action Short Film categories. Other qualifications (you may not need to accomplish all of these to qualify. Check the Academy website as their rules change almost every year) for entry are:

1. The movie must have been exhibited for paid admission in a commercial movie theater in one of six qualifying US metro areas:

   Los Angeles County.

   City of New York (any of the five boroughs).

   Bay Area (counties of San Francisco, Marin, Alameda, San Mateo, Contra Costa).

   Chicago (Cook County specifically).

   Dallas-Fort Worth (Dallas County, Tarrant County).

   Atlanta (Fulton County).

   The film must have a run of at least seven consecutive days, with at least one screening per day. The movie must also appear in the theater's public listings.

2. You must submit proof of your film's award-winning status from a film festival on the Academy's Short Film Qualifying Festival List (available online).

3. The film can't have been distributed in a non-theatrical manner until after its qualifying theatrical release.

The film must be submitted according to Academy technical guidelines and should be in English or have English-language subtitles. Once your film is submitted to the Academy, it will be voted on and an Oscar "shortlist" will be released. This is a powerful press opportunity that you should invest considerable time and money into. The Oscars are a popularity contest, much like everything else in Hollywood. You need to be comfortable making press appearances to speak about your film. This process usually comes toward the end of your film festival run anyway, so you should have already had plenty of experience speaking about yourself and your movie on the red carpet, with fans during Q&A sessions, or with press people and critics on podcasts or for written publications.

The shortlist for Oscar consideration is only 15 films deep and then is invited to be watched by all active and lifetime Academy members, and only five films can be chosen for the final awards consideration.

Making a short film has other advantages that don't include small golden statuettes at the end of a long and arduous press blitz. Short movies are a great way to hone your craft as a writer. Just like a GM might set up several one-shots when they're dipping their toes into the GM pool to get used to arbitrating rules and guiding players, a writer who is limited to the short film format can write small but powerful stories that move audiences in mere minutes.

Being able to tell a complete story in a small amount of space is a hard thing to do. To do it well takes practice, feedback, and patience. Short films, even ones that are made on the smallest of budgets, are efficient ways to test the waters as a writer. You can team up with eager new filmmakers who are looking to make their mark in the industry or write and direct the movie yourself. You can get feedback from family and friends, or you can wait until a crowd sees it in a darkened theater at a film festival and get your feedback that way. Either way, you are going to get the experience you need to move to the next level in your career.

GM, player, and charity stream producer Jes Wade discusses their foray into limiting the scope of a murder mystery story they ran:

> My second adventure was Murder in Mossbank, which got really popular, and was really cool and fun to be a part of. I've always liked mysteries. I've always loved murder mysteries. I think I got the idea when I was hiking with my partner (and talking) about just XYZ things that happen in this little town and how it affects the whole town. I felt that I'd be a little overwhelmed to have an entire town open (to the players). So, my premise, to make it a little bit easier on myself, was: This woman has just been murdered.

What if only a couple of stores are open because they feel like they have to be to protect the people of the town? So, it was a very closed environment.

As a new GM, as a new writer, it felt a lot easier to deal with than having a town of like, 50 places open and only a couple people that are going to have specific information for my players, who are fucking chaos goblins, that are going to want to go talk to every single person they can. Sure, you can break into the flower shop. Don't know why you want to do it. No one's there. You're not going to get anything out of it. Maybe you'll smell some roses and some lilies, I guess. But nobody's there.

Just because you're making a short film doesn't mean you need to limit the scope of your imagination. Many short films are scenes that can be extrapolated to larger themes. If you want to make Star Wars, you don't need to show the entire battle between the Rebels and the Empire. You can take a piece of it. Maybe a spy meeting with their contact, and all the things that go along with a story set that way. You can have suspense and intrigue and pack it into less than 15 minutes.

FROM THE AUTHOR

Short films are classified as any movie under 40 minutes. If you want a piece of advice from someone who has been in the industry for nearly two decades, don't make a 40-minute short film. Not because of any sort of quality concern, but because the majority of film festivals won't program a short film longer than 15 minutes (with 12 minutes being the "sweet spot"). If your film is exceptional, they might program it alongside other features or fit it into an overall shorter program, but if you want to set yourself up for success, be aware of how the system works.

Shorts are also a great way to experiment with genre. Film festivals often program short comedies but are hesitant to program feature-length ones. Science fiction and fantasy films can be extremely expensive to create, as are period pieces. Making these stories as short films allows you to make the art you want to make while still keeping a cap on your spending.

Maintaining healthy expectations as to what you hope to get out of your short filmmaking experience is key to keeping disappointment and depression at bay. Many filmmakers dream of making movies that will lead them to fortune and glory in Hollywood, and when those dreams fall short, they give up and never touch a camera again.

It doesn't have to be this way. If you go into your short filmmaking experience with an understanding of what your short- and long-term goals are up front, then you'll have an easier time meeting those goals and won't be as devastated when life throws its inevitable curveballs your way. Professional GM Jesse Jerdak speaks to his experience in the TTRPG community and folks who enter with unchecked expectations:

> What do you actually hope to get out of this? In AP right now, a lot of people are thinking that they're going to be Critical Role or Dimension 20. Well, that's all great, but if that doesn't happen, you could be disappointed, but I think you need to set an expectation of what your personal level of success is. What does success look like to you? Do you want to be famous, or do you want to make a living, or do you want to meet new friends, or do you want to be part of a community? Whatever those things are, I think that is a really important question to ask. Not everybody can be Matthew Mercer.

The latest generation of kids are already in the habit of making short films via social media. TikTok videos and Instagram reels are more informal examples of short films but are great practice for when they choose to branch out into more formal ways of storytelling. Kids are also familiar with audience building, a vital skill in the filmmaking world regardless of whether you're making shorts or features. These videos and followers are calling cards for these people's eventual careers. They can take the audience they've built with one video and carry them over to the next ones. This can be extremely attractive to potential reps and distributors who might be interested in putting additional time, money, or resources behind the talented people responsible for these miniature viral blockbusters.

FEATURE FILMS ARE MORE THAN JUST MARVEL BLOCKBUSTERS

We've addressed pilots and short films so far, but now it's time for the main event: feature films. All the work we've been doing in the previous chapters was to prepare you to write, and finish, your own screenplay. If you've already finished your first screenplay, then join us by starting your next one (the first question that you'll be inevitably asked if you're pitching your script is "what else do you have?").

What makes for an unforgettable feature? You can package together an undeniable director, have producers that can get you all the money in the world to finance the production, and you can have A-list talent attached up and down the call sheet. The movie can still be a flop. It all starts with the script.

While it's true that everyone has a story in them, not all stories are created equal, and most of them aren't cinema-worthy. Having an idea and developing that idea into a strong concept that you can take from page one to page 120 takes time, effort, and patience. There are going to be many times where you'll start your story, get 20 pages in, and realize that it just doesn't have the strength to make it to the end, and if you were to force it, it would just be a miserable slog.

When a rep sends your script to a studio, it's usually read by someone who is reading dozens of scripts per week, at the lowest levels of influence in the industry. Traditionally, they will only give your script between 10 and 15 pages of their time before throwing it in the trash. It's your job to make sure that those first several pages hook the reader so they'll keep going until the end. Jonathan Wilder, a TTRPG designer based in Los Angeles who went to Emerson for screenwriting, discusses his experience as a coverage reader:

> I think it's the same thing for screenwriting because another job that I had was doing script coverage, and for me because of my school background, and also from reading a lot of scripts, I can obviously recognize when a script is not like following the general conventions. There are plenty of very famous, well-regarded scripts that absolutely break the conventions. But it's clear when you read those that there's an understanding there, and there's intent behind doing it. I feel like there are a lot of times where I'd be reading a script, and I would know on a certain level…this is not how this should have been formatted, but I care about the story. I understand at least what they're trying to communicate visually, and so if I can understand that well enough, then when the director picks this up, they will know enough to interpret it.
>
> So many people touch the script. It's not just the writer, as long as the intent is clear enough. To me, it doesn't really matter how

much you followed the conventions, as long as it's not disorganized and hard to follow. What I was always looking for with the script coverage is within the first few pages. Did you give me a reason to care? Is there a clear hook there? Is it clear what type of story you're trying to tell? Is there a message here?

If there are two parts of your story it would behoove you to know before you start, it's the beginning and the ending. That first blank page is a bummer to look at, but if you know where your story begins, you'll have an easier time filling those first few pages. If the beginning's got you stumped, start from the end and work your way backward until you're comfortable going back and filling in the beginning.

Identify your feature script's key moments. Develop each act in your script around those scenes. Everything your characters do should be to get, organically, to those scenes, and those key moments should resonate and have consequences stemming from those key moments.

Even half-billion-dollar budgeted Marvel films follow this principle. It's not the big explosive set pieces that make those movies memorable; it's the small character moments before and after the huge battle scenes that matter the most. Those are the scenes you need to focus on, regardless of whether your script is the next big Disney opus or an indie feature bound for Sundance.

The big difference, outside of length, between a short film script and a feature film screenplay is that, in a short film, you might only have the time to deal with a single idea, event, or emotional moment. In a feature, you can explore broader narratives with layers of conflict, typically having room for subplots, more supporting characters, and broader worldbuilding.

EXERCISE 10X1

Write the first 12 pages of your feature script and swap them with another screenwriter. Get feedback for your work and give feedback on theirs. What are the strengths that you see in the other person's work that you feel you could learn from? Is their script something you'd consider reading more of? Why or why not?

Most feature screenplays adopt a traditional three-act structure, but don't feel you need to conform to this. Being different isn't always bad. The entertainment industry is a crowded mess filled with voices all aching for the next three-picture deal. Making your work stand out in your authentic voice should be something you strive toward.

There are a few sites on the web where you can showcase your work, but you should be careful to avoid places that are only looking to make a quick buck from having your work on their platform. One site in particular that is free to host your scripts on, was mentioned in the previous section of this book, and is frequented by industry people is Coverfly.

Coverfly gives you control over how people view your work while giving you the ability to showcase your talent to people who might look to option exactly the type of material you specialize in. They also have some integrations with popular screenwriting contests and postings for industry mandates (basically listings from producers looking for a specific type of script to option).

CHAPTER 11

Writing for Genre

WHY UNDERSTANDING GENRE MATTERS

Knowing the ins and outs of the genre you're telling your story in is more than just understanding the various tropes that comprise the genre. It's also about learning to subvert those tropes to come up with something truly original. On the surface, "Game of Thrones" is a standard fantasy filled with swords, kings, queens, castles, and dragons. But what makes it such a cultural phenomenon, and all credit to George R.R. Martin for basically creating a trope of his own, is that the show introduced a story world where even the main characters can die, horrifically and unexpectedly, despite audience popularity.

Avid TTRPG player and GM Brian Gray speaks about his experience shifting from the more walled-in D&D rules system to something a bit more open and playful, and how that shift in tone took some getting used to:

> I hate complex rule systems. The story for me is more important, and the collaborative story is the most important thing. I would like everybody to have a moderate level of buy-in to say, this is what we're going to do, and then find the system that best supports it, and hope that it's not too rules heavy or crunchy.
>
> Even D&D is restrictive in ways you don't really think about. D&D's rules wall you in a little bit, so I like systems that are more narrative and free flowing like what we did on My Little Pony.

DOI: 10.1201/9781003538202-11

The My Little Pony RPG, as a system, it was actually kind of difficult for all of us to get into, mostly because it's a tone shift. Anytime you do something, that's not the thing you play the most....You look for the commonalities, and if none exists, you're floundering for a moment. But once we all figured it out, the story it allowed us to tell, because it's aimed at players of all ages. It allowed us to tell a much more imaginative and whimsical story that leaned into the property and leaned into things the show had done. We just had a really fun time with it, being ridiculous.

Sometimes you might have a particular tone or genre in mind for a piece that you're working on, but it doesn't move the audience the way you expected it to, or the tone of the story doesn't quite fit the genre. Change it up! Don't be afraid to experiment.

Thinking about genre and convention, it's common in comic books to kill off and resurrect their heroes and villains all the time. It's very rare to have a movie or a show where the main character bites the bullet (or meets their end at the tip of a blade) mid-show and then fades to black and rolls credits. Shows like the CW's *Arrow* tried to kill off its main character, Oliver Queen, multiple times during the show's eight-season run, but it was always fairly understood that the character would come back in due course. It's also a bit spoiler-y that, in the age of the 24-hour entertainment news cycle, a person could assume that a character would be returning to a show once an announcement that their contract had been renewed hit the news wire. Killing off your titular character on a television show is very different from doing it in a different medium like comics. Do you feel they succeeded in telling that story?

EXERCISE 11.1

Give three examples of comic book television or film adaptations that did right by their source material. What are the reasons you feel your choices were successful? Is there anything you would have changed to make the adaptation more faithful to the source material?

Understanding how to write for the genre you are presenting to your audience will make it easier for you to sell that story in a variety of ways. You might write a novelization or a feature script and try to find representation on your way to eventual publication or option. Knowing your genre inside and out will aid you in pitching, querying, and creating excitement around your intellectual property.

You may write a short script intending on shooting it yourself for the film festival circuit as either a calling card or proof of concept for future work. If you understand your genre, it allows you to better select the festivals that are more likely to screen your work and put your film in front of audiences that are most likely to rave about it.

Even after the writing is done, knowing your genre will help you in the marketing and sales processes of your work. If you can identify your niche audiences, it will give you a leg up on building communities around yourself and your work, while also putting your work directly in the line of fire of those most likely to pay money for it.

Genre matters. Every genre has its own formula, tropes, arcs, etc., to consider. Sometimes subverting these normalities can cause your audience to take an immediate dislike of your work, even if what you're doing is a purposeful subversion of the genre. Audiences are fickle like that sometimes. This is especially true with movies where the marketing doesn't match the final product. For example, the 2011 Liam Neeson wilderness film *The Grey* promised a nail-biting man versus wolf fight that never occurred, which disappointed some audiences. It instead cut to black, and the credits rolled right as the fight between the wolf and Neeson's character begins. There's a brief after-credit scene that gives a hint as to the aftermath, but that wasn't what audiences were sold when they watched the trailers for the film.

The Grey is a brilliant film that explores some deep philosophical themes and features outstanding performances by Neeson and the rest of the cast. These factors helped it gross $81 million at the box office, and positive critical reviews gave the film more longevity than the marketing dollars they spent deserved.

Jason Bulmahn, the creator of the Pathfinder TTRPG, shares his thoughts on how subverting audience expectations with genre may not always be a good idea:

> There's a social contract nature to these games, and to these forms of entertainment. I knew what I was getting into when I started this. I know this is an action-adventure flick. That's what I'm here to watch. It doesn't suddenly turn into a horror flick. I think we've

all watched movies that are in one genre, that have the pacing of another genre, and we all just kind of go, why didn't I like it? It's because it was a horror movie that was paced like an adventure film, and as a result, it didn't really feel like a horror movie. I think ALIENS falls into that category. I love ALIENS, but it's not a great sequel to ALIEN.

I don't want to short sell ALIENS, because I love the movie. The characters in it are amazing. Some things that are built there are great, but it's not a good sequel, because, frankly, it breaks that covenant. If I watched the first one and then I came to watch the second one, I kind of go, huh? It wasn't what I expected. You can have varying degrees of that when people are playing your home game. You've started by running an action-adventure module you bought, and then you switch gears over to a horror module. I think that's one of those things you talk to everybody about, because first, maybe they haven't built their characters for that. Their characters might be thinner facade characters designed to go on adventures and have hardships and stuff, and they may not have the deep characterization and introspective necessary to really even enjoy a horror story, right? I think that is a challenge with a home group, and it's not insurmountable, but it is something where it all comes down to agreeing and understanding the stories you're trying to tell together.

When you're writing, I believe you kind of have to make some of those decisions in absentia, right? The other people aren't there. When I'm writing an adventure, I have to kind of figure out what it's going to be and I'm going to write it. When I'm writing a published adventure, I kind of have to decide what that is, and then I have to kind of follow that covenant. Speaking of ALIENS, we (Paizo) did a hardcover book called "Book of the Dead" for Pathfinder, Second Edition, that includes an adventure in the back that I wrote and that is my homage to ALIENS, but it's with the undead.

You arrive at a town where everyone's gone, you don't know where they went, and it looks like there were fights everywhere, and it's really bad. It's supposed to be spooky, creepy, and scary, but then it turns into an action thing. That's the covenant of what

I set up to do, right? Understanding how that fits in with everything. I wasn't doing a follow-up to ALIEN, so I have a bit freer rein to menace those poor villagers.

It just boils down to understanding that these, in one way, shape or form, are a story we are sharing with each other. Everybody's going to approach that from their own biases, their own perspective, their own understanding, and as a storyteller, as somebody building the narrative, you have to be aware of that power, that you're going to grab these people's attention and do something with it and show them a thing. Be responsible for that. I don't mean to make it sound weighty, but it is.

Film and literary genres are very similar in their execution. Most rely on the same four elements:

1. Characters.

2. Setting.

3. Story/themes.

4. Plot structure.

Once you've decided what genre your next project is going to be, you can start with these four elements as part of your outlining process to begin the worldbuilding within the genre you've chosen.

The rest of this chapter will cover several popular genres and how to write for them effectively based on your desired outcome. It will go over some obvious tropes of those genres and also give some direction on how to manage audience expectations within those genres should you decide to exercise your creativity beyond what a particular genre offers.

ACTION/ADVENTURE

Subgenres Include

Survival

Set in a world after a catastrophic event or in a dystopian society, often emphasizing survival.

Examples: *Mad Max: Fury Road*, *The Hunger Games*, *I Am Legend*.

Spy

Involves espionage, high-tech gadgets, and international intrigue.

Examples: *James Bond Series, Mission: Impossible, The Bourne Identity.*

Superhero

Features protagonists with superhuman abilities or unique skills, often based on comic books.

Examples: *Avengers: Endgame, The Dark Knight, Spider-Man: Into the Spider-Verse.*

Disaster

Focuses on characters trying to survive natural disasters, man-made catastrophes, or extreme conditions.

Examples: *San Andreas, The Day After Tomorrow, 127 Hours.*

Martial Arts

Focuses on hand-to-hand combat, often showcasing specific fighting styles or philosophies.

Examples: *Enter the Dragon, Crouching Tiger, Hidden Dragon, The Raid.*

War

Features battles and military operations, often with a strong emphasis on heroism and strategy.

Examples: *Saving Private Ryan, Black Hawk Down, Fury.*

Buddy Cop

Thrives because it combines universal themes of friendship and teamwork with action and comedy, making it appealing to a broad audience.

Examples: *Lethal Weapon, Rush Hour, Bad Boys*

Action Comedy

Blends action-packed adventures with humor and lighthearted moments.

Examples: *Pirates of the Caribbean, Jumanji: Welcome to the Jungle, The Mummy.*

Action/Cyberpunk/Techno-Thriller

Explores the intersection of action and technology in dystopian or futuristic settings.

Examples: *Blade Runner 2049, Ghost in the Shell, Upgrade.*

Action Horror
Offers the thrill of action-packed heroics while maintaining the tension and unpredictability of horror.
Examples: *Resident Evil, Predator, Overlord.*

Heist
Involves elaborate plans to steal or outwit adversaries, often with action-packed chases or confrontations.
Examples:*Ocean's Eleven, Heat, Baby Driver.*

Monster/Kaiju
Features battles against giant creatures or monsters.
Examples: *Godzilla, King Kong, Pacific Rim.*

Revenge Thriller
Centers on characters seeking justice or vengeance, often with intense fight sequences.
Examples: *Kill Bill, John Wick, Taken.*

Action/adventure movies are a lot of things. Loud. Filled with explosions. They have main characters that are larger than life and villains to match. What are some of the other characteristics of this genre? What makes action/adventure so appealing? Let's take a closer look at what makes this genre tick.

Looking at movies like *Raiders of the Lost Ark, The Matrix,* or *Terminator 2: Judgment Day,* what do they all have in common? They all feature stories with world-ending or defining consequences. The protagonists are on a very distinct mission against a well-defined threat. Whether the hero is trying to stop Nazis from acquiring and using the Ark of the Covenant, free their world from the tyranny of the machines, or stop an uncertain future from ever happening (oddly enough, also about freeing humanity from the threat of machines). Action and adventure films go over the top, with pronounced action and physical punishment from beginning to end upon the heroes.

You might see these films taking place in exotic locations. Look at the James Bond series of movies, for instance. One day 007 is in Monaco playing Baccarat Chemin de Fer. Later in the film, he's back at the MI6 headquarters in London, only to globe trot again to Venice for a showdown with the movie's antagonist. The varied locations give the movies a grand sense of scope that gives the audience a broader sense of global stakes and uses the allure of exotic locations and cultures to keep the air of mystery in the film. They also give a sense of escapism for the audience, showing locations and lifestyles that the audience wishes they could visit or an alternate life they wish they had. At no point is the concept of Bond's expense account really given any credence, nor do any civilian casualties (people or property) ever get addressed in any way where the hero would later face consequences for their actions.

The protagonists of action and/or adventure films are above the law in most ways. They can kill a room full of spies, be in the vicinity of a deadly bomb that kills hundreds, steal cars with reckless abandon, and more, yet never see the inside of a jail cell for more than a scene. The heroes are skilled, resourceful, and often courageous (even though the Hero's journey story structure might portray them initially as reluctant heroes). The character rarely grows beyond the paragon they're representing, and if they do, it's part of the B-plot of the story.

The villains are distinct. Depending on the era, many action/adventure movies will focus their villain on a single region of the world, calling that person and the government they represent "evil." The villains usually aren't working alone but are supported by a network of henchfolk, secret world-shaping cabals, or a patron that remains hidden throughout the story.

Action/adventure stories are also defined by their moments of suspense and tension. Sometimes this comes as a ticking clock. A hero might need to get an antidote to a poison before the villain releases it into the city. There might be a bomb about to go off somewhere in the world, and the hero needs to reach it in time to avert a larger disaster. Sometimes it's that the hero needs to identify who the villain is, as they might have infiltrated the organization the hero works for and need to stop them before they use that organization's resources for nefarious purposes. The goals and objectives are as clear as the hero's motivations for achieving them.

With action comes stunts. These stories use martial arts, feats of impossible physics, and sometimes a lot of bullets to achieve their story goals. In a novel, an author might spend a paragraph or two describing how the hero might take on an assailant. In movies like *The Bourne Identity*, the director, cinematographer, and actors use camera movement to help create the action. They use the environment the actors are in, adding to visceral hits and landings (e.g., broken tables, windows, etc.), and elaborate hand-to-hand and gunplay to make a simple takedown of one villain into an entire scene where, for a moment, you might believe the hero could fail. Couple all of this to a pulse-pounding soundtrack that punctuates the action you're seeing, and the scene leaps off the page.

More often than not, these movies end with the hero coming out on top. The villains, defeated, go into hiding to fight another day, or are dispatched by the hero in a final confrontation. Sometimes the hero is rewarded with power. Sometimes they fall in love, or they learn something, but usually they are still the same core person they were at the beginning of the story.

FANTASY

Subgenres Include

Dark Fantasy

Blends fantasy with elements of horror, creating a darker, more sinister tone.

Examples: *Pan's Labyrinth*, *The Witcher* (Netflix), *Hellboy.*

Low Fantasy

Low fantasy resonates because it bridges the gap between the ordinary and the extraordinary, making its stories feel more grounded and relatable.

Examples: *Harry Potter* series, *The Golden Compass*, *The Shape of Water.*

Grimdark

Set in worlds that are brutal, oppressive, and unforgiving. Societies are often corrupt, violent, and on the brink of collapse.

Examples: *The Northman*, *The Witcher* (Netflix)

Sword and Sorcery

Focuses on individual heroes, often warriors or rogues, in fantastical settings with battles, magic, and personal quests.

Examples: *Conan the Barbarian, Willow, The Beastmaster.*

High Fantasy

Set in entirely fictional worlds, often with epic battles, magical creatures, and a clear good-vs-evil storyline.

Examples: *The Lord of the Rings, The Hobbit, The Chronicles of Narnia.*

Comic Fantasy
Combines humor with fantastical elements for a lighthearted take on the genre.
   Examples: *Shrek, The Hitchhiker's Guide to the Galaxy, Ella Enchanted.*

Urban Fantasy
Combines magical or supernatural elements with a modern urban setting.
   Examples: *Harry Potter, The Mortal Instruments: City of Bones, Bright.*

Epic Fantasy
Grand, sweeping stories with large-scale stakes, often involving multiple characters, kingdoms, and wars.
   Examples: *Game of Thrones* (TV series), *Dune* (blends sci-fi and fantasy elements), *Eragon.*

Historical Fantasy
Offers the best of both worlds: the immersive detail of historical settings and the imaginative freedom of fantasy. By combining the two, it allows audiences to explore familiar historical periods through a fresh and speculative lens.
   Examples: *Stardust, The Illusionist, Penny Dreadful.*

Contemporary Fantasy
The unique thrill of blending the familiar with the extraordinary creates a sense of wonder by showing how the magical or supernatural exists just beneath the surface of the real world.
   Examples: *Doctor Strange, The Matrix, Men in Black.*

Science Fantasy
Combines science fiction elements like futuristic technology with traditional fantasy elements.
   Examples: *Star Wars, Avatar, The Dark Crystal.*

Juvenile Fantasy
Focuses on young protagonists discovering magical worlds or powers as they grow and mature.
   Examples: *Harry Potter, The Spiderwick Chronicles, A Wrinkle in Time.*

Fairy Tale

Adaptations or reinterpretations of classic fairy tales or folklore, often with whimsical or dark twists.

Examples: *Cinderella* (2015), *Maleficent*, *The Princess Bride*.

Magical Realism

Incorporate magical or fantastical elements into otherwise realistic settings and stories.

Examples: *The Shape of Water*, *Big Fish*, *Life of Pi*.

Romantic Fantasy

Focuses on romantic relationships within a fantastical setting, often involving magical obstacles or connections.

Examples: *The Shape of Water*, *Stardust*, *Twilight*.

Steampunk

Merges Victorian or industrial-era aesthetics with magical or fantastical elements.

Examples: *The League of Extraordinary Gentlemen*, *Stardust*, *Mortal Engines*.

Alternative History

Allows authors and creators to reimagine history while maintaining an anchor in the real world, making it feel both familiar and fresh.

Examples: *The League of Extraordinary Gentlemen*, *Watchmen*, *The Man in the High Castle*.

Mythological Fantasy

Inspired by myths, legends, and ancient deities, often rooted in real-world cultures.

Examples: *Clash of the Titans*, *Percy Jackson & the Olympians*, *Immortals*.

The fantasy genre is the default setting of games like Dungeons & Dragons and Pathfinder. But what are some of the defining characteristics of the fantasy genre? What makes it so prevalent in storytelling across mediums like TTRPGs, books, and movies? GM, voice actor, and AP performer Kelly (thekellhop) was asked those questions. She had this to say:

I think we have properties like Lord of the Rings to thank for that and growing up with those epics. These beautiful tales of love and friendship and hardship and war prevailing through the toughest times anyone can imagine. I think you grow up watching that and you think, God, damn, I want to do that. I think there's just something about a world that has its challenges, of course, but is also an equal measure, filled with wonder at the same time. I think, more than anything, people are looking for magic, and fantasy is a genre that easily lends itself to that. You think back to when you were a kid and you pick up a stick on the ground and you're waving it around like you're casting spells, or your sword fighting, or you're this, or you're that. You have been doing that since you were three. I think there's this beautiful rediscovery within this space of not wanting to let go of that. It's kind of like a superpower. I love that we grow up, and we play so hard when we're little, and maybe somewhere along the line, you might lose that a little bit. But then there's a portion of us that actually managed to rediscover that and the joy that's so abundant in that, and fantasy is really everything we wanted when we were kids. That's why when we go to reclaim that power of playing pretend, that's the first thing we reach for, and we keep reaching for it.

One of the first characteristics that helps us identify the fantasy genre is an invented world. This is also common in science fiction. An invented world, like Pern from the award-winning Anne McCaffrey series of science fiction/fantasy novels, The Dragonriders of Pern, has defined itself over the course of many books as a widely diverse and detailed work of fantasy. Pern has an established planetary orbit within a solar system. It has two moons, three continents, four oceans, and many islands. It has ecosystems, class systems, social constructs, and everything else that makes up a living, breathing society.

Alternately, but also related, fantasy can also delve into parallel or hidden worlds like those within the Chronicles of Narnia series. The Chronicles of Narnia is structured to allow children to believe that a fairy tale world is just beyond their grasp or vision, while a far-off world like Pern feels real, but resides in a galaxy beyond ours.

Another key feature of the fantasy genre is the heroic quest. This is most often depicted in games like Dungeons & Dragons and Pathfinder.

Adventure and heroism are what the fantasy genre is all about. It usually involves a journey, a quest, or some other task that takes the protagonist from their home to some faraway place. Many times, these quests are coming-of-age tales that see their protagonists go through a formative phase during the arc of their journeys.

The concepts of good vs. evil are also a large part of fantasy. Heroes are often struggling with moral clarity while the villains are usually clearly defined as being bad. The villains in fantasy are larger than life, and far stronger than the protagonist, who is often depicted as a commoner, a weakling, or an otherwise underdog to the villain. Think of Sauron from Lord of the Rings, ever watchful from his castle. The amount of detail given to him in the movie depictions of Tolkien's novels doesn't begin to do his legend justice. Sauron is a villain that has been killed no less than three times over the ages of Middle Earth, and he is credited with defeating champions like Elendil and Gil-Galad.

Magical and supernatural elements are also incredibly pervasive in fantasy. The image of a wise wizard locked up in their tower, surrounded by tomes of untold power, is a common image in the genre. Spells and curses have been used in fairy tales like the Brothers Grimm's Little Briar Rose (aka Sleeping Beauty) and Hans Christian Andersen's the Little Mermaid to add stakes and drama to the hero's (or in this case, heroine's) stories.

GM, player, sensitivity reader for TTRPGs, and Paizo employee Rue Dickey also chimed in about why they feel the fantasy genre is a staple in our storytelling traditions, often a starting point in gaming:

> I think it's because fantasy stories are something that everyone has some touchstone they can pull from, like whether it's Harry Potter or Lord of the Rings, or Eastern fantasy. There're loads of dragons and things in Chinese mythology. There are vampires in mythology, basically anywhere. And so, fantasy has touchstones that basically anyone can relate to, and it's way easier to dive into a game or a storyline, if you at least have some point you can hold on to.

Mythology and folklore are stalwarts in fantasy stories. A key attribute to many fantasy books and movies is to have large, epic stories with sweeping narratives featuring titanic battles between rival armies while the heroes fulfill ancient prophecies while the fate of the world hangs in the balance.

Many times, these "chosen one" prophecies are tied back to something ancient in the world the story takes place in, and something related to the protagonist's culture or heritage.

Considering the moral and ethical implications pervasive within the fantasy genre, there is also a lot of symbolism and allegory present. Whether shown as a shining sword gifted to the hero, or some other trinket or bauble, the items the characters carry are often a sign of their morality, true strength, or their place in the world.

While not fantasy per se, one could look at the Teenage Mutant Ninja Turtles as an excellent example of allegory through their weapon choice. Leonardo (the one with the blue bandanna) wields two katana swords. Arguably the deadliest weapon out of the four turtles. He is also the most mindful and disciplined of the four, and the least likely to use them out of anger. His counterpart in the foursome would be Raphael (the red bandanna), who uses two sai, which look fearsome as three-pointed short-range weapon, but are traditionally used for defense and disarming of bladed foes. Michelangelo (the orange bandanna) uses nunchaku. Known as "the party dude" and the one to engage in the most tomfoolery, he is given the weapon that requires the most focus and training to use, as it's an easy weapon to hurt oneself with. Last is Donatello (the purple bandanna), who is given the bo staff. Donatello is the most mechanically gifted of the turtles and uses the least sophisticated weapon, technologically speaking.

This leads to the last aspect of fantasy that we'll address here: escapism. Fantasy is a genre that is easy to get lost in. There are awe-inspiring settings involving castles, great forests, floating islands, and ancient ruins. Fantasy holds something for everyone. It offers a sense of wonder for people of all ages and backgrounds. With these characteristics, it's easy to see why fantasy is so prevalent across multiple types of media. The immersive and timeless narratives that someone can create in this genre traverse the gaps in our realities and offer universal human experiences.

HORROR/SUPERNATURAL

Subgenres Include

Slasher

Focuses on a killer (often masked or mysterious) who stalks and kills victims, usually in gruesome ways.

Examples: *Halloween, Friday the 13th, Scream.*

Supernatural Horror
Centers around otherworldly beings or phenomena such as ghosts, spirits, or demons.
 Examples: *The Exorcist* (1973), *The Conjuring* series, *The Ring* (2002).

Found Footage
Presented as if the events were captured on amateur video or surveillance, creating a sense of realism.
 Examples: *The Blair Witch Project, Paranormal Activity, Cloverfield.*

Survival Horror
Focuses on characters trying to survive against horrifying odds, often in isolated or confined settings.
 Examples: *The Descent, A Quiet Place, Bird Box.*

Body Horror
Explores grotesque transformations or mutilations of the human body.
 Examples: *The Fly, Tetsuo: The Iron Man, Videodrome.*

Folk Horror
Draws on folklore, rural traditions, or pagan beliefs to create fear.
 Examples: *The Wicker Man* (1973), *Midsommar, The Witch.*

Comedy Horror
Blends horror with comedic elements to create a balance of scares and laughs.
 Examples: *Shaun of the Dead, Evil Dead II, Tucker and Dale vs. Evil.*

Monster Horror
Revolves around terrifying creatures such as vampires, werewolves, zombies, or giant beasts.
 Examples: *Godzilla* (1954), *An American Werewolf in London, The Thing* (1982).

Psychological Horror
Focuses on the mental and emotional fears of characters rather than physical threats.
 Examples: *The Babadook, Black Swan, The Shining.*

Zombie

Centers on the undead, often as a result of a virus or a supernatural cause.

Examples: *Night of the Living Dead* (1968), *28Days Later, Train to Busan.*

Haunted House

Centers on characters trapped in or exploring a house with a sinister or supernatural presence.

Examples: *The Amityville Horror* (1979), *The Others, The Haunting of Hill House* (2018, TV).

Gothic Horror

Combines horror with romance and a dark, moody atmosphere, often set in haunted castles, manors, or other ominous locations.

Examples: *Crimson Peak, Dracula* (1931), *The Haunting* (1963).

Paranormal Horror

Explores phenomena beyond the realm of normal experience, often involving poltergeists, mediums, or psychic abilities.

Examples: *Poltergeist, Insidious, Hereditary.*

Fear. Dread. The darker side of the human experience. That's what the horror and supernatural genres evoke. Horror films aren't always blood and gore, though. Often, they explore the inequities of society, hold a mirror up to injustice, and comment on our innermost desires. Horror is a far more complex genre than many people give it credit for. The themes explored are complex, and the talent it takes to pull off those scares that make us hide our eyes from the movie screen and turn away in fear or disgust requires years of training and skill. But what makes up a horror (or supernatural) movie? How can you create the same type of existential terror that horror masters like John Carpenter, Wes Craven (RIP), or Stephen King churn out with such consistency?

Suspense is the first step to creating fear. The key is knowing how to build suspense and when to release it to get the most bang for your buck. Sometimes seen as cheap tricks, jump scares aren't easy to pull off. The timing of a good jump scare is everything. In a film, the lighting, mood, music cues, and suspenseful lead-up are all integral to the process of delivering the scare that gets the audience's pulse-pounding. Suspense can be created by achieving a sense of unease through a number of different methods. Putting your characters in a familiar place that is slightly and eerily different from how they remembered it is one way to start. From there, building on that tension, you might introduce a legend, a curse, or they might discover that there is a killer among their number. The fear of the unknown is a huge motivator in tension and suspense. The longer you can carry on building tension, the more effective the release will be.

There is such a thing as too much tension, and not giving the audience a moment of either levity or other release can actually work to your detriment. There are many horror filmmakers who are excellent at creating and dissolving tension by using humor or other distractions before delivering their suspenseful coup de grace. These include Sam Raimi (*The Evil Dead, Darkman, Spider-Man*), Alfred Hitchcock (*Psycho, The Birds, Vertigo*), and Edgar Wright (*Shaun of the Dead, Hot Fuzz, The World's End*). If you want to explore resources that are master classes in the form of tension, suspense, and horror, these are the filmmakers who will show you the way.

Monsters and creatures hiding from your protagonists and strategically striking from the darkness are another hallmark of the horror genre. Ghosts, demons, vampires, werewolves, and zombies are common enemies faced in the horror and supernatural genres. All of them are relentless, and all of them have weaknesses for your heroes to exploit.

In the TTRPG world, monsters have stat blocks that give the GM and the players an idea of the lore behind fangs and withered fingers. It also gives the players information on their weaknesses and strengths (usually initially kept hidden from the players by the GM, but available for discovery with the right dice rolls and questions). This allows the players to strategize or use a process of elimination to determine how they can best defeat their monstrous foes. If a screenwriter were to use the same approach of writing out the strengths and weaknesses of their antagonists, they would then be able to more effectively give their characters the tools and knowledge they'd need to defeat them by the end of the script, doling out that knowledge at specific intervals in relation to the pacing of the overall plot.

Gore and violence are another aspect that is hit or miss for some people in the horror genre. Some horror films contain no blood at all, sometimes relying on what is off-camera to scare the audience. The theory behind that is that there is nothing that the filmmaker can conjure on the screen that the mind can't make even more horrific. One of the most popular horror films of all time, *Rosemary's Baby*, uses psychological horror instead of blood and gore to achieve its goals.

The reason blood and gore work so effectively in movies is because when you immerse yourself in the story and connect with the characters, the sight of those characters suffering and in pain connects back to you subconsciously. You feel a piece of that pain.

Of course, too much gore can lead to desensitization and sometimes even parody, creating the opposite effect that horror is meant to achieve. Tone, in this case, is everything. There is a huge difference in audience reactions to the bedroom blood flood in *A Nightmare on Elm Street* after Johnny Depp's character is pulled into his bed and killed off-screen, the elevator blood flood in *The Shining*, and the hole-in-the-wall blood flood in*Evil Dead II*.

The timing of the violence used in relation to events happening in the real world can ruin the escapism that movies create. Even films that set the proper expectations regarding the gore and violence contained can metaphorically shoot themselves in the foot if their film releases on the same day as a gun-related tragedy.

Looking at the success of movies like those in the *Saw* franchise or *The Descent*, leads one to examine the effectiveness of isolation and helplessness in horror films. Keeping a character trapped, either physically or emotionally, can make your audience feel those same feelings, even when they're in a theater full of other people. The sense of powerlessness is a horror staple, and keeping things beyond the control of your characters is a great way to keep suspense and tension rising until you release it. If you are looking for a prime example of a character feeling powerless and having it affect them psychologically, watch *The Fall* (2024). Just be considerate of yourself if you have an innate fear of heights.

We wrote about death and disease in the worldbuilding chapter of this book, and that is a theme that horror forces viewers to confront constantly. The idea of mortality is pervasive throughout horror, especially in the supernatural genre. Morbidity and dark foreboding atmospheres are often coupled with ghosts, haunted houses, and other isolated locations serving as either a Hell or Purgatory for characters. Stories that revolve around the unknown after death deal with some of humanity's most primal fears.

In the vein of films like *Battle Royale*, *The Texas Chainsaw Massacre*, and *Friday the 13th*, the theme of moral transgression and punishment is put on full display. Movies in the slasher genre are part of what coined the term "final girl" and is usually because the last person left alive in those movies is the one who didn't sin or morally transgress during the film. The character is the virgin, or the innocent, and is left alive once the credits roll specifically because of their moral upstanding. These sins aren't always relegated to sex but can also be attributed to any of the so-called seven deadly sins. These character deaths reflect a form of either karmic or cosmic justice.

It's not that the horror/supernatural genres have the most tropes associated with them, but they certainly are the most cited and often copied. The slasher film usually contains an unstoppable killer hunting down teens. If those teens split up, you can guarantee that they will be killed one by one by the pursuing masked slasher.

Other tropes like creepy clowns, twist endings, and unsettling children are also used fairly unsparingly throughout the horror and supernatural genres. One more that is used frequently is the "one last scare" trope, where the killer, who was thought to be vanquished, comes back for one last stab at the surviving hero/heroine. A lot of these tropes were so obvious and overused that Wes Craven's *Scream* franchise devoted an entire scene to "the rules of surviving a horror movie."

ROMANCE

Subgenres Include

Action Romance

Combines romance with high-stakes action, where the protagonists find love amid danger.

Examples: *True Lies, Mr. & Mrs. Smith* (2005), *Speed.*

Historical Romance

Set in historical periods, often featuring lavish costumes and societal norms that challenge or shape the romance.

Examples: *Pride and Prejudice, Atonement, Bridgerton* (TV).

Paranormal/Horror Romance

Combines romance with horror elements, where love often blooms amid terrifying circumstances.

Examples: *Crimson Peak, Warm Bodies, Bram Stoker's Dracula.*

Forbidden Romance

Centers on love that is considered taboo or socially unacceptable due to external circumstances like family, class, or societal rules.

Examples: *Romeo + Juliet* (1996), *The English Patient*, *Brokeback Mountain*.

Romantic Comedy

Blends romance with humor, focusing on lighthearted, often humorous situations leading to romantic resolutions.

Examples: *When Harry Met Sally, 10 Things I Hate About You, Crazy Rich Asians*.

LGBTQIA+ Romance

Focuses on romantic relationships within the LGBTQ+ community, often exploring themes of identity, acceptance, and love in different contexts.

Examples: *Call Me by Your Name, Carol, Moonlight*.

Romantic Musical

Romance is central to the plot and is expressed through music and song, often blending heartfelt lyrics with dramatic storytelling.

Examples: *La la Land, West Side Story* (1961/2021), *Moulin Rouge*!

Young Adult Romance

Focuses on the romantic experiences of teenagers or young adults, often exploring first love and coming-of-age themes.

Examples: *To All the Boys I've Loved Before, The Fault in Our Stars, Love, Simon*.

Romantic Fantasy

Combines romance with fantastical or supernatural elements, such as magic, mythical creatures, or alternate worlds.

Examples: *The Shape of Water, Twilight, Stardust*.

Romantic Thriller

Blends romance with suspense, danger, or crime, often involving love interests in perilous situations.

Examples: *Mr. & Mrs. Smith* (2005), *The Bodyguard, Out of Sight*.

Romantic Adventure

Combines romance with action and adventure, often featuring couples on thrilling or dangerous journeys.

Examples: *The African Queen, Romancing the Stone, The Princess Bride.*

Erotic Romance

Focuses on the passionate and sensual aspects of love, often exploring themes of physical intimacy alongside emotional connections.

Examples: *Fifty Shades of Grey, 9½ Weeks, The Lover.*

Science Fiction Romance

Explores romance in futuristic or speculative settings, often dealing with technology, space travel, or alternate realities.

Examples: *Her, Eternal Sunshine of the Spotless Mind, Passengers.*

Romantic Road Films

A love story that develops during a journey, often involving self-discovery and adventure.

Examples: *Before Sunrise, The Longest Ride, It Happened One Night.*

The romance market and genre are especially interesting because they can be incredibly specific and fruitful for creative folks in multiple disciplines. For screenwriters, The Hallmark Channel churns out dozens of low-budget (for Hollywood) happy endings per year. There are novelists you've probably never heard of that have tens of thousands of mailing list subscribers who write four or more fade-to-black works of fiction per year. While mainstream comic books might not feature overtly in the romance genre, indie comics like Fresh Romance, a collection of romance comics from fantastic writers and artists.

The romance genre has some very specific things that its audiences look for, and often, if those things are not present in the media they're consuming, the audience leaves disappointed. That doesn't mean those audiences are fickle. In fact, they are incredibly discerning in their taste and know exactly what they want in their romantic stories.

So, what are the aspects of this genre that make it what it is? How can you tell a romance story that will resonate with audiences? Here are some elements you should include in your next romance book or script that will make your viewers and readers happy.

The first thing is that love should be the central theme of your piece. The primary focus of romance pieces is relationships. Those relationships can come in many styles and types. The tension and resolution of the story should hinge on whether the couple will end up together. While physical connection in romance is often a focus, you also want to develop a strong emotional connection between your characters. Affirm this by showing scenes of intimacy, attraction, and emotional growth as part of the core of the story.

One thing that many consumers of romance stories insist on is a happy ending. The primary couple should overcome obstacles to end up together in the end. A bittersweet ending can also be acceptable but is not traditionally the norm in this genre. If the story is told well, sometimes it's acceptable for the two main characters to not end up together, as long as there is significant personal growth achieved through love and/or heartbreak.

The conflict in a romance story differs from that in an action story and actually can have more in common with the comedy genre. Tension in a romance story comes from obstacles standing in the protagonist's way of getting together with their love interest. Many times, this can lead to comedic misunderstandings, which are very common in movies like *Pretty Woman, Sweet Home Alabama*, and other films in the romantic comedy subgenre. These conflicts, along with social and class differences, previous relationships popping up unexpectedly, and other external pressures, can give you a lot of different options when telling the particular story you're trying to achieve.

Other frictions in romance stories stem from emotional or situational conflicts where the main characters might suffer internally with feelings of fear of commitment, past trauma, long-distance relationships, family disapproval, or cultural barriers.

Romance is often about grand gestures, and these stories feature memorable and dramatic acts of love that express deep emotions and commitment on behalf of the characters. There's the age-old trope of one partner running through an airport to catch the other before they get on a plane and leave forever. It's a simple and effective story device that works every time, even when a discerning eye can see it coming a mile away. The entire story builds to this scene of emotional climax. This is the turning point that leads toward the happy ending.

Other tropes that you'll see in romance novels and movies are love triangles, enemies to lovers, friends to lovers, forbidden love, and second chance at love storylines. It's not uncommon to find these stories taking place in fantasy realms, the real world, and even a combination of both (sometimes referred to as isekai, a Japanese term that translates to "different world"). These romance stories are often found in manga, anime, and video games, as well as movies and novels.

Romance as a genre is successful, dynamic stories aside, because of the way it idealizes romance as an idea. It offers escapism to its consumers by offering a heightened version of love and relationships, whose arcs fulfill needs inside people for perfect love and acceptance. Romance, when done correctly, can have an emotional intensity that can leave the audience completely spent as they ride the roller coaster of love, joy, heartbreak, passion, longing, and vulnerability. Because the conflicts are focused inward, the audience can relate to and understand the characters' feelings and motivations easier. The audience internalizes the conflict and experiences much of the story through their own worldviews and current life situations.

This genre also offers optimism about love and leads with a hopeful tone even when the characters are experiencing obstacles or dramatic moments. The transformative power of love and finding meaningful connection is always present and taps into the fantasy of "the one," and that love conquers all.

These themes are universal, and while it is sometimes hard to look at the world around you and find these heartfelt stories, they are the workhorses of the entertainment industry and, like the horror genre, will always have an audience and will almost certain to make a return on an investment in them.

COMEDY

Subgenres Include

Slapstick

Relies on physical humor, exaggerated actions, and visual gags to create laughter.

Examples: *The Pink Panther* (1963), *Dumb and Dumber*, *The Mask*.

Romantic Comedy

Combines humor with romance, focusing on the comedic aspects of love and relationships.

Examples: *When Harry Met Sally*, *Crazy Rich Asians*, *Notting Hill*.

Farce

Focuses on exaggerated, improbable situations and misunderstandings that lead to comedic chaos.

Examples: *Noises Off, The Birdcage, Death at a Funeral.*

Action Comedy

Combines humor with action-packed plots, often featuring comedic heroes in thrilling scenarios.

Examples: *Rush Hour, Men in Black, The Nice Guys.*

Dramedy

Blends comedic and dramatic elements, focusing on lighthearted situations while addressing deeper emotions and themes.

Examples: *Silver Linings Playbook, Crazy, Stupid, Love, About Time.*

Adventure Comedy

Combines humor with action or adventure, often featuring humorous protagonists navigating perilous situations.

Examples: *The Goonies, Jumanji: Welcome to the Jungle, Tropic Thunder.*

Gross-Out

Relies on crude, vulgar, or outrageous humor that often involves bodily functions or awkward situations.

Examples: *American Pie, There's Something About Mary, Superbad.*

Screwball Comedy

Features absurd or farcical situations, often involving a battle of the sexes or witty repartee.

Examples: *It Happened One Night, Bringing up Baby, His Girl Friday.*

Mockumentary

The term is a combination of "mock" and "documentary." These films use the documentary format to tell humorous, absurd, or exaggerated stories, often parodying real-life events, societal trends, or actual documentaries.

Examples: *This Is Spinal Tap, Best in Show, Lake Mungo.*

Deadpan Comedy

Relies on dry humor, with characters delivering jokes or humorous situations in an emotionless or serious tone.

Examples: *The Grand Budapest Hotel, Napoleon Dynamite, What We Do in the Shadows.*

Observational Comedy

A cornerstone of humor, especially in stand-up and sitcom formats. Its ability to find humor in the ordinary helps connect audiences, making them feel seen and understood.

Examples: *Curb Your Enthusiasm, Seinfeld, The Office.*

Road Trip Comedy

Centers on characters embarking on a journey, often leading to comedic adventures and mishaps.

Examples: *National Lampoon's Vacation* (1983), *Road Trip, Planes, Trains & Automobiles.*

Sports Comedy

Revolves around humorous situations in the world of sports or athletics.

Examples: *Dodgeball, Happy Gilmore, Talladega Nights.*

Teen Comedy

Focuses on the humorous aspects of teenage life, often in school settings.

Examples: *Mean Girls, Ferris Bueller's Day Off, Superbad.*

Musical Comedy

Features humor interwoven with musical performances, often in light-hearted and whimsical stories.

Examples: *The Producers* (2005), *Singin' in the Rain, Pitch Perfect.*

Workplace Comedy

Centers on the comedic dynamics and absurdities of a work environment.

Examples: *Office Space, The Intern, 9 to 5.*

Parody

Imitates and pokes fun at other genres, films, or real-life events in a humorous way.

Examples: *Airplane!, This Is Spinal Tap, Scary Movie.*

Satire
Uses humor to critique or ridicule social, political, or cultural issues.
Examples: *Dr. Strangelove, The Death of Stalin, JOJO Rabbit.*

Family Comedy
Aimed at audiences of all ages, it focuses on family relationships and everyday life humor.
Examples: *Cheaper by the Dozen, Mrs. Doubtfire, Home Alone.*

Dark Comedy
Deals with serious, morbid, or taboo topics in a humorous way.
Examples: *Fargo, The Lobster, In Bruges.*

Comedy of Manners
Satirizes the behaviors, customs, and social norms of a particular group, often with witty dialog.
Examples: *The Importance of Being Earnest, Clueless, Emma.*

Horror Comedy
Blends horror and comedy, using scary situations to create laughter.
Examples: *Shaun of the Dead, Scary Movie, Zombieland.*

Fish-Out-Of-Water
Focuses on characters placed in unfamiliar or uncomfortable settings, creating comedic situations.
Examples:*Borat, Coming to America, Elf.*

Comedy, whether highbrow or low, is an essential cultural pillar in our society. Like horror, it holds a mirror to us, reminding us not to take ourselves too seriously, and that even the most high and mighty of us are, in our most lonely moments, just regular people.

People who poop.

Comedy on television trends well and goes through cycles in Hollywood for what style of comedy is the new "it" subgenre. When comedy is popular and making money, it prints it like the US mint. When a comedy misses, it spoils the genre for the rest of the folks out there trying to get their films made and goes into hibernation until the next big comedic actor hits or a breakout screenwriter emerges.

Because of the subjective nature of comedy, it's a tricky genre to work within. The film festival circuit will program comedy short films all day long, but when it comes to features, they will err on the side of drama. Genre festivals (e.g., horror festivals) will program comedy, but it usually need to fall in line with a horror subgenre. As a standalone genre, comedy is probably the toughest one to break into. Screenwriting contests and fellowships are even harder on comedy. Feedback from these tends to skew negative because there is so much that the reader needs to interpret themselves, and if the work doesn't reflect the reader's own sense of humor, then the premise of your jokes will be lost.

Stand-up comedian and writer Dash Kwiatkowski discusses their take on comedy as a performance piece, the agreement between the audience and the comedian, and how this relates back to their time at the D&D table:

> I've been talking to a lot of people about stand-up lately as I've just been doing a lot of reflecting on the life that I've led, and I actually think that this is very applicable to DM'ing too, in that DM'ing is a style of storytelling that has to be deeply conversational. I think that's what I was looking for in both stand-up and DM'ing. It is conversational storytelling. The reason I was thinking about that is that stand-up is conversational storytelling. Many people don't think of a stand-up comedy performance as a conversation, but it is. You'll see people get up and try to monologue, and that doesn't work, because that's not the performance. That's not what people are going there to see. People are coming to a stand-up show to pretend that the things you're saying are things they're thinking of on the fly in the moment, having this conversation. It's a conversation where only one side talks, but the other side responds with laughter and groans and noises and energy. You have to meet people where they are in that conversation for stand-up to be successful.
>
> I think DM'ing, to me, is exactly the same where you can have your magnum opus story or this great narrative constructed, and if you just try to push a bunch of players through it, they're not going to have a good time.

If you were trying to break into television, you have your choice of late-night TV, dramedy, situational or sitcom programs (single-camera or multi-cam), improvisational comedy shows (usually either sketch or variety shows, which have become less common), parody newscasts like "The Daily Show," or animated comedy shows. Each of these leans on more than just being able to make consistent witty turns of phrase. These operate with very strict formats, and you need to write within those formats effectively, and many times, quickly.

Sometimes even good writing can turn a worthy piece of comedy into a studio filled with silence if the wrong actors are handling the dialog. Comedy is as much about who is saying something as it is about what they are saying.

Comedy can be a powerful weapon in a writer's arsenal. When times are bad in the world, people look to comedy to ease their pain and make them forget for a while. Right after 9/11, when firefighters and other first responders were digging through the rubble of Ground Zero, stand-up comedians were packing clubs trying to do their part to add levity to a horrible and traumatic event. Comedians did the same thing during the outset of the COVID-19 epidemic, resorting to doing gigs on rooftops, parking lots, and drive-ins to give people a small sense of normalcy during a time when they were stuck indoors or unable to see their loved ones.

So, what are the things that make up a comedy? What are the elements to watch out for when you're writing or reading something in the comedy genre? Here are some characteristics that define it.

First and foremost, you are looking to make your audience laugh or amuse them. This might be presented as physical humor or through humorous situations, dialogs, or characters.

A lot of humor is done through exaggeration and absurdity. Taking the mundane, stretching it out, twisting it, and making something new from it is a trick that comedians use all the time, and is part of where observational humor comes from. Characters are portrayed as absurd themselves in a normal world, or they "play it straight" in an exaggerated world around them. Comedy thrives in chaos but does best when rooted somewhere in reality. It gives the audience something to grab onto, giving them the chance to relate the situation back to themselves.

Like the romance genre, many comedic stories are told in a lighthearted manner. They often end with happy or optimistic endings. Even dark comedies like the Farrelly Brothers' *Me, Myself, and Irene* or Ben Stiller's *The*

Cable Guy end with the main characters in better places than where they started.

Comedy uses playful conflict and misunderstandings as a way to move its stories along. Mistaken identity stories, unlikely pairings (e.g., *Beverly Hills Cop*'s carefree Axel Foley and the more straitlaced Sgt. Taggart), and farce are very effective ways to tell stories and lend themselves well to franchises if the premise doesn't wear itself out with audiences up front. A couple of examples of farce leading to successful series would be the Zucker Brothers' *The Naked Gun* (which was actually spun off from the "Police Squad!" television program). Surely you remember the couple of Airplane! films they made? Yes, this was an attempt at the "don't call me Shirley" joke. Did it work?

Dialog and wordplay are where comedy sings. Puns, gags, double entendres, and witty banter exchanges create Monday morning water cooler exchanges and lines recited ad nauseam in bars and locker rooms. In addition, sarcasm and irony are powerful ways to poke fun at societal norms and those in power.

Comedy often finds humor in everyday life. Television shows like *The Drew Carey Show* went on for years because everyman Drew Carey's portrayal of a working-class schlub alongside his misfit friends was endearing and relatable to millions of people. People enjoy watching characters like "30 Rock" Liz Lemon trying to excel at their jobs and their romantic relationships. The audience sees themselves in their struggles. These flawed individuals bumble their way forward through their shows, and their quirky misadventures provide hours upon hours of quality entertainment.

Physical comedy, like pratfalls and other forms of slapstick, when done well, is the jump scares of the comedy genre. Nothing hits like a well-timed moment of physical comedy. A dramatic exit after a tearful speech giving way to the character bumping clumsily into the wall—Perfection. Late-night television still occasionally delves into the world of physical comedy during their shows, and sketch television makes it a staple, but no one has ever matched the comedic chops, slaps, and gouges of shows like "The Three Stooges."

Like dialog, timing is an essential component of what makes comedy work. Literally shaving a second in the editing room for a reaction shot after a one-liner can be the difference between a theater full of people full-on belly laughing and dead silence. Comedy is about give and take. It has a rhythm to it like music, and the beats between a setup and a punchline can be measured like sheet music. One second too late or too early in an awkward pause can ruin the entire gag. Timing is critical, and it's also half of what the writer of a comedy script can control. That goes back to why having the right comedic actors in place is just as essential as good writing in this genre. Both have to work together seamlessly to pull off magic.

With so many subgenres, comedy is a versatile genre to work within. While you may have difficulty getting recognized for it with awards or other accolades, it's still a genre worthy of your time. Write a couple of spec scripts and have them in your war chest for when you're pitching and they ask, "what else have you got"? If you are pursuing writing comedy as a career, take the time to learn the craft from experts. Go to stand-up shows and listen to how comedians handle crowds and land their jokes. Listen to the polished delivery of veteran comedians and compare them to newcomers. Watch copious amounts of comedic television and films to understand how timing and pacing work in comedy. Understand why something is funny and not just accept that it got a laugh. Delving into the psychology of comedy is going down a rabbit hole, but it can help you better understand how to form jokes and witticisms that will get laughs.

THRILLER/MYSTERY

Subgenres Include

Psychological Thriller

Focuses on the psychological state of characters, often exploring themes of paranoia, obsession, and manipulation.

Examples: *Se7en, Black Swan, Gone Girl.*

Political Thriller

Explores political conspiracies, government corruption, or power struggles.

Examples: *All the President's Men, Argo, The Manchurian Candidate* (1962/2004).

Crime Thriller

Combines elements of crime films and thrillers, focusing on criminal activities and the pursuit of justice.

Examples: *Heat, The Girl with the Dragon Tattoo, Prisoners.*

Supernatural Thriller

Incorporates supernatural elements like ghosts, curses, or unexplained phenomena into the thriller format.

Examples: *The Others*, *The Ring* (2002), *It Follows*.

Mystery Thriller

Centers on unraveling a mystery, often with a focus on uncovering the identity of a killer, the cause of an event, or hidden secrets.

Examples: *The Da Vinci Code*, *Knives Out*, *The Sixth Sense*.

Conspiracy

Revolves around uncovering hidden plots or conspiracies, often involving powerful organizations or shadowy figures.

Examples: *The Parallax View*, *Enemy of the State*, *The Bourne Identity*.

Revenge Thriller

Focuses on characters seeking revenge, often driven by personal loss or betrayal.

Examples: *Oldboy* (2003), *Kill Bill*, *John Wick*.

Disaster Thriller

Centers on catastrophic events, either natural or man-made, with characters struggling to survive.

Examples: *Contagion*, *The Day After Tomorrow*, *Greenland*.

Survival Thriller

Focuses on characters fighting for their lives against dangerous odds, often in isolated or hostile environments.

Examples: *The Revenant*, *127 Hours*, *The Shallows*.

Spy Thriller

Focuses on espionage, covert operations, and international intrigue.

Examples: *Casino Royale* (2006), *Tinker Tailor Soldier Spy*, *Mission: Impossible* series (1996–present).

Legal Thriller

Centers on the legal system, often involving courtroom battles, lawyers, and moral dilemmas.

Examples: *A Few Good Men*, *The Lincoln Lawyer*, *Primal Fear*.

Action Thriller
Merges intense action sequences with suspenseful storytelling.
Examples: *Die Hard, Mad Max: Fury Road, Taken.*

Techno-Thriller
Focuses on advanced technology, cybercrime, or futuristic themes combined with suspenseful storytelling.
Examples: *The Matrix, Ex Machina, Enemy of the State.*

Erotic Thriller
Combines elements of suspense and erotica, often focusing on passion, betrayal, and dangerous liaisons.
Examples: *Basic Instinct, Fatal Attraction, Eyes Wide Shut.*

Medical
Blends elements of suspense, danger, and intrigue with the world of medicine, science, and healthcare.
Examples: *Contagion, Outbreak, Awakenings.*

Gothic Thriller
Combines suspenseful storytelling with gothic elements like old mansions, dark secrets, and a foreboding atmosphere.
Examples: *Rebecca (1940/2020), Crimson Peak, The Others.*

Cozy Mystery
A lighter, more relaxed form of mystery storytelling that often involves amateur sleuths, quaint settings, and crimes that are typically free of graphic violence, gore, or explicit content.
Examples: *Murder, She Wrote, Knives Out, Agatha Raisin.*

Noir
Classic mystery with dark, gritty tones and morally ambiguous characters.
Examples: *The Maltese Falcon, The Big Sleep, LA Confidential.*

Neo-Noir
A modern take on film noir, featuring morally ambiguous characters, dark atmospheres, and complex plots.
Examples: *Chinatown, Drive, Blade Runner.*

Police Procedural
Focuses on the step-by-step process of law enforcement officers investigating a crime.
Examples: *Zodiac, LA Confidential, The Silence of the Lambs.*

Locked-room Mystery
Where a seemingly impossible crime, often a murder, occurs under circumstances that suggest no one could have entered or exited the scene.
Examples: *The Last of Sheila, Gosford Park, Knives Out.*

Heist
Revolves around the planning, execution, and aftermath of a high-stakes theft or robbery.
Examples: *Heat, Ocean's Eleven* (2001), *The Italian Job.*

Hard-boiled
A gritty, tough-as-nails branch of crime fiction and film characterized by morally ambiguous characters, bleak urban settings, and a cynical worldview.
Examples: *The Maltese Falcon, Double Indemnity, Chinatown.*

Whodunit
A classic mystery format where the audience is invited to solve the crime alongside the characters.
Examples: *Murder on the Orient Express* (1974/2017), *Clue, Knives Out.*

Paranormal Mystery
Blends elements of supernatural fiction and traditional mystery or crime genres.
Examples: *The Skeleton Key, The Frighteners, The Others.*

Driven by suspense and intrigue, mystery stories can intimidate writers who aren't comfortable creating puzzles for their characters to solve. Some great tips for creating a compelling mystery come from Jennifer Kretchmer, a film/TV producer, actor, and consultant:

> It has to be justified. You can't just say this dungeon has traps, because it does. That makes no sense. Let's say it's a temple. You

wouldn't have traps because then your worshipers couldn't get in. It defeats the purpose of the place existing. So why would these things exist? What's a reason that I could give to put these things in? Could it be a test? I think the times we get mad at puzzles, the times we get mad at mysteries are when they don't feel like they connect, when they don't feel justified and when they also don't feel like they're set up to let someone know there's a puzzle there. It should let you know what it needs from you, and it lets you know when you've solved it. Because if you don't have those three things, and I say this having been a puzzle designer as well, if you don't have those three things, each of those steps will be a problem. If your players don't know that there's a puzzle there, they're never going to know there's a puzzle there. They will not try to solve it. If they don't know what the puzzle is asking of them, they won't know how to approach it. So if you give them a bunch of dots on a page and there's nothing to cue them, that they're in a certain type of pattern, and that they have to find a pathway through the dots weaving around the ones that don't have the centers filled in, then they will not know what to do with these dots, and then they're going to move away from the puzzle. And if don't when they've solved it, then they'll just keep going around in circles forever, and there's no satisfaction in doing the puzzle.

It's also better to go too easy than it is too hard. You want people to feel satisfied with what they're doing. And I think this is true when you put riddles in games too. What's really fun in tabletop games is, and I feel like we're speaking heavily on the D&D side of things, but this is true in any game where you can put puzzles in. The wonderful thing about tabletop games is if your players come up with a better answer than what you have, there's nothing stopping you from changing on the fly and saying, yes, that's correct, because it lets everyone feel good about what happened. Unlike television, where so often people are iterating to make themselves feel like they were ahead of the audience, even if the audience cracked the mystery they want to be like, "no, you didn't solve it. You didn't figure this out", which is often a terrible choice at a table. The correct choice is to let people feel like they succeeded, even if that wasn't the original plan. They might come up with something better than anything you could have planned, and when that happens, that's the magic of being at a table. Let that happen, let that be. That suddenly becomes reality. You can change on the fly. You can rewrite things if they need to be rewritten. That's what's unique about this medium and art form that it's incredibly flexible and can be better than whatever you had planned for it to be.

Everyone has a different approach to solving mysteries and puzzles. Some people are going to be faster at it than others simply because their brains work differently. Rue Dickey, a cultural and sensitivity consultant, voice actor, and game designer, speaks to their experience with solving puzzles.

As a neurodivergent person, how I experience the world differs from the way a neurotypical person does. What is a clue that a neurotypical person will pick up on that I wouldn't, or vice versa? I ran a game once, and I thought I was running a very well laid out mystery, but because the people I was playing at the table with do not experience the world in my particular autistic field of view, they were all like, what are the clues? How do I find them? That was a really interesting moment for me, where I realized, oh, I should make sure that my mystery makes sense to someone who isn't me before I run it at a table.

Like game creation, writing a story or a script will go through an iteration process, where you can rewrite as much as you need to get it to where you want it to be. The key here is to be patient and get feedback from people in a variety of circles and circumstances to ensure that your mysteries and puzzles can be solved by the majority of the people in the marketplace.

What are some of the other earmarks of puzzles and mysteries? In stories centered on the crime or detective genre, you're going to start with a central mystery for the protagonist to solve. This is central to the classic whodunit story where an investigator is trying to hunt down the culprit of a murder or theft. These mysteries are paced in such a way that you aren't meant to know who the antagonist is until the end of the story. They may also introduce unsolved puzzles at the beginning of the story that lead to conclusions that open the door for more puzzles for the reader or viewer to solve, leaving a trail of breadcrumbs to either a red herring (a false antagonist), the real antagonist, or the victim of the crime (usually in the case of a theft, murder, or kidnapping).

Having your protagonist be a hard-boiled and seasoned detective might seem like a fun character to introduce to your audience, but that also means that the stakes and the mystery, need to be equal to or higher than the ability of the detective to solve. One of the reasons that the relationship between Sherlock Holmes and Doctor Watson works so well is that the story is told through the eyes of Watson and his observations on the genius sleuthing of Holmes. This allows Watson to make mistakes, be a bit slower than Holmes, and allows the reader to marvel at Holmes as he solves the harder puzzles that aren't meant for the audience to catch on to.

Thrillers and mysteries are an art form unto themselves. They have a specific type of pacing that needs to be addressed throughout their stories. They need to build tension, know when to dole out clues, revelations, suspects, and motives, and know when to ratchet up the stakes for the main characters. There is a precision to knowing exactly when to throw in a plot twist and throwing a surprise ending at an audience without them seeing it coming a mile away.

The characters in thrillers and mysteries are often complex. There might be the occasional stereotypical goon or suspect thrown in, but often the characters need to be fully fleshed-out people to get audiences to connect with them emotionally. The creators of these characters need to play on the audience's emotions to lead them down the path toward dead ends or, ultimately, a satisfying conclusion.

Police procedural shows are very popular on television. This is due to a number of factors including the audience's connection to the main characters, but also because of the predictability of the format. In that predictability, the writers of these shows are able to come up with a new mystery for their protagonists to solve every week. They present a crime, clues, suspects, and false leads, then the protagonists interrogate suspects for information leading them further down the case's rabbit hole. Each week, the show creates a unique atmosphere centered around the location of where the crime was committed, the victim of the crime, and the main suspects. All of this leads to a (usually) logical resolution. Sometimes these conclusions are arrived at through an investigation of the evidence through forensics (autopsies, fingerprints, and DNA analysis are popular ways of achieving this), and profiling of the suspects using a psychological approach. Can it become predictable? Yes. Is the main culprit usually the one person with the least amount of screen time? Yes. Does it keep us engaged and entertained? Also, yes.

The sheer number of ways to present a mystery to an audience seems daunting, but like any other genre, there are tropes that you can rely on to that will get you started. A good locked-room mystery, for instance, is a classic way to present a mystery. A crime committed in a room where no one could have possibly gotten in or out is a challenge for the protagonist and the audience to solve. Other tropes can involve the suspect or victim suffering from amnesia due to the trauma they've endured, or perhaps they were knocked unconscious when the initial crime was committed and are unable to account for vital information during critical moments of the mystery. Characters leading double lives are a fun way to introduce intrigue into your stories. Secret identities have been a staple of the superhero world for decades, and these can work just as well for your protagonists or your antagonists in your stories too.

If you are looking to add complications to your mystery, you might try adding an unreliable narrator to your story. An unreliable narrator sees the story from their perspective, but the audience might question the truthfulness of their version of events. Additionally, you can add flashback scenes or tell the story from multiple perspectives, giving the story a larger sense of scope and leaving the audience to wonder whose version of the story is the accurate one.

The themes most mysteries and thrillers tend to explore are reflections on society, or the pursuit of justice, including morality, truth, and the consequences of crime. Popular expressions of these themes include societal issues such as class divisions, corruption, or abuse of power.

Unlike many other genres, mysteries and thrillers offer the opportunity to engage directly with the audience, allowing them to solve the puzzles and clues along with the protagonist. This can be a great way to build audiences if you are clever enough to keep them guessing. The only downside is that if you don't meet the audience's expectations or fail to keep them engaged with your mysteries and puzzles, you can lose them in lieu of your competitors.

SCIENCE FICTION

Subgenres Include

Cyberpunk

Explores a dystopian future dominated by high-tech advancements and low-life characters. It often includes themes of corporate control, AI, and cybernetics.

Examples: *Blade Runner, The Matrix, Altered Carbon.*

Steampunk

Blends science fiction with Victorian-era aesthetics, often incorporating steam-powered technology and alternate histories.

Examples: *The City of Lost Children, Steamboy, Wild Wild West.*

Soft Science Fiction

More focused on speculative elements and human or societal aspects than on scientific accuracy.

Examples: *Star Trek, Minority Report, The Time Traveler's Wife.*

Alternate History

Explores what might have happened if key events in history had unfolded differently.

Examples: *Inglourious Basterds, The Man in the High Castle, Red Dawn.*

Genetic Engineering

Focuses on the scientific and ethical questions surrounding genetic modification, cloning, and the creation of genetically engineered organisms or humans.

Examples: *Jurassic Park, The Island, Never Let Me Go.*

Apocalyptic Science Fiction

Focuses on the end of the world or a post-apocalyptic future, often caused by nuclear war, environmental collapse, or other catastrophic events.

Examples: *Mad Max: Fury Road, The Book of Eli, Snowpiercer.*

Parallel Universe/Multiverse

Explores the existence of parallel universes or alternate realities, where different versions of the world or characters exist.

Examples: *Doctor Strange in the Multiverse of Madness, The One, Sliding Doors.*

Space Opera
Emphasizes grand, epic adventures in space, often featuring intergalactic wars, political intrigue, and large-scale battles.
Examples: *Star Wars, Guardians of the Galaxy, Dune.*

Hard Science Fiction
Focuses on scientifically accurate or plausible depictions of the future, with attention to the details of real science and technology.
Examples: 2001: *A Space Odyssey, Interstellar, The Martian.*

Alien Invasion
Centers around extraterrestrial beings invading Earth, exploring themes of first contact, survival, and the fear of the unknown.
Examples: *Independence Day, War of the Worlds, Arrival.*

Time Travel
Involves characters traveling through time, exploring the consequences of altering past events or the paradoxes created by time manipulation.
Examples: *Back to the Future, Looper, Predestination.*

Biopunk
Focuses on biotechnology, genetics, and the implications of biological advancements on humanity and society.
Examples: *Gattaca, Elysium, The Island.*

Dystopian Science Fiction
Explores societies that are undesirable, oppressive, or corrupt, often because of technological advancements or political systems.
Examples: *The Hunger Games, Children of Men, The Road.*

Kaiju
Refers to stories that focus on giant monsters, often originating from nature or space, that wreak havoc on cities or battle other gigantic creatures.
Examples: *Godzilla, King Kong, Pacific Rim.*

Science Fiction Comedy
Blends the imaginative and speculative elements of science fiction with the humor and absurdity of comedy.
Examples: *The Hitchhiker's Guide to the Galaxy, Spaceballs, Men in Black.*

Dieselpunk

Blends historical and imagined elements, creating alternative realities where advanced technology, art, and culture evolve differently from our own.

Examples: *The Sky Captain and the World of Tomorrow, Iron Sky, The Rocketeer.*

Afrofuturism

Centered on imagining futures where African diaspora communities play a prominent role, often blending traditional African cultural elements with futuristic technology, space travel, and speculative worldbuilding.

Examples: *Black Panther, Space Is the Place, Come Back, Africa.*

Space Exploration

Focuses on the exploration of outer space, often dealing with the challenges of long-term space travel, encountering new worlds, and the potential for extraterrestrial life.

Examples: *Apollo 13, Gravity, Contact.*

Space Western

Combines the elements of space exploration and space opera with the thematic and aesthetic influences of the Western genre.

Examples: *Serenity, Cowboys & Aliens, Outland.*

Body Snatcher

Where extraterrestrials or other forces take control of human bodies, often through parasitic or transformative means, leading to questions of identity and trust.

Examples: *Invasion of the Body Snatchers* (1956, 1978, 1993), *The Faculty, The Invasion.*

Science Fiction stories take on many forms. The most common cultural touchstones we have for sci-fi stories in our own media are from superb storytellers like Isaac Asimov, Philip K. Dick, Ray Bradbury, H.G. Wells, and Ursula K. Le Guin. Stories like Asimov's *Foundation, I, Robot,* and *The Bicentennial Man* challenge humanity's assumptions about ourselves in the present while exploring how our future paths could unwind.

Science fiction stories can be grounded in a current reality with a small subversion to show us how a minor change can have massive effects, or they can show us distant galaxies and worlds far in the future with technology that is far beyond our current scientific abilities. These stories are sometimes centered on time travel, like in Wells' The Time Machine, which also does a wonderful job of highlighting other social woes, like the dangers of capitalism and social inequalities. The implications of science gone wrong (also a trait in many horror stories), and the importance of versatility in a person's way of thinking.

Like horror, sometimes science fiction is used as a mirror of our society. When George Lucas' Star Wars was released in theaters in 1977, and the world was treated to a struggle between the Rebel Alliance against the evil Galactic Empire in a galaxy far, far away, the subtext within that space opera filled with aliens and laser swords was a commentary on the Vietnam War.

In an appearance on "James Cameron's Story of Science Fiction," George Lucas expanded on his stated overarching theme of Star Wars being about "a large technological empire going after a small group of freedom fighters." He states, "It isn't the science, aliens, and all that kind of stuff that I get focused on. It's how people react to all those things." And that, "the little guys won. The highly technical empire—the English Empire, the American Empire—lost. That was the whole point."

What are some of the other traits inherent to science fiction stories, and how can you incorporate these elements into your own stories? The hallmark of the science fiction genre is the exploration of scientific concepts. This can be through speculative science, using hypothetical advancements in areas like genetics, AI, physics, or looking to the stars at extraterrestrial life. The "science" in sci-fi can fit into a more logical and real-world model in describing the worlds your characters are visiting, or it can use made-up methods of science that you create on your own to describe the worlds and technology in your work. The various "Star Trek" television shows do well with creating their own scientific explanations and technology to bring their ships and alien worlds to life. "Doctor Who" is another example of a television show that sometimes takes leaps of logic when describing their own methods of getting the Doctor out of impossible situations (never underestimate the power of just "reversing the polarity" to solve a technical problem when the clock is against your characters in a sci-fi setting).

Space travel and colonization can be a spectacular backbone to a story while also carrying the possibilities of discussing the effects of real-world colonization in ways that will get your audience thinking about their own world history in a subversive manner. Alien planets and solar systems give you so many ways to have your characters interact with whatever awaits them in the stars. Will they meet friendly faces? Are your characters seen as invaders? Will the planets they visit be able to sustain life, or will your protagonists be forced to create and sustain a shelter for themselves?

Space is dangerous and inherently hostile to life, making it a worthy adversary for your adventurers without them even having to step foot outside their ship. Part of the reason the movie *Alien* is so scary isn't just the Xenomorph lurking in the shadows of the ship, but it's that there is nowhere to run in the blackness and infinite depths of airless nothingness.

Science fiction has a long history of using technology to comment on humanity. Looking at artificial intelligence in books and movies and comparing it with what we are seeing today, and its both positive and negative effects on our current capitalistic culture can feel alarming. On one hand, having a computer be able to act as a tool in your daily life, helping you with mundane tasks sounds wonderful, but there are some people and companies that feel that AI can take over the jobs of creators by absorbing and iterating on previous work, or have decided that a computer should write the script for their great idea. They are supplementing technology for talent and hard work. Being a brilliant writer isn't about just having solid ideas, it's about how you execute those ideas, and that comes from constant practice, trial and error, and occasional failure. Talent isn't something that a computer can replace; it can just take what other talented people have done and regurgitate a simulacrum to an audience.

One trait of science fiction that has been popular recently is parallel and alternate realities. This is currently most common in comic books and comic-based movies. Perhaps the James Bond movies are a series of adventures set in alternate realities based on the changing of the actors every few years and how many of the chronologies of the films rarely line up with a solid, un-branching timeline.

Sometimes creating a multiverse scenario is something you're forced to do because you wrote yourself into a corner (this is the easiest thing to do for comic book films when a character/actor drops out of a franchise, dies, or falls out of public favor). It might also be something to consider if you are having a collaborator write about characters that exist in your universe, but you don't want their work to become canon within your main storyline to avoid potential character and story conflicts.

From a story creation point of view, writing a series of "what if" stories about your characters can be a fantastic exercise in understanding your characters' motivations and how they would react differently under different circumstances in your story.

EXERCISE 11.1

Take a story you have written, regardless of genre, and create five different scenarios that would occur to your main character if you were to change one detail or plot point in your story. Does your character's story become stronger? How do these new scenarios change who your character is at their core?

Disasters can make for great films and stories. A catastrophe that leads to an end-of-the-world scenario can be an interesting backdrop to a personal character arc for your protagonist. When looking at a potential world-ending tale, how do you imagine the world falling apart? Is it going to be because of an environmental disaster? Will it be a pandemic that kills most of the world's population? Will the end of the world come from an unstoppable invading alien species? Science fiction has given us countless frameworks for how we, as humans, meet our doom. Some examples of films that handle apocalyptic stories include *Mad Max*, *I Am Legend* (which is actually a remake of *The Last Man on Earth*. Both are based on the novel written by Richard Matheson in 1954), and Roland Emmerich's *The Day After Tomorrow*. These movies have world-ending storylines but approach the cause and after-effects of world devastation differently.

Another subgenre in science fiction is post-apocalyptic. Once the world ends, how do any survivors carry on? This deals with not only the rebuilding of society but can often question what makes up a society in the first place. Is it the rule of law? High standards, morals, and ethics? Firm belief and religious systems? These points can be turned into interesting stories that explore humanity when we are at our lowest and most vulnerable. Excellent examples on television that visit these storylines are *The Walking Dead* (based on the wildly successful comic book) and *The Last of Us* (which is based on a hit video game).

Writing science fiction can feel complex and unapproachable to some writers who think that their stories need to be chock full of aliens and exotic locations. The important thing to remember when writing science fiction is that it's about the people. Whether human or alien, the experiences we all share are what makes for an excellent story. When the alien on Star Trek meets the Federation captain, both characters share similar feelings of fear, trepidation, and more. Through the course of the show, we see them begin to understand and trust each other. On the canceled show Firefly, the crew of the Serenity are hesitant to trust their new passengers at first, but because of their shared distrust of the Alliance, they aid River Tam and her brother as they evade the people who want to take River back to the research facility and harness her power for their own machinations. Despite there being a "Verse" of possibilities to explore on Firefly, you never see an alien, and the plot focuses on the interpersonal relationships within the crew of the Serenity.

Science fiction isn't just about aliens and crazy space adventures. It's a genre that explores the intersection of imagination, technology, and human experience. It reflects on our futures and realities while questioning what we're doing with the resources we have in the present.

FAMILY/KIDS

Children's stories are their own animals, and as such don't really conform to the subgenre model used in the other areas in this chapter. This is because children's stories are the subgenre of each of the previously mentioned genres. Almost any genre can be adapted to fit a child- or family-appropriate narrative.

Stories made for children are crafted to entertain, educate, and resonate with younger audiences. They often prioritize accessibility, simplicity, and themes that align with children's perspectives and developmental stages. Stories for kids and families are written differently than other stories and can be considered a genre unto themselves.

Stories for children have more simplified structures and language (and not just by eliminating cursing). These stories use simple, clear, and concise language that works with the target age group that the story is crafted for. For younger children, you'll often find the use of repetitive phrases being used to reinforce morals or lessons. The reason for using simplified language and plots is not to talk down to children, but to keep their attention and to communicate intention and feeling, which children respond to better than flowery language filled with nuance, idiom, or subterfuge. Most children's picture books are shorter than 32 pages, and middle-school-aged children's books are written with brief chapters.

There are many stages that children go through, developmentally speaking. Each stage shows an increase in speech and language skills, fine motor and visual-motor skills, and their ability to self-identify and be increasingly independent in their day-to-day tasks. Shows that reinforce the importance of these skills, as well as adventures and bonds with family and friends at that age, include Bluey, Caillou, and Sesame Street. These all have bright, fun, and engaging characters with little actual drama and problems that are solved easily by using lessons learned within that show's episode or with the help of the characters' friends and family, reinforcing teamwork and community.

Another identifying characteristic of children's stories is other children as the main protagonist, and/or an animal protagonist that is the friend of the child or the main character themselves. In fact, anthropomorphism is a large part of many children's stories and movies (the talking door knockers in the movie *Labyrinth* are one example). Sometimes children's television shows will even involve the viewer and invite them to take part in solving a puzzle within the show (i.e. Dora the Explorer, Blue's Clues), empowering the viewer to face the same challenges, struggles, and triumphs as the heroes on TV, fostering a sense of capability and confidence in the viewer.

Other themes present in many children's programs are growth and morality. Stories often incorporate clear moral lessons or teach values such as kindness, honesty, courage, or perseverance while also addressing universal childhood experiences like dealing with loss (usually found in middle-grade stories) and helping children process increasingly complicated emotions as they grow older. An example of a film that many people can point to that deals with the complications of a child dealing with the loss of a close friend would be *My Girl*.

Coming-of-age stories are focused on character's personal growth, discovery of themselves, and the world around them (usually involving a journey or larger adventure outside their home or territory, taking on a "quest-like" plot structure). Movies like *Now and Then* and *Stand By Me* are two examples of movies for pre-teen boys and girls that deal with the difficulties of growing up and the close bonds they form with their friends can relate to. A lot of the media made for teens and pre-teens tends to focus on friendships and exploration, but also often includes a heavy dose of anti-authoritarian (not necessarily anti-parent) subplots in them. Movies like *The Iron Giant*, *School of Rock*, and TV shows like *Steven Universe* and *Adventure Time* might make the list of media that follows that trend.

Children's television programing and films use bright imagery and often take place in whimsical worlds (especially true with children's films directed by Hayao Miyazaki like *My Neighbor Totoro*, *Spirited Away*, and *Princess Mononoke*) that include elements of fantasy, magic, and make-believe. These allow children to explore their imaginations and other creative possibilities. They also engage with children using humor, silliness, and absurdity, and give children (for the most part) happy resolutions that are positive and reassuring, providing a sense of safety at the end of the journey for the characters and closure to their personal growth plots.

Children's stories are rarely cynical. Most stories, even those addressing serious topics, maintain a hopeful and uplifting tone. Even when a character is at their low point, there's usually a friend or secondary character cheering them on with a "we/you can do it" speech that sets the protagonist back on their path. These stories are steeped in empathy and understanding, both for the main character and for the world around them. Even if the protagonist starts their journey being closed off and grouchy, by the end they will most assuredly have opened their heart to their friends and their community, having learned to open their mind to differing opinions and perspectives. These stories often emphasize inclusivity and diversity by featuring characters from all kinds of backgrounds, shapes, colors, abilities, and experiences.

These characteristics ensure that children's stories are engaging, developmentally appropriate, and meaningful, often leaving a lasting impact on young readers by sparking their imaginations, teaching valuable lessons, and nurturing a love of storytelling.

CHAPTER 12

Breaking the Rules

THERE ARE NO RULES

POINT OF INSPIRATION

"In the front of the D&D Player's Handbook, it says these rules are here as guidelines, and if you don't want to follow them, the ultimate decision-makers at the table are the DM, players, and having fun."—Rowan Zeoli

One common theme that you've seen throughout this book is that, despite the mountainous volumes of rule books for hundreds of TTRPGs out there, and an equally significant number of books written about screen-writing and storytelling, it is good to understand and become proficient with the rules as written, but it is also just as important to write for yourself first. Don't become hung up on dangling participles and passive verbs, or whether a specific story beat is appropriate for a scene. Certainly, don't stress over whether your slug lines are bolded or not. Get through to the end of your story. Tell it your way. The chance to revise it is always there, but the opportunity to write it only happens once.

Podcast producer, composer, and founder of the podcast studio Fortunate Horse, Taylor Moore discusses his feelings about rule-breaking, and how sometimes the structures we build around us are artificial and can be pushed through, and how the only things limiting us are the laws of physics:

DOI: 10.1201/9781003538202-12

Have you ever heard someone say, did you know that the bumble-bee should not be able to fly according to the laws of aerodynamics, that it breaks the laws of aerodynamics? That was something somebody would say, just one of those factoids like you eat seven spiders a year. It's just one of these things that we just absorb like dumb facts, (from) pre-internet days. It's much worse now. Now it's a civilization-destroying conspiracy theory that you buy into. But I think about that bumblebee thing a lot because it's bullshit. You don't have to know any facts to hear that and know it's bullshit, because if the laws of aerodynamics are about how flight works, then nothing that flies can break the laws of aerodynamics. It just means we didn't understand the rules, right? So, when people talk in art about breaking the rules, if you break a rule and it works, then that wasn't a rule, was it? Right? But you know, we adapt all these frameworks to work within, because it makes working within much easier in so many ways. Like if a painter decides the canvas is going to be three by five, and that's it. You give yourself these frameworks because it helps to start. It helps judge the work. It helps the process. But every once in a while, it's the framework you bust out of, and you discover something wonderful. You can't break a rule and win, for the same reason that you can't say a bumblebee defies the laws of aerodynamics.

When you're hired to write something, or you're in a collaborative writing situation like a television series writer's room, the situation is different, and your expectations of the story you're expected to tell versus the story you want to tell need to be managed. You might not get to have all the cool dramatic character moments you want. Or you might need to reel in your story for a specific budget range. This is something that even game designers for TTRPGs deal with.

Jason Bulmahn, the creator of the main D&D competitor Pathfinder, talks about his experience writing Pathfinder adventures and working within budgets that include dollars, time, and story economy.

I think that often it's less about the actual cost value, because a lot of that is locked in by contracts and how big the product can actually be. It's a game book. It's going to be 64 pages, 96 pages, or it could be 120. There are set sizes that we work with, and as a result, that means you can only put X number of things in it. The biggest thing for me whenever I'm planning any of those things out, the budgeting comes down to using my words in my space effectively to make sure the plot and the story have the right kind of push/pull elements I want, and that it's telling the narrative I want; that it has the story structure.

I'm a very firm believer in building tabletop adventure stories very similar to how you might build a novel or a script. It has to have pacing. There are different models of how you build out the scenes and the chapters to kind of convey the right feeling. Right? You don't want the players to ease through five combats in a row, because, frankly, it gets boring. Narrative tension comes from the one that was really close. Now they are confronted with a mystery, and they don't have the answer. Then, aha! They found the thing they needed and now can progress the story. It's a push/pull of drama, and you have to make sure that you know all of your ideas fit within the framework in the space that you have.

The same goes with an actual play. When you're building an actual play and you're trying to figure it out, okay, I've got eight three-hour episodes. I know what I can include in these, and I want to make sure each one ends on a satisfying note. I want to make sure that each one has a reason for folks to come back for the next time. They don't have to be cliffhangers, but they can be moments of drama or tension. How do I make sure I get my combats and all the other things to fit into a tidy box? It's not different. It's just a different format. I'm dealing with pages or minutes on the screen. So ultimately, I approach it from a very budgeted mindset. I know how much space an encounter takes up, and how long it takes to play combat if I'm the one running it. I can make it go faster, or I can drag it for a while. I know how to manipulate those variables if I'm writing it, trimming out encounters I don't need, or minimizing their impact on the space so that the players can have their moment in the text, but they're not overpowering.

It takes a conscious, deliberative approach, and most of it flows from the outline. I'm a pretty meticulous, outline-driven designer, especially with narrative. I like to map it out and say, "all right, how does this start? How can I get the players engaged and hooked right away?"

I wrote the very first standalone adventure for Pathfinder called The Fall of Plaguestone, and I think one of the biggest sins of adventure design is not starting and immediately pulling the players into action. I think for a roleplaying game, you've got to get those dice rolling. If it's an hour of people talking before anybody rolls a die at the very start of an adventure, there's just something you need to do there.

So, you're in the back of a wagon, you're getting to know each other, and you're on your way, you're between two towns, and then some wolves, and these aren't normal wolves, there's something wrong with them. Immediately there's action, because there's a fight with wolves. There's tension, because they outnumber you and attack you unawares. There's a mystery, because these aren't normal wolves. One of them has acid dripping from its mouth and looks mangy. There's a tangible reward that carries the plot forward, and that the caravan master is so impressed that you stepped forward to protect his caravan, he invites you to dinner later that night once you get to town. He promises a sumptuous feast. The story proceeds and spoilers here, I designed it in such a way that you have that fight, you have some other role-playing encounters, maybe some skill checks as you talk to other members of the caravan and arrive in town and learn a bit about this town called Plaguestone, and then you go to dinner with the caravan master, good old Bort, and in the middle of the dinner, he begins to choke, sputter, change color, falls over, and dies. That is designed specifically to be your first session. It should be about two to three hours' worth of game time. You got one fight, you got a bunch of skill checks, you got some people you can role play and interact with. You got your chances to get to talk to other people. There's another kind of secondary fight if you have more time with a bit of a bar brawl after a misunderstanding, and then you've got your cliffhanger to hook you in for more of the session.

"That was planned from minute one to be how the opener of this adventure works. From there, I know where all my major story beats are. I want to make sure I'm building around those, and then after that, you've got your kind of denouement moments where folks can kind of decompress, spend their money, heal up, gear up for their next adventures. I think writing adventures works very much like building any story or narrative. You're just setting the stage for the players, who are your protagonists and the main points of the story."

If reading this, in more of a television format, sounds familiar to you, it's probably because what Jason describes above is very similar to how a TV pilot episode would be laid out, setting the scene for future episodes in the season to come. If he were to take his Pathfinder adventure, the Fall of Plaguestone, to say, Netflix, and pitch that exact pilot, there is an excellent chance that something with that level of narrative design would be interesting to them (especially if they try to compete with other streamers and their own sword and dragon shows).

Notice how Jason understood that while he was writing an exciting adventure, ultimately, he was writing for the audience it was intended for: players and GMs.

A lot of creatives don't like to think about their stories as products that have shelf lives. They want to see their work as a book or a movie, not as a unit. But unless you have a generous patron (or Patreon in the more modern sense) funding your ability to create freely without the stench of capitalism wafting a malodorous breeze under your nose, then you're probably going to capitulate occasionally to someone else's demands.

Write for yourself. Edit for whomever is paying you.

Take the classes. Learn the rules, but don't see them as obstacles to creation. See them as guidelines you can break with impunity. It might not result in the most salable material, but it could be the script, the novel, or the audio drama that changes how people perceive that medium for a generation.

CHAPTER 13

Fade Out

THERE ARE NO RULES

Writing and completing a script or a novel is no effortless task. Sure, you may crank out 90 pages in a weekend if inspiration strikes you the right way, but truly getting to the core and heart of your piece is something that takes time, constant practice, refinement, and outside validation. To be clear, you aren't searching for an "atta boy" from your peers, but you are looking to make sure that the work you are submitting to contests, festivals, fellowships, and more importantly, to reps and industry professionals, is of equal caliber to what is expected from a professional screenwriter, novelist, or any job writing in the creative arts.

That doesn't mean it has to be perfect.

A script is written, rewritten, and re-rewritten over and over during the pre-production and production process. Even the finished film or television show gets "re-written" again during the editing process. Film and television is a highly collaborative career, and keeping in mind that the tabletop gaming world is also a collaborative way of storytelling might keep you in the right frame of mind when you're sitting next to your keyboard, alone on a Friday night, struggling with how to transition from act II to act III in your screenplay. Actively seek the counsel and advice of others. Form writing groups. Attend writer retreats, meet-ups, and conferences. If money is an issue (and it definitely is for many writers, so don't feel shy or any shame), look at grants or request fee waivers.

DOI: 10.1201/9781003538202-13

How do you "break in" to the industry? That's a complicated question, as the answer is different for everyone. Some people are born into the industry because their parents work in it, and before you cry "nepo baby," understand that not everyone's parents are mega-movie stars. Some people have parents that work hard as PAs, transportation captains, or in offices maintaining accurate guild paperwork and payroll for the hundreds of people who work on films. Filmmaker and author Jamie Nash talks about his experiences in the industry and how he has kept his foot in the door over the years:

> It's tricky to say. I mean, I definitely think there is a heaping dose of luck that factors into some of it. Things have to go the right way in order for things to happen. But what I've noticed from every single person that made a career of this, whether they're at my level, which is low on the totem pole, compared to some. Deep down, there's a tenacity there, and there's relentlessness; they eat and sleep and breathe it. I've really found that relentlessness. I'm constantly churning out stuff.
>
> There's some level of network(ing). Some people are just relentless networkers. They're constantly spinning gold out of everybody they meet. It comes more naturally to some of us and maybe it's born out of passion. We just want to do it so much that we channel the hardships of it into whatever that thing we're relentless about.
>
> Most of the people I've met that have broken in, it's taken at least 10 or 12 years. When people say it's going to take a long time, I think a lot of people assume, oh, yeah, two years. It's like 10 or 12.
>
> I have had moments where things dropped in my lap. They're very few and far between, and they're the best days of my career when somebody just calls up and says, "I have a thing for you. We're going to write you a check. Call your agent. It's done." It might have happened to me, and again, I'm a low-level guy in the totem pole, maybe four or five times over the course of the last 15 years. Usually it's like, hey, do you want to pitch for the next month trying to get the job? That's the call. Usually it's like, we'd like to hear your take, we'd like you to read, we'd like to have a meeting with you about and usually it's very rare that anything ever drops in anybody's lap. It's going to take 10 years to get the lucky breaks. That's the problem. If you only do it for one year,

odds are you're not going to get the lucky break. Odds are you're not going to be ready for the lucky break.

Dimension 20's main Dungeon Master, Creator, and Executive Producer Brennan Lee Mulligan gives context to what some people refer to, mistakenly, as impostor syndrome, when what they really mean is that they are new to the process and still need to learn how the systems work, and how to refine their craft until it's the best they can make it.

> The term imposter syndrome is very specific, and I've begun to hear it in the way that internet language tends to take psychological terms and broadly apply them past the point of utility. I had someone come up to me one time in a one-on-one improv class and be like, I'm really experiencing imposter syndrome. And I said, no, you're not. You're a novice. And what I was saying was that you have a lack of confidence because you're learning a new skill and are developing muscles that don't exist from the ground up.
>
> Welcoming the experience of wrestling with an unfamiliar set of new skills is amazing. And that's not imposter syndrome. That is, you are getting discomfort and joy of getting good at something brand new. If someone comes up to me talking about being a dungeon master, and they're like, I just feel like I have imposter syndrome about running my first game. And I was like, your relationship to your nerves around doing a good job is a good thing. It doesn't mean that you misapprehend yourself or that you are an imposter. It means that you want to be good, but you should make peace with it's going to be a journey to get there. That's a positive thing. That's not bad, that's not inaccurate.

You don't need to live in Los Angeles or New York to be a successful writer or screenwriter. It helps, of course, to have immediate and regular access to people in your industry for networking purposes, but you can always save up to visit and block-book meetings for when you're in town. This is a common practice for many writers, and it also sets an expectation on behalf of the people you're meeting with that your time is limited and precious (and possibly already full of other meetings with competing studios or agencies). More important than living in a major city is learning how to play "the game." Going back to TTRPGs, it helps to know the rules, for instances, where the situation calls for a more refined approach rather than brute force. That's when you know to roll a charisma check instead of an attack. Learn to charm. If you can't charm (maybe you're neurodivergent and not naturally able to deal well with social situations), learn to write compelling emails instead. Use your strengths to get your foot in the door.

FROM THE AUTHOR

This is going to be a bit of a tirade, so bear with me. If you do decide to make the move to Los Angeles to make a go of being a screenwriter or filmmaker, let me tell you the same thing that I tell everyone based on my own experiences of living in LA (and corroborated by many other creatives I've spoken with who made the same move I did).

It's going to take a solid two years for you to be completely comfortable living in LA. It might even take longer. Some of it depends on how quickly you find the three most essential things to nail down. You need to find your neighborhood, your friends, and your job. This might seem like a series of small tasks, but they are vital to your ability to thrive in LA.

Los Angeles is big. Bigger than you probably think it is. It is filled with millions of people, and it can sometimes feel like the loneliest place to be in the world. This is where having those three elements in place early comes into play. Once you have your neighborhood (where you live), and you've had the chance to explore it, finding your favorite food spots (don't skip the food truck scene, it will be some of the best food, especially late-night after a couple of after-party beverages, that you'll ever have), hangout places, and ways to get around without having to jump on any of the major freeways, you'll then be able to focus on finding your friends. I would encourage you, if you live in Highland Park, to avoid having your core group of friends be from Santa Monica, because you'll likely never see them.

Los Angeles is a lot like New York in that once you've landed in your borough, you'll likely stay in that general area more than the rest of the city. In LA, because of the traffic and how spread out the city is, most people stay where they live and where they work. For me, it was Highland Park and Hollywood (with some regular trips to North Hollywood and Culver City). I can count on one hand the number of times I've seen the Pacific Ocean in the six years I lived and worked in Los Angeles.

If I wanted to make like the Miley Cyrus song and hop off the plane at LAX (with a dream and my cardigan), it would take me over an hour, maybe longer, to see the Hollywood sign (which would actually be on the left contrary to the song coming from that direction). Most of that time is spent sitting in traffic (it's only 21.2 miles from LAX to Hollywood).

Having steady work lined up providing a steady income will also make your time in Los Angeles feel less stressful. Considering the last few years that have been filled with a pandemic, multiple strikes, and other issues that have affected the creative industry, finding steady work is something that has been difficult for people who have been there for decades, never mind being a fresh face trying to "make it." Take jobs where you find them. Get in the habit of saying "yes" more than "no" to work you might otherwise turn a blind eye to. Be strategic. Put yourself in front of the people you want to work around (for networking) or take jobs that give you the time to write or create without exhausting you beforehand. Los Angeles is expensive. Learn to look for deals (don't sleep on the Mexican grocery stores for discount ingredients and quick meals). When I was at my most lean money-wise, I was spending $25 per week on food and making it last from one payday to the next. Not a simple thing to do.

Once you've got those three things in line, LA will feel a bit more like home. The rest of the time in those two years is spent convincing people, and sometimes yourself, that you're not leaving anytime soon. Los Angeles is a very transient town with people coming and going all the time, so people who are established there are sometimes hesitant to give their time and energy to new people that might be gone in a month or two. That's why, if you're lucky enough to get a meeting, you'll often hear the phrase, let's follow up in a couple of weeks (which is really six months). This isn't a method of ghosting or anything malicious. They just want to make sure that you're still going to be around by then. Once people can see that you're a somewhat stable fixture around town, you'll find that those meetings will bear fruit more often.

Like many careers, there are naturally talented people who will excel with little outside instruction. Some of those people will show innate writing talent but might struggle with networking or the business side of the industry. Others will struggle to get from page one to Fade Out but will be charismatic enough to garner the attention of industry pros everywhere they go. Find the people who aren't like you. Make connections with folks who don't have similar skill sets and use each other's strengths to make inroads into the industry.

Most of all, enjoy what you do.

You do it because it's fun and you love it, and you are part of the story. You're scratching your creative itch. Whether the audience is ever going to know it or not. Some people need acclaim, adulation, they need people to know they did it. Other people don't need that. They just need to be part of the process, to be invited to the party, to be in the room, and that's enough. They felt okay because I was in the room. I did that, I was there.

ED GREENWOOD, AUTHOR AND WORLD BUILDER

One reason for writing this book was to give you a set of guidelines for telling better stories, managing your characters' backstories, and creating more consistency in the worlds they inhabit. TTRPGs are the perfect framework for inventive storytelling for screenwriters. But TTRPG systems are ultimately a set of rules for a game. Games should be fun. Doing what you love should have an element of fun to it as well. If the method presented in this book doesn't work for you, that's fine. Try a new one. If Save the Cat is more to your liking, use that. Use anything that gets you to the end of your script.

As you journey through the industry, you will come across many people who will tell you the "right" way to write. The only correct way is the way that works for you. Everything else is formatting.

Good luck, and happy writing.

ONE LAST EXERCISE

Write the script. Write the book. Write the article. Just write...and finish.

Contributors

Ashley Warren (she/her)—Ashley Warren is an award-winning writer and narrative designer who has developed, produced, and co-authored numerous best-selling titles for Dungeons & Dragons including the Uncaged Anthology series, Icewind Dale: Rime of the Frostmaiden, Heckna!, and Legendlore. She is the lead designer and developer of Loreloop: The World We Live In, The World We Create, an original tabletop role-playing game supported by the National Endowment for the Humanities. She serves as the director of the Storytelling Collective, a global online writing program for independent creative storytellers. Ashley is best known for her immersive, atmospheric storytelling that she lends to both games and fiction. She holds a Master's in Literacy Studies from the University of Nevada, Reno, NV. Connect with her at Scribemind.com.

Banana Chan (she/they/he)—Banana Chan is a Cantonese Canadian game designer, writer, and publisher living in the US. Her most notable work has been on Forgery, Jiangshi: Blood in the Banquet Hall, The Revenant Society, Pathfinder 2E: Tian Xia World Guide, Dungeons & Dragons 5E: Van Richten's Guide to Ravenloft, and Betrayal at House on the Hill: 3rd Edition. They won Dicebreaker Awards' Game Designer of the Year 2022 and two Silver ENNIE Awards in 2022.

DOI: 10.1201/9781003538202-14

B. Dave Walters (he/him)—B. Dave Walters (@ BDaveWalters) is a storyteller and proud Scoundrel American. Best known as the host and DM of Invitation to Party on G4 TV, and DM for the cast of Stranger Things on Netflix Geeked. He is the writer and co-creator of D&D: A Darkened Wish for IDW comics, and creator and DM of the Black Dice Society for Wizards of the Coast, and DM of Idle Champions Presents. He is the Lead Designer for Into the Mother Lands RPG.

Brennan Lee Mulligan (he/him)—Brennan Lee Mulligan is a multi-talented actor, comedian, writer, producer, and showrunner, as well as a partner at the acclaimed comedy streaming platform, Dropout TV. Brennan's career began with formal training in acting and improv, eventually leading him to join the cast of CollegeHumor Originals. He has since become one of the most prominent figures in the Dungeons & Dragons community. As executive producer, showrunner, and host of Dropout's hit series Dimension 20, Brennan helms the highest-performing subscription-based D&D show on the market, which recently made headlines by selling out Madison Square Garden in under five minutes. The latest season, Dungeons and Drag Queens, recently premiered to widespread acclaim.

In addition to his work on Dimension 20, Brennan expanded his role in the Dungeons & Dragons universe by serving as Dungeon Master for Critical Role's celebrated campaign, Exandria Unlimited: Calamity in 2022, and has recently announced that he will serve as DM once again for Exandria Unlimited: Divergence, premiering this February. Brennan is also deeply engaged in the podcasting world with his latest creation, Worlds Beyond Number, which quickly became the most pre-subscribed podcast on Patreon and ranks in the top ten of all Patreon creators. Upon its release, it claimed the #1 spot as the top fiction podcast in the United States.

Together with his wife, Izzy Roland, Brennan performs in Bigger! With Brennan and Izzy, a live improv show that has delighted audiences on both coasts by transforming quirky real-life stories into hilarious improvised scenes.

Brennan currently resides in Los Angeles.

 **Brian Gray (he/they)**—Brian Gray, aka urbanbohemian, is a Black Queer writer, gamer, foodie, streamer, TTRPG player (and sometimes GM), charitable fundraiser, comic book lover, cocktail connoisseur, stalwart brunch supporter, disco music aficionado, and all-around Generation X geek having grown up through the introduction of video games—from arcades to home consoles to computer gaming—and loving every innovation along the way.

As a streamer, he showcases a variety of game genres, dabbles in food and drink streams from the kitchen, takes part in virtual panels and roundtables, and has been in several tabletop role-playing games (TTRPGs) from charity one-shots to starring as Virgil in "Rivals of Waterdeep," one of the longest-running Dungeons & Dragons actual play shows, and De Ross in "Cyberpunk: Independence," a Cyberpunk RED actual play podcast and stream.

His approach to gaming and streaming is that everyone should have fun, whether it's GMs and their players or streamers and their viewers! With a focus on finding games where representation and diversity are prominently woven into the content instead of being an afterthought, he enjoys showcasing and featuring a wide variety of gaming genres and creative voices.

He's been honored on Rainbow Game Jam's Queer In Games List, identifying 50 people in the industry whose efforts have made the industry a more welcoming and safer space for the LGBTQIA+ community. He's spoken on panel topics ranging from streaming as a hobby or career, streaming as a member of a marginalized community, avoiding racism and fostering inclusivity in your TTRPG campaigns, charity streaming and fundraising, parasocial relationships while streaming, finding your place in TTRPGs as an LGBTQIA+ player, and imagining a better world and future through the medium of gaming.

When you stop by Brian's streams, you'll be made to feel at home, welcomed, and respected. While he might go on chatty tangents about brunch, disco music, comic books, sci-fi, TTRPG memories, or the latest anime to grab his attention, the focus is always on having a good time, playing some great games, and spreading immaculate vibes.

Brogan Kelley (he/him)—Brogan "Nonat" Kelley has played TTRPGs for over a decade now and has talked about them professionally for almost five years. He always puts the group experience and storytelling first and foremost in his games, whether as a player or a GM. He loves that these games can bring so many people together to share adventures with friends and strangers alike. He's got no plans to stop enjoying these fantastic games anytime soon.

Carlos Cisco (he/him)—Carlos Cisco is a film and television writer with produced credits on "Star Trek: Discovery," "East Los High," and the horror film *Black Demon*. He's also a writer and narrative designer for tabletop role-playing games with credits on Star Trek Adventures (Modiphius), Flee, Mortals! (MCDM), Candela Obscura, and Daggerheart (Darrington Press).

Cate Osborn (she/they)—"Catieosaurus" is a certified ADHD sex educator, mental health advocate, and full-time content creator. As a professional streamer and TTRPG influencer, she is passionate about opening conversations about neurodiversity and accessibility in the gaming community.

Christian Nommay (he/him)—Christian Nommay is a French RPG designer, freelance writer, and screenwriter living in Quebec City, Canada. He is the creator of Titan Effect, an espionage and sci-fi role-playing game and transmedia universe. Christian is passionate about animation, RPGs, video games, mythology, and photography.

Connie Chang (they/he/she)—Connie is a trans, Chinese American, ENNIE-winning RPG designer, screenwriter, and actual play Game Master who's been featured on Polygon, *The New York Times*, and Dimension 20's Adventuring Academy. You can find them running the ENNIE-nominated Transplanar RPG, working on GODKILLER RPG, a Top Physical Games bestseller on itch.io, or making videos for their 176,000 TikTok followers.

Dan Hernandez (he/him)—Dan Hernandez is a writer-producer who recently served as co-showrunner and executive producer of the upcoming "LEGO Star Wars: Rebuild the Galaxy," as well as Hulu's adult animated comedy Koala Man. Along with his writing partner Benji Samit, Hernandez also created the Disney Channel original show Ultra Violet & Black Scorpion. Other television credits include the Peabody-nominated One Day at a Time, The Tick, Central Park, Super Fun Night, and 1600 Penn. He and Benji are developing multiple shows under their overall deal at Disney.

In film, Dan and Benji's credits include the critically acclaimed *Teenage Mutant Ninja Turtles: Mutant Mayhem*, *Pokémon Detective Pikachu*, and *The Addams Family 2*. They are currently working on the recently announced *Spaceballs* sequel for Amazon/MGM, which they are co-writing with Josh Gad, the *Figment* movie for Disney, and features for multiple studios including Paramount and Skydance. In 2019, he was spotlighted as one of *Variety's* "10 Screenwriters to Watch."

Dash Kwiatkowski (they/them)—Dash is a writer, podcaster, and paranormal investigator currently living in Providence, RI. They spent a decade as a touring stand-up comedian and have been featured in comedy festivals around the country and are one-third of a comedy special featured on Amazon Prime called "Brash Boys Club" in spite of not being brash, a boy, or in any notable clubs. They've been investigating the paranormal for several years and are pretty convinced Bigfoot is some sort of ghost.

Ed Greenwood (he/him)—Ed Greenwood is a Canadian writer, game designer, voice actor, and librarian best known for creating The Forgotten Realms® fantasy world, starting at age six; he still works on the Realms every day, more than 50 years later. Over those years, he has created or co-created dozens of other settings, such as Stormtalons and Mornmist, and contributed to the fantasy settings of others, including Oz and Middle Earth.

Ed's 450-plus books have sold over 60 million copies worldwide and have been translated into over 40 languages. Ed was elected to the Academy of Adventure Gaming Art & Design Hall of Fame in 2003 and the Canadian Fantasy and Science Fiction Hall of Fame in 2022. He has won multiple ENNIE, Origins, and other awards.

Ed has been the narrative designer for Mages of Mystralia (Borealys) and Unforetold: Witchstone (Spearhead), and has voice-acted and consulted on many computer games. Ed has also judged the World Fantasy Awards and the Sunburst Awards, hosted radio shows, acted onstage, explored caves, jousted, and been Santa Claus—but not all on the same day. He is likely the only Canadian to have scripted comic books for multiple companies and appeared as himself in the pages of comic books published by several imprints.

Ed shares a house in the Ontario countryside with over 400,000 books, not counting the secret book room.

Follow Ed on Twitter @TheEdVerse for daily doggerel, watch his weekly Realmslore videos on his YouTube channel, visit Greenwood's Grotto on Discord for his Realmslore replies and to chat with many Realms contributors and creators, and subscribe to his Patreon for deep dives into Realmslore.

Grant Howitt (he/him)—Grant Howitt is a tabletop role-playing game designer, publisher, and journalist. He won six ENNIE Awards for his game Heart: The City Beneath. His game Honey Heist, which inspired an online trend of self-published games with one-page rulesets, has been featured on Critical Role, The Adventure Zone, and Friends at the Table. Through his publishing company Rowan, Rook, and Decard, Howitt is a co-designer on Kieron Gillen's DIE: The Roleplaying Game.

Howitt has worked as a freelance writer for mainstream publications such as the *Daily Mirror* and *The Guardian* and indie organizations such as Video Brains. He has described his style as "Gonzo Tech Journalism".

Harlan Guthrie (he/him)—Harlan Guthrie is a Canadian writer, editor, director, sound designer, musician, and voice actor. He is the sole creator and talent behind Malevolent, the Lovecraftian horror audio drama which is part of the Rusty Quill Network and runner-up to the 2021 Discover Pods awards, and Deviser, the sci-fi horror podcast.

As a writer, he has been featured as a guest writer on Season 1 of The Magnus Protocol and has had a number of his works featured on the multi-award-winning NoSleep Podcast. As a sound designer, he's worked on The Town Whispers, SEANCE: High Falls, and many more. His creation credits include founding the weekly streaming channel The INVICTUS Stream as well as the Actual Play D&D podcast Dice Shame, which he also acts in and edits. As a musician, he's composed the main musical themes of Malevolent, Deviser, and the music for Season 2 of Dice Shame.

Though he's a lover of all things nerdy and has a passion for storytelling in all its forms, his heart belongs to his son Henry, his daughter Marie, and his wife Jo; with whom he produces a yearly satirical Christmas radio show.

Jason Bulmahn (he/him)—Jason Bulmahn is the Director of Games at Paizo Inc., responsible for creating new board games, card games, and role-playing games for the company. He is the creator of the Pathfinder RPG and led the design for its second edition. He is also the publisher at Minotaur Games, creator of the Hopefinder RPG and other game accessories. He is a regular streamer on Twitch and a gaming content creator on YouTube.

James Introcaso (he/him)—James Introcaso is MCDM Productions' lead game designer, the co-creator of Roll20's Burn Bryte RPG, author of multiple best-selling products for the Dungeon Master's Guild and DriveThruRPG, and coauthor of seven official Dungeons & Dragons books. At MCDM, James has worked on the upcoming RPG Draw Steel as well as Flee, Mortals! The MCDM Monster Book, Where Evil Lives: The MCDM Book of Boss Battles, Kingdoms & Warfare, Beastheart and Monstrous Companions, The Talent and Psionics, and Arcadia.

Jamie Nash (he/him)—Jamie Nash is the director of the new horror comedy Last Night at Terrace Lanes. Jamie has written and sold almost every type of story under the sun, including the horror films Exists, V/H/S/2, The Night Watchman, Altered, and Lovely Molly, as well as the family films Santa Hunters and Tiny Christmas. He recently wrote and directed the podcast Black Velvet Fairies. He is also the author of Save the Cat! Writes for TV and the Save the Cat! Beat Sheet Workbook and co-hosts the podcast Writers/Blockbusters.

Jeff Cannata (he/him)—Jeff Cannata has been working in the tech and entertainment field since the young age of 14 when he parlayed a Bay Area creative writing award into a job at the *Contra Costa Times newspapers*, reviewing computer and video games in a weekly syndicated column. His column even embraced the pre-internet world of online interaction with a feature called Cannata ON-Line, which allowed readers to submit questions by dialing into a homebrew bulletin board service.

Jeff's column continued until he moved to Santa Barbara to attend UCSB, where he earned a BFA in Theater, graduating with Honors. As an actor and comedian in Los Angeles, Jeff has built a resume that illustrates his range and versatility. On television, he has been seen on The Mentalist, Scandal, Shameless, Rake, and Stalker, had recurring roles on soaps like The Bold and the Beautiful, General Hospital, and The Young and the Restless, as well as family fare like Nickelodeon's Just for Kicks. His numerous national and regional commercials include products as varied as Coors Light, Dodge, Coldwell Banker, Disney, and the Apple iPhone.

As co-creator and host of the wildly successful net talk show, The Totally Rad Show, Jeff became a recognized web personality and an authority on movies, video games, television, and comics for the hundreds of thousands of fans who watched the show. TRS was honored with Webby and Podcast awards and was called "the best weekly video podcast—period" by *Wired* magazine.

Jeff was the LA correspondent for Reviews on the Run, the G4 network's daily media review program, for over 300 episodes, and has guest hosted on Daily Tech News Show, This Week in Tech, Techzilla, Breaking it Down with Catherine Reitman, and Attack of the Show, among many others.

Currently, Jeff can be heard every week on The Filmcast, a movie review and opinion show recently named one of the "30 Best Podcasts" by Complex.com, as creator and host of DLC, the video game industry talk show on the 5by5 Network listed in Entertainment Weekly's 20 "Must Listen" podcasts, and on the comedy podcast We Have Concerns, named one of iTunes' "Best of 2014" and winner of a 2016 Podcast Award for Best Entertainment Podcast.

Finally, Jeff is considered one of the internet's preeminent Dungeon Masters, as the driving force behind the highly regarded improvised storytelling show, The Dungeon Run. His incredibly popular storyline ran for 115 episodes, comprising over 400 hours of pulse-pounding, emotionally powerful fantasy adventure.

Jennifer Kretchmer (she/her)—A producer, writer, and actor who has worked in front of or behind the camera on over a thousand episodes of television. She is also a *New York Times* best-selling author and game designer (D&D's Candlekeep Mysteries, Modiphius' Dreams and Machines, Paizo's Starfinder, the ENNIE-Award-winning Haunted West), a Twitch streamer, and a disability consultant. She performs as a DM and player on numerous tabletop actual play series, including Demiplane's Children of Éarte. Jen is a Diana Jones Emerging Designer Award finalist and the creator of the Accessibility in Gaming Resource Guide and helped create Dungeons & Dragons' accessible D&D For All kit.

 **Jesse Jerdak (he/him)**—Jesse is an actor, cosplayer, professional Dungeon Master, voice actor, 3D modeler, and martial artist.

Jesse spent his early career working in mixed martial arts but soon transitioned to film. Jesse has several SAG-AFTRA credits for principal roles starring alongside great actors like Nick Nolte, Renee Russo, and Morgan Freeman. His creative energy led to costume and prop making, and his costumes have been featured on HBO, Cartoon Network, and Critical Role.

These days, Jesse can be found at the D&D table, telling stories, building detailed terrain, and using the acting skills he developed over the years. His outlandish D&D terrain has been featured on Critical Role and Roll 4 initiaGive.

 **Jes Wade (they/them)**—Jes Wade is a TTRPG charity content creator who specializes in producing TTRPG streams and creating TTRPG bundles. Since 2021, their charity efforts have raised over $256,000. Jes also writes D&D adventures like the Mithral Best Seller on the DMs Guild: Murder in Mossbank which was featured in issue 37 of *Dragon+* magazine. Jes has been playing TTRPGs since 2019 when they were introduced to D&D on a rugby camping trip.

 **Jonathan Wilder (he/him)**—Jonathan Wilder (he/him) is a TTRPG designer based in Los Angeles. He became fully immersed in the world of TTRPGs in college, where he was studying Writing for Television. He now works at one of the entertainment unions. In the TTRPG space, Jonathan was most recently the Project Director and co-designer of The Trust Dossier: Dungeons of Sharn on the DMs Guild. He is now working on his own TTRPG called Tabula Rasa.

Joshua M. Simons (he/him)—Joshua is the founder of Broken Door Entertainment, an indie game publishing company in the tabletop games industry. His professional career included pit stops in IT, healthcare, and Big Tech along the way to the games industry. He believes life is full of lessons to be learned, and at each stop on his journey, he has been an eager student. Josh is known for his work with nonprofits like Take This and Jasper's Game Day, as well as the writing he has done with Mage Hand Press, on bestselling DM's Guild titles, and now at Broken Door Entertainment. He has been featured in articles on *Forbes* and *Polygon* and has appeared on the official D&D Twitch channel before, among other popular Twitch and YouTube gaming channels. You can learn more about him and his work at www.joshuamsimons.com.

Justin Miller (he/they)—Noir hosts GenCon's Tabletakes, a news show about all things tabletop. Noir is a stand-up comedian, musician, and Second City Alumni. You can find them on TikTok or Twitch ranting and raving about a number of nerdy topics.

Katie Downey (she/her)—Katie "Goblinkatie" Downey (Patron of the Pact of the Polyhedral) is a TTRPG and variety streamer/podcaster, dice goblin, and Take This Ambassador. Katie is best known for playing Saesha Valispard on Elder Eye Entertainment's "D4" 5e D&D campaign. She has streamed with Kobold Press, Nerdarchy, Rivals of Waterdeep, The Dawnbringers, Mage: As Above, So Below, Players And Book, and numerous other shows/networks. She is known to podcast here and there as well, playing Zale on Stellar Arcanum and Gigi on The Loot & Dagger Sidequest. She even occasionally appears as herself on shows like Sidekicks & Sidequests, Psyched To Be With You, and Dungeons & Dragons' official podcast: Dragon Talk.

Kelly (she/her)—Kelly is a voice actor, content creator, and actual play performer. She sat down to roll dice with some new friends one evening, and the rest is history. With over a decade of experience in this hobby space that she loves, Kelly (also known as "thekellhop" online) is an enthusiastic member of the TTRPG community. She treasures tales told around the table with good friends and has a passion for collaborative storytelling in all of its many forms.

Margaret Borchert (she/her)—Blacklist recommended writer Margaret Borchert is a proud "vintage gay" who firmly believes her parents should have predicted her coming out years in advance because the only part of Star Wars she cared about was Princess Leia's metal bikini. She still holds a deep affinity for beautiful women in elaborate costumes and plans to include them in everything she makes. An LA native who's lived all over the world, she's worked as a Writers' PA on Freeform's The Bold Type, a writer/researcher on the Webby Award-winning podcast An Oral History of: The Office with Brian Baumgartner, and as the assistant to TV writer Scarlett Lacey (Magnum P.I.; The Empress). In her free time, Margaret loves to play D&D and can be found DM-ing multiple campaigns for her friends.

Meghan Cross (she/her)—aka meghanlynnFTW, is a queer, neurodivergent, New England-based TTRPG designer and content creator with a passion for telling rich, collaborative stories through games. She is an indie TTRPG designer specializing in GM-less and solo TTRPGs under the name Siren's Song Games. In addition to her design work, she also appears in TTRPG actual play productions—having been featured on several productions across various Twitch channels and podcasts such as Protean City Comics, Party of One, and WebDM. Not only is she an experienced player, but she is also an experienced host—having hosted her own streaming series Unprepared, where she showcased a variety of GM-less games with a rotating cast of players. When not working on TTRPGs, she can be found on the couch with her partners, watching Taskmaster and making up songs about her dogs.

Ned Donovan (he/him)—Ned is an executive producer of and cast member on the official Dungeons & Dragons TV show Encounter Party, and the Director of Audio Fiction for the New Jersey Web Festival. He works professionally as an actor and producer in theater, TV, film, and podcasting: ned-donovan.com.

Patrick Perini (he/him)—"Storyteller" is probably the fastest way to summarize Patrick Perini. A more nuanced breakdown would lead to a ridiculous moniker like writer–composer–game-master–actor–director–producer–organizer–game-designer–and–former–technologist. "Storyteller" is easier.

And it provides a nice through-line for a journey with almost as many hyphens as that ridiculous moniker. Patrick grew up in the story-craft of the stage, learning to act, improv, stage management, and technical skills. Thrust into adulthood, he cut his teeth on video game and tech companies, where he learned how to recruit amazing teams and build impactful projects from nothing (as it happens, you do both by telling great stories). And through struggles with chronic illness, he learned how to harness patience, advocacy, and empathy. As Miyazaki says, one cannot tell good stories without understanding pain.

All the skills Patrick has picked up along the way have culminated in a multi-faceted career of experimentation, narrative, and play. He has contributed to a variety of projects from a weird-west TTRPG setting to an epic, low-fantasy audio drama. He also occasionally fiddles with the design for Grimm Games, his wife's TTRPG design studio.

He's an Appalachian in body, a San Franciscan in soul, and resides in Portland, Oregon. His current primary project is Unbalanced Encounters, a multi-award-nominated narrative play podcast.

Rah Rah (he/they)—Rah Rah runs The Heart is a Dungeon Podcast and enjoys playing games with friends.

Rowan Zeoli (she/her)—A journalist covering the intersection of progressive thought and niche cultural movements. Her work has appeared in Polygon, Tripsitter, Autostraddle, and The Fandomentals, where she's covered gender, psychedelics, and the largest developments in actual play, from award-winning indie programing to big-budget productions. She is also co-founder of the convention/non-profit WriteHive. She can be reached at rowan@rascal.news.

Rue V. Dickey (they/he)—Rue is a Roma-Indigenous-Welsh nonbinary disabled creative based out of Oregon, US. Rue organized the TTRPGs for Trans Rights in Texas bundle, raising over $ 400,000 for charity. They are a 2022 ENNIE Fan Award for Best Publisher and Diana Jones Emerging Designer Award Nominee and Hugo-Nominated Event Organizer. He is proud to be a recipient of the Gen Con Participation Grant, as well as the Story Synth & Big Bad Con Game Design Microgrant.

Sara Roberts (any/all)— Sara Roberts is a queer, neurodivergent YouTuber, performer, and AP producer best known for her detailed TTRPG character costuming. Sara grew up with a love of sewing and theater, which they have used as the backbone of their digital content creation since 2018. You can currently find them as the Producer and Game Master of a dating sim loosely disguised as a 5e Dungeons & Dragons campaign called Luck & Chaos. L&C is streamed live Thursday nights on Twitch and available now on YouTube and all podcasting platforms.

Tatiana Gefter (she/they)—Found in the PNW, Tatiana Gefter can be found haunting fiction podcast and ttrpg spaces all over the internet. You may recognize her as the creator and lead voice actress of Soul Operator, an audio drama and actual play fusion. You also catch her as Violet Lull in The Department of Variance of Somewhere Ohio, Marigold in Tales from the Fringes of Reality, Helen Hartley in Woe. Begone, and beyond.

Taylor Moore (he/him)—Taylor Moore is a producer, composer, and performer who founded Fortunate Horse, the podcast studio behind *Worlds Beyond Number*, *Rude Tales of Magic*, *Fun City*, and *Oh These Those Stars of Space*. Formerly a union organizer and Head of Comedy and Podcasts at Kickstarter, he is also an award-winning sound designer and has been a guest lecturer at colleges and universities around the world regarding new media production and co-operative business models.

Zachary Vaudo (any)—Zachary Vaudo is your omnipresent Jewish-Domari player and GM wherever tabletop games are played. His performances are spread across the TTRPG multiverse, roaming around channels and games in numerous guest appearances and limited-run games. You can also hear his music on select games and most music streaming services as Sneakernet; hear his voice (and sound effects) on the horror audio drama The Blood Crow Stories; and read his words in multiple indie TTRPG game scenarios.

Appendix A

GLOSSARY OF TTRPG TERMS

Actual Play (AP)—Also sometimes referred to as live play, is when a TTRPG is played either in front of or for an audience.

AOE (Area of Effect)—An RPG and TTRPG term that usually refers to a spell or condition that has an effect that is cast over a wide area around or in front of the player. For instance, a cleric or a wizard might cast a healing spell that covers a broad area to heal the entire party all at once.

BBEG (Big Bad Evil Guy)—The principal antagonist or ultimate boss of a TTRPG game. Not always a "guy," not always bad or evil, and not always big.

Campaign—Made up of several adventures or sessions that the players embark on to complete one or a series of quests. Campaigns can be long or short but are typically at least four or more sessions long.

CC (Crowd Control)—The way a player uses game mechanics to control the flow of their enemies on the battlefield or during an encounter. For instance, using abilities that slow, stun, or silence enemies and make them unable to act normally on their turns.

Character Sheet—This is where a player character's stats, history, hit points, inventory, and more are collected and kept track of for a session or campaign of a tabletop game. Sometimes this is written on a physical piece of paper but can also be a digital character sheet if the player is using a VTT.

Class—This determines the primary abilities that a player's character might have and gives insight into their backstory. Popular examples include paladin, bard, wizard, and rogue.

Critical Hit—Also called a "crit". This is a successful attack that does more damage than a normal hit. In a game like Dungeons & Dragons, a critical hit is accomplished when a player rolls a 20 on their d20.

Crit—(see Critical Hit)

Critical Failure—The opposite of a Critical Hit. In Dungeons & Dragons, a critical failure occurs when the player rolls a 1 on their d20. It is an automatic failure to the player for whatever action they were attempting to take.

DC (Difficulty Check/Class)—A number set by the Game Master (and often enumerated in their rule books) for a player to meet or beat with their dice rolls. For example, if a player wants to drive a car, the GM might set a DC of 15 to do it successfully. If the player rolls a 15 or higher, they do it. If they roll lower, they either fail or there are other complications that arise at the GM's discretion.

D20—A type of die that has 20 sides commonly used for TTRPGs. Also, a shortened form of the title for the show *Dimension 20* on Dropout.

XP (Experience Points)—Points gained by players for accomplishing quests, missions, or feats given to them by the GM. These points are usually tied to goals, allowing the players to level up their characters.

GM (Game Master)—Also sometimes known as the Dungeon Master. Game Master is a system-agnostic term for the person who runs the game for the players. They are the person setting the players on their quests, and the person the players interact with for all non-player characters and entities they encounter along the way.

Glass Cannon—A nickname given to a character that has strong offensive power but is weak defensively, or a character that hits hard and for a lot of points but is easily defeated because they have a low amount of hit points.

DM (Dungeon Master)—(see GM (Game Master))

Homebrew—A name given to elements, settings, and other parts of a game that aren't strictly created by the original game creators. This is often done to add flavor to a game, balance or fix an overlooked part of the game as it was written, or to give the players a fresh experience outside of the typical adventure they would usually play.

HP (Health/Hit Points)—The lifeline of a character or monster. Usually lower when characters are just starting their adventures. Health/Hit points get higher as players progress in level. Also used as a measure of toughness for a player's character separately from their (in the case of D&D) constitution score.

Module—An adventure that is fully formed, which a GM can pick up and run with their players with less preparation than a homebrew game.

NPC (Non-Player Character)—Characters that players encounter on their journey that are played by the GM. They might be integral to the story or might just be a random person the players meet on the street.

One-Shot—An adventure that can be completed from start to finish in one session.

OOC (Out of Character)—When the player breaks character to speak to the other players or the GM. Also sometimes called an "Above the Table" conversation.

PHB (Player's Handbook)—A rulebook specifically given to players that contains all the rules, feats, and information necessary for players to create and play their adventuring characters effectively.

PC (Player Character)—Characters controlled by the players at the table.

PvE (Player vs Environment)—Gameplay where players are fighting against enemies controlled by the GM (or in video games, computer controlled).

PvP (Player vs. Player)—Gameplay where players can fight with each other. Often discouraged in TTRPGs as this type of combat can create tension or resentment between players.

Railroading—A game type where no matter what the players decide during their adventure, it follows along a predetermined path set by the module or GM.

Rule of Cool—An unofficial rule in TTRPGs that refers to allowing players to break the rules in service of making the story better for the rest of the table.

Rules Lawyer—A person who plays or runs a TTRPG that only uses the rules as written and does not deviate from them. A person who feels passionately that the rules be followed in the service of fairness and balance to the game.

Safety Tools—A set of policies set by the GM and mutually agreed upon by all players before a game to make sure that everyone has a safe and comfortable time during their game so they can focus more on the fun elements and stay clear of topics that may make other players uncomfortable.

Session—A period when the TTRPG is being played. Often a few hours long, sometimes longer.

Session Zero—A session that takes place before the game starts where the players and GM can discuss characters, story, and handle any mechanical or rule questions or changes before the game begins.

TotM (Theater of the Mind)—A type of TTRPG that has no physical elements for the players to look at or handle. All the scenes, characters, and items are described by the GM, and the players need to imagine the world in their minds.

TPK (Total Party Kill)—A scenario where all the players' characters have been killed by the GM in a single encounter.

TTRPG (Tabletop Role-Playing Game)—A game where players assume the personae of characters they create and interact with a world as described and run by a Game Master, who leads them through an adventure in which the player characters experience growth through experience, eventually leading to a conclusion that sometimes takes years to achieve through multiple sessions.

VTT (Virtual Tabletop)—A way to experience a TTRPG via a digital interface on a computer or even a touchscreen display. A VTT might include maps of the locations the players are in, tokens to represent the players, monsters, or other elements, and even include music to set the mood of the adventure.

Appendix B

GLOSSARY OF SCREENWRITING TERMS

Action—The paragraph in a screenplay that comes after the location information and describes the character's physical movements at the beginning of the scene. There may be additional action lines in between dialog as characters move around the scene's location.

Aerial Shot—An overhead shot that is traditionally done with something as a tall building but can also include shots from a helicopter or via a drone. It can sometimes be used as an establishing shot, but it can also add frenetic action to set a tone for a scene.

Allegory—A type of story that contains hidden meanings, usually with moral undertones. It differs from a metaphor by not being overt, but by allowing the reader or viewer to interpret the story and symbols in it.

Angle On—A shot direction to the cameraperson to point the camera in a different direction in the same scene.

Antagonist—The thing, usually a person, that is set against the protagonist in the story. Not always a villain, but someone or something with opposite ideals, viewpoints, or goals to the protagonist.

Backstory—A character or plot's history or background.

Back To—When a camera reverts to its original position after moving within a scene.

Beat—A structural narrative element that marks a shift or pause in story or tone.

B.G. (Background)—Used to describe action or anything of interest happening in the background of a scene that is out of the focus of the foreground shot.

Character—A person in a story. Some are main characters, which are the focus of a story, and some are background characters, which support the main characters in their endeavors.

Character Arc—The transformation (internally or externally) a character goes through in a story.

Climax—The point of the highest point of tension in the central conflict of a story.

CU (Close Up)—A close (tight) shot on a person's face or an item to make the audience focus on something specific (i.e., a face, fist, a tear, a ticking clock, etc.)

Close On—A shot that suggests a close up.

Closer Angle—An angle closer to the subject from a previous shot on the same subject at a farther angle.

Conflict—The primary challenge to the main character in a story. This can be internal, external (from another character), or environmental.

CONT'D—An abbreviation of the word "continued" and shows that a character is still speaking from the previous page.

Continuous—A series of shots that all occur in succession without any gap in time or story.

Crawl—Text that moves around the screen superimposed over a moving image. For example, the opening crawl to the original 1977 *Star Wars* film.

Credits—In a script, this can be a signal as to where to place the opening credits. Otherwise, this is the list of people who worked on a film that generally scrolls on the screen at the end of a movie.

Crossfade—Not quite a dissolve, as this involves a fade to a black screen, but generally involves both a fade in and out together.

Cut To—A quick change from one scene to another as opposed to a fade out or other narrative cut.

Dash—Shows an interruption in dialog, but can also be used as a narrative flow device.

Dialogue (Dialog)—Conversation occurring between two or more characters within a scene of a story.

Director—The person in charge of making a movie. Sometimes the director is also the writer. They are assisted by the 1st Assistant Director who handles many of the more "hands on" aspects of making a movie, allowing the director to make many of the major decisions, work with the actors, and run the film set.

Dissolve To—A type of fade cut but generally is seamless from one scene to the next, blending one or more elements into the cut.

Dolly—A device on wheels or rails that has a camera mounted to it, allowing the camera smooth freedom of movement in a direction.

Ellipsis—A narrative device created by using three dots to denote a trailing thought or dialog. Implies an intentional pause.

Establishing Shot—The shot at the beginning of a scene that gives context to the location the scene takes place in. It might show the constrictions and initiations of where the actors can go and is usually a wide shot and might include signs or other significant details of the location relevant to the characters or story.

EXT (Exterior)—Used in a screenplay to show that a scene takes place outdoors.

INT (Interior)—Used in a screenplay to show that a scene takes place indoors.

XLS (Extremely Long Shot)—A shot taken from a very long distance, sometimes used as an establishing shot in a movie.

Fade In/Out—A gentle fade from one scene to a new one. Sometimes this is from/to black.

Favor On—A shot focused on a specific person for the duration of a scene regardless of other people/things within the scene.

Feature Film—A movie that is longer than a short film. Defined as a film over 40 minutes, but can be three hours or longer depending on the filmmaker's intent.

Flash Cut—A shot insert into a scene, as quickly as one frame, sometimes as a subliminal message to the audience.

Flashback—A moment in a story where a character mentally goes back in time to reveal a plot detail or remind the audience of something important to the story. This can also be used by an off-screen narrator in the same way.

FG (Foreground)—A shot that focuses on the elements closest to the camera lens.

Freeze Frame—A pause in the movie where the picture stops moving and holds for a period of time.

Insert—A specific shot cut into a scene for emphasis.

Intercut—Also sometimes written as INTERCUT BETWEEN. This cuts two scenes back and forth between each other for a few moments each to make a narrative point or show a passage of time.

Iris Out—A stylistic shot similar to a wipe but is done from the center of the frame flaring out in a circle to the rest of the frame, revealing the next scene.

Isolate—A technique that draws attention to a person or object in the scene by focusing on them either through the lens focus or lighting within the scene.

Jump Cut To—A transition between scenes that shows a passage of time from one scene to the next, obviously omitting unimportant narrative in-between.

Lap Dissolve—A transition between scenes that fades one scene out while the next scene comes into focus.

Match Dissolve To—Similar to a match cut, this transition is a dissolve where the next scene, by design, dissolves to the next one seamlessly while some elements blend together.

Monologue—A speech made by one (hence the prefix mono) character either to other characters or directly to the audience.

Montage—A series of shots cut together (often to a soundtrack) to create a sense of character advancement and mark a passage of time. For instance, a training montage in movies like *Rocky* or *The Karate Kid*.

(More)—Used when a character is speaking, but you hit the end of the page before they're finished. Use this at the bottom of the page and (CONT'D) at the top of the next.

MOS (Mit Out Sound)—A German phrase meaning moment of silence.

OC/OS (Off Camera/Off Screen)—Refers to something happening or a character speaking off screen or off camera. This is marked in a parenthetical next to the character's name in the script.

Pan—A camera movement where the camera turns while maintaining a stationary position.

Parenthetical—This is a character direction that comes before or within the dialog.

Plot—The sequence of events that makes up a story using cause and effect.

POV (Point of View)—A shot meant to be from a character's eyes within a scene.

Protagonist—The main character of a story. Also the character who drives the action and plot.

Pull Back—The camera movement where the camera physically pulls away from a subject using a zoom or a dolly action.

Pull Focus—A camera function (sometimes done by a focus puller or automated system) where it changes focus from one subject to another.

Scene—A portion of a film or script that takes place in one location or time.

Push In—The camera movement where the camera physically moves toward a subject.

Reverse Angle—A 180-degree move by the camera to show something out of view or from the reverse POV of a character.

Script Doctor—A person hired to "punch up" or rewrite a script. Usually not credited as a writer unless a WGA minimum is reached.

Shooting Script—The draft of a screenplay that is used as the main script while shooting a film. This is the copy that is sometimes annotated by the director and other crew members for production. Further edits are denoted by different colored pages when given to cast/crew.

Shot—An image of a person or thing.

Short Film—Loosely defined as a film less than 40 minutes in length that tells a complete story.

Slugline—Often debated by screenwriters whether they should be bold or not, the slugline is the scene heading in your script. They communicate location and time of day.

Smash Cut To—A sharp transition sometimes done in conjunction with a sound to create a jump scare or for comedic effect.

Spec Script—A screenplay written but not commissioned. Sometimes a writer will take existing IP and write a story set within that property to showcase their ability to do similar work.

Split Screen Shot—A shot containing images from two separate scenes to convey two parts of the story happening at the same time.

Steadicam—A camera that remains stable regardless of movement by the cinematographer.

Stock Shot—Footage for a film that has been previously filmed and sold to a stock footage company that a filmmaker can use for a licensing fee.

Super—Indicates that a line of text is supposed to be on the screen within the scene. Most often used when showing a date or a ticking clock situation in a film.

Swish Pan—A camera pan that blurs the frame and mostly used as a transition to a new scene.

Tight On—A close-up shot.

Time Cut—Meant to connote a passage of time within a scene.

Trailer—A series of cuts of scenes of a movie meant to entice people to watch the entire film. An advertisement for a movie.

Tracking Shot—A shot where a non-stationary camera follows a person or object through a scene.

Transition—The movement from one scene to the next. Can be accomplished in a variety of ways.

VO (Voice Over)—A narration over events and scenes in a film. A voice over can give basic narration as to what's happening in a scene, or act as an omniscient storyteller speaking directly with the audience.

Wipe To—A scene transition that where the new scene "wipes away" the old one.

Zoom—A movement that closes in on a person or object within a scene. Sometimes done slowly for dramatic effect.

Appendix C—Blank World Map

Appendix D—Blank Character Sheet

character sheet

character profile: ☐ protagonist ☐ antagonist

Name

Age

Are they the narrator?

Appearance:

Personality traits:

Languages spoken or specific speech patterns:

Behaviours and mannerisms:

Life altering experiences:

Interests:

Motivations:

Values:

Attitudes:

Strengths:

Weaknesses:

How do others percieve them?

character development

How does this character change throughout each part of the story?

beginning	middle	end

Who is this character in conflict with?

How does this character change from the beginning of the story to the end?

character stats

☐ Str   ☐ Wis

☐ Dex   ☐ Int

☐ Con   ☐ Cha

These character stats are meant to be updated for consistency as your character progresses through the story.

As your character grows, their stats might increase in applicable areas.

Feel free to add any stats you feel your character might have or need that are not listed.

supporting characters (friends and enemies)

List the supporting characters in the story and briefly describe them (personality, appearance, actions, role or purpose etc.).

name	character affiliation and description

Index